The Michigan Affirmative Action Cases

LANDMARK LAW CASES

AMERICAN SOCIETY

Peter Charles Hoffer
N. E. H. Hull
Series Editors

BARBARA A. PERRY

The Michigan Affirmative Action Cases

UNIVERSITY PRESS OF KANSAS

Published by the University Press of Kansas (Lawrence, Kansas 66045), which was
organized by the Kansas Board of Regents and is operated and funded by Emporia
State University, Fort Hays State University, Kansas State University, Pittsburg State
University, the University of Kansas, and Wichita State University

Library of Congress Cataloging-in-Publication Data

Perry, Barbara A. (Barbara Ann), 1956–
The Michigan affirmative action cases / Barbara A. Perry.
p.   cm. — (Landmark law cases)
Includes bibliographical references and index.
ISBN 978-0-7006-1548-3 (cloth : alk. paper) — ISBN 978-0-7006-1549-0
(pbk. : alk. paper)   1. Grutter, Barbara — Trials, litigation, etc.
2. Gratz, Jennifer—Trials, litigation, etc.   3. Bollinger, Lee C.,
1946 — Trials, litigation, etc.   4. University of Michigan — Trials,
litigation, etc.   5. Affirmative action programs in education — Law and
legislation — United States.   6. Universities and
colleges — Admission — Law and legislation — Michgian.   I. Title.
KF228.G78P47   2007
344.73'0798— dc22
2007017873

British Library Cataloguing-in-Publication Data is available.

Printed in the United States of America

10 9 8 7 6 5 4 3 2 1

To the memory of my parents, Lillian and Louis Perry,
and my mentor, Paul Weber

CONTENTS

EDITORS' PREFACE

With few exceptions, the world of modern American constitutional law is one of balancing tests, a world of gray tones rather than sharp lights and darks. Bright-line boundaries in moral philosophy, political ideology, and social advocacy blur and bend in courts of law. Affirmative action cases are prime examples; though some jurists insist that no distinctions can be made on the basis of suspect categories like race, sex, religious affiliation, and national origin, the law is full of such distinctions. Some may be benign, aiding one group over another, precisely because, in the past, bright-line rules barred one group from jobs, education, political participation, and other basic civil rights. Case law and legislation qualify the distinctions, making each occasion of their application even more gray shaded.

The University of Michigan's undergraduate admissions policies and the university's law school recognized such distinctions. Perhaps even more important, as educational institutions, they recognized that diverse student bodies, like diverse faculties and a diverse governing board, were a pedagogical value in themselves. Although the guidelines for the two admissions procedures differed, one based on points assigned to certain minority applicants, the other on a rough percentage for admission of certain minorities, both aimed at the goal of a diverse student population. For a major state university in a state whose population was similarly diverse, such weighting had democratic as well as educational value.

But since *Bakke v. California Board of Regents* (1978), educational affirmative action programs have become lightning rods for various groups strongly opposed to any racial set-asides, goals, or quotas. These legal action groups have solicited cases, watchdogged schools' admissions policies, and in general won their suits. The University of Georgia's policies giving some weight to minority status, the University of Texas Law School's similar procedures, and other state schools' attempts to increase minority presence have fallen before court challenges. As we write this preface, seventeen states have approved either constitutional amendments or legislative enactments barring any consideration of applicants' race in public higher education or professional school admissions.

The two Michigan cases, *Jennifer Gratz v. Lee Bollinger, President of the University of Michigan*, and *Barbara Grutter v. Bollinger* (2003), argued for the petitioner undergraduate and law school students by the Center for Individual Rights, began in 1997 and resulted in two of the most complex and yet revealing affirmative action cases that the U.S. Supreme Court has decided. But the cases were more than dry constitutional law. And the story of the cases reveals even more than the decisions did.

Barbara Perry has followed these cases from their inception. She has gained the inside story from interviews with the key participants. With keen insight into the issues, and a deeply caring and high-minded regard for all the participants and their arguments, she has brought the affirmative action story up to date. She follows with unerring accuracy the twists and turns of the district, appellate, and high court cases, explaining how counsel for the two sides planned their arguments and how the judges and justices came down where they did. Perry explores as well how academics flocked to defend diversity as a value, for, as she reminds us, the educational issues were as important as the legal ones.

In their winding course, nothing could stop the cases from going political. With the late president Gerald Ford defending the university, and President George W. Bush speaking out against the affirmative action plans, it was no wonder that every eye in higher education was focused on Ann Arbor, and then on the Marble Palace.

Sometimes a case has a hero or a heroine. These cases had many. One of these stands out: Justice Sandra Day O'Connor understood what was at stake. Her jurisprudence of simple justice, of attention to facts and outcomes, of humanity, was never more in evidence than in her role on the Court in these cases, and in her opinions in both of them.

For general readers, specialists, and students interested in affirmative action in higher education, this book is must reading. It does not hurt, either, that Perry writes with verve, a wonderful eye for anecdote, and real compassion.

PREFACE

Americans over the age of eight or so on the historic dates of December 7, 1941, November 22, 1963, and September 11, 2001, can remember exactly where they were when they heard that the Japanese had attacked Pearl Harbor, that President Kennedy had been assassinated, that terrorists had crashed highjacked jetliners into the World Trade Center, the Pentagon, and a Pennsylvania field. I suspect very few Americans can recall what they were doing when they received word about the *Regents of the University of California v. Bakke* decision on June 28, 1978. I, however, distinctly recall standing outside a pub in the shadows of Oxford University's "dreaming spires" when I heard the news from fellow Americans with me on a summer study program in England.

The U.S. Supreme Court's first affirmative action decision had attracted my attention during my senior year of college in 1977–1978. Having just completed a two-semester constitutional history course at the University of Louisville, a short time after my initial visit to the majestic Supreme Court building, I was already intrigued by the litigation when my composition professor assigned the *Bakke* story to our class as a topic on which to write an essay. Unbeknownst to me as I stood on the Oxford sidewalk in 1978 was that in just a few months I would accept my first job out of college as an affirmative action compliance officer at the Louisville–Jefferson County Human Relations Commission.

At twenty-two years of age, and with a newly minted political science degree in hand, my task was to inform contractors doing business with the city of Louisville that they had to comply with a new ordinance, requiring them to file workforce data with the commission, which could request an affirmative action plan from them if minorities and women were "underutilized." From Procter and Gamble, to local companies with as few as sixteen employees, I received a variety of responses. Long used to complying with similar federal laws, P and G sent its inch-thick, bound employment data report and affirmative action plan without hesitation; small-business owners complained bitterly and were often recalcitrant. The stock answer from the latter was "I already *have* a black employee. He's been with us for years and is the best darn janitor we've ever had!" That statement was usually followed by, "I'll hire anyone who's qualified. I don't care if he is pink, purple, or polka-dotted!" Most employers eventually submitted the data and a plan, if necessary; others chose not to do business with the city in order to avoid the law.

Although the job offered lessons on how to deal with the public, I was eager to leave in 1979 and return to Oxford, where I received my master's degree in politics, philosophy, and economics. I could never have imagined that, when the next affirmative action case in higher education was heard at the U.S. Supreme Court on April 1, 2003, I would be seated in the front row for oral argument, thanks to my dear friend, General William K. Suter, clerk of the Court. On June 23, 2003, at the Court's "Opinion Day," when the decisions came down, I was in the courtroom again, this time with teachers from the Supreme Court Summer Institute in which I lecture each year. Everyone knew that *Gratz v. Bollinger* and *Grutter v. Bollinger*, the two cases challenging affirmative action policies at the University of Michigan's undergraduate college and law school, respectively, were destined to be landmarks. A quarter century had passed since *Bakke*, when the Court approved consideration of race as a "plus" in higher education admissions but invalidated the use of fixed quotas to achieve racial balance. No matter which way the Court decided the Michigan litigation, it was sure to garner headlines and influence educational and societal outcomes.

This book begins with an examination in chapters 1 and 2 of civil rights politics leading up to the *Bakke* decision, judicial precedents from *Bakke* to *Gratz* and *Grutter*, and historical contexts in the state of Michigan prior to the affirmative action cases, particularly busing disputes in the 1970s. Chapter 3 presents the personalities and public litigation interest groups behind the lawsuits. Lower court decisions in the cases, and political controversy surrounding them, are the subject of chapter 4. The critical influence of legal briefs presented to the Supreme Court, including from business, military leaders, higher education, and interest groups, is chapter 5's focus. Chapter 6 recreates the atmosphere of the oral arguments in *Gratz* and *Grutter*, with play-by-play and "color commentary" of the debate at the U.S. Supreme Court. All the opinions issued in the cases are analyzed in chapter 7 and linked to the justice who authored them. Finally, chapter 8 discusses the ramifications flowing from the rulings.

Although Jennifer Gratz and Barbara Grutter were the two lead plaintiffs by whose names the UM cases became known, and their stories are crucial to the launching of the litigation, another woman is at the center of its outcome. Sandra Day O'Connor achieved a victory in her *Grutter* opinion for the Court. My study explains how her personal, professional, and judicial backgrounds brought her to that pivotal moment in legal history.

I would like to thank Michael Briggs, Senior Editor at the University Press of Kansas, for his supportive guidance on this project. He and his colleagues at UPK — Director Fred Woodward, Assistant Director and Marketing Manager Susan Schott, and Production Editor Larisa Martin — I now consider friends, as well as the finest publishing team an author could ever imagine. Howard Ball and Mel Urofsky provided helpful reviews of the proposal. M. Christopher Brown II's and Terry Anderson's comments on the manuscript helped to improve the final product. As always, Henry Abraham offered substantive and moral support throughout my research and writing. His "clipping service," going all the way back to *Bakke*, was invaluable. My colleague and friend Steve Bragaw was a reliable sounding board for conversations about affirmative action, and he shared his immense expertise on litigation history, particularly the art of interviewing. Gary Kemp, Assistant Clerk at the U.S. Supreme Court, generously assisted me in tracking down briefs. Maureen Mahoney, who successfully argued for Michigan in *Grutter*, and Nathaniel Vitan, who contributed to the Michigan brief, both of Latham and Watkins in Washington, offered to provide answers to my questions about the case. As a nonlawyer, I was particularly grateful for responses to my technical queries. Kirk Kolbo, of the Minneapolis firm Maslon, Edelman, Borman, and Brand, who was the winning oral advocate in *Gratz* and who also argued *Grutter*, generously responded to my inquiries. Professor Carl Cohen of the University of Michigan, whose principled opposition to racial preferences was crucial in launching the Michigan cases, kindly offered background information to enliven my narrative. I also want to thank Gary Gregg II, Director of the McConnell Center at the University of Louisville, for understanding that I needed a full summer prior to assuming my senior fellowship at the center to complete the book. Laura Chai, my brilliant and delightful graduate assistant at the University of Louisville, industriously tracked down material for revisions. The Kenmore Fellowship, established by the Newman family at Sweet Briar College, provided funds for expenses associated with the project. Cathy Sobke, my student and research assistant at Sweet Briar, gathered data and articles that jumpstarted my early work in 2004.

Special friends in Charlottesville have made my labors much easier. The Bragaws (Steve, Wendy, Elinor, John Marshall, Adelaide, and Quentin) and the Capons (Rose, Rob, Howard, and Miriam) are my surrogate families. They have sustained me with love and laughter (and wonderful meals!).

Usually the completion of a book project is cause for celebration. My happiness and relief over reaching the finish line for this study are bittersweet. For all of my previous seven books, three very special people cheered me as I completed the assignments: my dear parents, Louis and Lillian Perry, and my "lifetime mentor," Professor Paul J. Weber of the University of Louisville. In the span of ten months, I lost them all to cancer. Each was brave to the end and continued to bolster me with love and encouragement, even as their time in this life drew to a close. Their courage and wisdom continue to guide me — and will to the completion of my days. To them, with deepest affection, I dedicate this work.

CHAPTER I

"An American Dilemma"
Racial Politics in the Pre-*Bakke* Era

The clock had just struck midnight. It was April 1, 2003. In the darkness surrounding the U.S. Supreme Court building, a few voices whooped and shouted. Could it be young revelers engaging in some sort of April Fools' prank? Hardly. Several thousand demonstrators from across the country were amassing around the high court. They encircled the edifice and began marching around it. "Jim Crow, hell no!" "Two, four, six, eight, we don't want to segregate!" "What do we want? Affirmative action! When do we want it now? Now!"

What had possessed these young people of all races and ethnicities to congregate at the witching hour for a parade around the Supreme Court? They knew that in exactly ten hours the nation's highest court would hear oral arguments in two landmark affirmative action cases from the University of Michigan. The nine justices' decisions would determine the fate of admissions policies promoting racial and ethnic diversity throughout American universities. Undoubtedly, the members of the Supreme Court were long home by that late hour, but lights burned brightly in their court chambers. Law clerks, working long into the night, could not escape the display of public opinion at their doorstep.

Nor could the justices when they arrived for work that morning. After dispersing for a few hours' rest, the demonstrators were back at the Court by daybreak. Despite the April date, spectators waiting to enter the building, including the University of Michigan president, Mary Sue Coleman, shivered in the unseasonably cool temperatures. The cold did not deter the protesters. An elderly black woman, bundled in her winter coat and knit hat, held a handwritten placard directed at one judge in particular. It read, "Clarence Thomas — How did you get into law school?" Luke Massie, of the Coalition to Defend Affirmative Action and Integration and Fight for Equality by Any

Means Necessary, which organized the rally, remarked to a reporter, "This is the first march of the new civil rights movement." The throng of several thousand completed their protest at the Supreme Court and then marched along the Mall to the Lincoln Memorial, site of Martin Luther King Jr.'s "I Have a Dream" speech nearly forty years earlier. The 2003 event climaxed with an emotional rendition of the spiritual "Lift Ev'ry Voice and Sing," recognized by many as an African American anthem.

If "the Negro problem and modern democracy" was "an American dilemma," as Swedish sociologist Gunnar Myrdal identified it in his 1944 book, then affirmative action would become a dilemma within a dilemma two decades later, and no less so in 2003. By the mid-1960s, Negroes were embracing "black" or "African American" as their preferred racial label, a symbolic representation of the earth-shaking social change that the United States experienced during the later half of the twentieth century.

Although the 1950s are often viewed in retrospect as a quiescent decade, it was anything but where race was concerned. The Supreme Court's *Brown v. Board of Education* decisions calling for school de-segregation, and the South's recalcitrant reaction; President Dwight Eisenhower's sending troops to Little Rock, Arkansas, to integrate its schools; Rosa Parks's refusal to relinquish her seat on a segregated Montgomery bus and the boycott that ensued, led by Dr. King, were all harbingers of what tumult the next decade would bring. As political scientist Irving Bernstein has noted, the population of black Americans had grown by 6 million between 1940 and 1960, prompting a demographic shift from the rural South to urban ghettos in the North among blacks searching for jobs. The Negro unemployment rate was nearly double that for whites, with African American men and teenagers suffering even higher rates. In 1960 almost half of black families lived on annual incomes below $3,000, while a young, white, male middle management worker alone could expect to earn at least twice as much.

The sixties, which witnessed such unprecedented upheaval in American politics, began with each of the two major political parties pledging its support for civil rights. Knowing that they could not ignore the racial powder keg forever, and recognizing that the anemic Civil Rights Acts of 1957 and 1960 would not quell blacks' insistent demand for full

{ *Chapter 1* }

citizenship, the Democratic and Republican parties' 1960 presidential platforms both called for an end to discrimination based on race, color, national origin, or religion in employment, education, transportation, housing, and voting. The Democratic platform, grandly titled "The Rights of Man," added the administration of justice to areas of proposed nondiscrimination. The Democrats also specifically mentioned that they would support the establishment of a fair employment practices commission "to secure effectively for everyone the right to equal opportunity for employment," and that the president should eliminate racial discrimination in the federal government and federal contracts. Moreover, the U.S. Commission on Civil Rights should aid communities, industries, and individuals in securing rights. The GOP platform commended the President's Committee on Government Contracts, established by Eisenhower and chaired by Vice President Richard Nixon, and vowed to create a permanent commission on equal job opportunity. The Republicans also supported a law to ban discrimination in labor union membership.

Yet both political parties suffered from schisms that political scientist James MacGregor Burns observed constituted two parties within each. The fault lines in both parties were along the same regional, social, and ideological boundaries. Northern, urban, progressive liberals among Democrats and Republicans eyed the White House as their ultimate prize, with the hope of using federal government (especially executive) powers to solve the nation's ills. Southern (or southwestern), rural, states' rights conservatives in both parties made Congress and governors' offices their power bases and looked to block federal initiatives (particularly in civil rights). Thus, no matter which candidate won the 1960 presidential election, Senator John F. Kennedy (D-MA) or incumbent Republican vice president Richard Nixon, he would face schizophrenic political parties (his own and the opposition), as well as a separation-of-powers battle between the presidency and Congress, and a federalism conflict between the national and state governments. In no policy area were these tensions more obvious or raw than civil rights. No wonder that neither candidate made civil rights for Negroes a centerpiece of his campaign strategy or rhetoric.

A host of issues, in addition to civil rights, impinged on the 1960 presidential race: the Cold War, a "missile gap" (alleged by Kennedy) between the United States and the Soviet Union, nuclear proliferation and testing, Communist gains in Southeast Asia and Cuba (ninety miles from America's shore), the flash point of Berlin and other pressures behind the Iron Curtain, periodic economic recessions, pockets of abject poverty, urban decay, suburban sprawl, health care (especially for the elderly), and aid to education. JFK's Roman Catholicism was also a factor in the election, as were his charisma and telegenic persona in the new television age that produced the first televised presidential debates.

Although he usually did not emphasize the Democratic Party's platform plank on civil rights while on the campaign trail, Kennedy did not neglect it completely. In his acceptance speech at the Democratic National Convention in Los Angeles, Kennedy's theme was the challenges of the New Frontier and how he was up to the task of confronting a world that was inexorably changing. Emphasizing his youth (he had just turned forty-three), JFK noted that "here at home, the changing face of the future is equally revolutionary. The New Deal and the Fair Deal were bold measures for their generations — but this is a new generation. . . . A peaceful revolution for human rights — demanding an end to racial discrimination in all parts of our community life — has strained at the leashes imposed by timid executive leadership."

In the first televised Nixon-Kennedy debate, which concentrated on domestic issues, JFK's opening statement skillfully tied Lincoln's famous question on whether the nation could exist half slave and half free to both the international Cold War and the domestic civil rights movement. He proclaimed the question in 1960 to be "whether the *world* will exist half slave [Communist] or half free." Kennedy responded to his own rhetorical inquiry: "I think it will depend in great measure upon what we do here in the United States, on the kind of society we build." To convince voters to reject the Republican status quo, the Democratic candidate cited a litany of conditions that should be changed in order to strengthen America at home and abroad:

I'm not satisfied until every American enjoys his full constitutional rights. If a Negro baby is born, and this is true also of Puerto Ricans and Mexicans in some of our cities, he has about one half as much chance to get through high school as a white baby. He has one third as much chance to get through college as white students. He has about a third as much chance to be a professional man, about half as much chance to own a house. He has about four times as much chance that he'll be out of work in his life as the white baby. I think we can do better. I don't want the talents of any American to go to waste.

His thinly veiled subtext: How could the United States win the hearts and minds of third world nations (most with nonwhite populations) if America, the leader of the free world, treated its people of color as second-class citizens?

Nevertheless, trying to walk the fine line between the two factions of his party, and knowing that his religion diminished his chances of winning southern states, Kennedy rarely addressed civil rights on the campaign trail, though he met with the Reverend Martin Luther King Jr. twice. One action that JFK took just ten days before election day, however, may have increased his appeal to Negroes and given him enough votes to capture a razor-thin popular-vote victory over Nixon. King had been arrested and jailed for trespassing during a sit-in demonstration at an Atlanta department store's segregated restaurant. Authorities later dropped the charges, and all the arrested demonstrators were released from jail, except for King, who was held for violating a probated sentence in a previous arrest for operating a vehicle in Georgia with an Alabama driver's license. (King's car had been pulled over initially because a white woman was a passenger.) King was transferred to a county jail and then brought before a segregationist judge, the one who had originally heard his traffic violation case. Looking to stymie the civil rights leader, the judge sentenced him to six months' hard labor at a state penitentiary, to which he was transferred in handcuffs and leg irons through the backwoods of Georgia in the dead of night. At the urging of his civil rights advisers, JFK made a brief personal phone call to King's pregnant and distraught wife, Coretta, expressing his concern. King was released on $2,000 bond after Robert Kennedy intervened, despite stewing over the potentially damaging effect on his brother's electoral chances among white voters in the South. King publicly thanked Senator Kennedy, "who served as a great force in making my release possible." The story of JFK's concern for King and his family spread through the black community. Kennedy's outreach even converted King's father, also a Baptist cleric, who had been dubious about voting for a Catholic for president. As Jack Kennedy, son of the domineering and anti-Semitic Joseph P. Kennedy Sr., noted wryly, "Imagine Martin Luther King having a bigot for a father! Well, we all have fathers, don't we?"

Kennedy's famous inaugural address is noted for its Cold War rhetoric, not as a call to arms in the domestic war for civil rights. Indeed, through his first two years in office, President Kennedy refused to send any sweeping civil rights proposals to Congress for fear that the southern Democrats would not only defeat them but also stall his other New Frontier policy proposals. Without congressional authority to attack segregation in private business, Kennedy turned to executive action for addressing equal opportunity in federal service and in contracts let by the national government. After observing that the Coast Guard honor guard in his inauguration parade had no Negro cadets, JFK discovered that the Coast Guard Academy had never graduated a black student. Merle Smith Jr. entered the academy in 1962 and became the first African American to graduate four years later. He had a successful twenty-year career in the Coast Guard, rose to the rank of commander, earned a law degree from George Washington University, and served as a legal officer. After retiring from the military, he became general counsel for General Dynamics. Kennedy used the Coast Guard Academy example to request that each of his cabinet heads examine the racial profile of his department's employees. Perhaps not surprisingly, the number of blacks was pitifully low. Among the 3,674 foreign service officers at the State Department, only 15 were African American; of the 1,692 attorneys employed by the Department of Justice, a mere 19 were black. Most of the 13 percent of the federal workforce who were African American were concentrated in lower GS ranks. Roy Wilkins, director of the National Association for the Advancement of Colored People (NAACP), commented with some amusement "that Kennedy was so hot on the Department heads, the Cabinet officers, and the Agency heads that everyone was scrambling around trying to find himself a Negro in order to keep the president off his neck."

Similar to presidents beginning with Franklin Roosevelt, Kennedy would create a Committee on Equal Employment Opportunity

(CEEO). Headed by Vice President Lyndon Johnson, the CEEO offered a report and executive order to President Kennedy shortly after his inauguration. LBJ's report declared: "The Government of the United States cannot remain in a position where equal opportunity for employment and advancement is denied to citizens employed on the Government's own work, because of their race, creed, color, or national origin." Echoing Myrdal's identification of the "American dilemma," Johnson argued, "This is an intolerable paradox in a democratic society." Along the lines of British political philosopher Isaiah Berlin's dichotomy between negative and positive liberty, the vice president noted that it was not enough for the federal government simply to ban discrimination. Rather, Johnson, the skillful Texas pol who had made civil rights a focus of his successful career in the U.S. Senate, proclaimed, "It is necessary that *affirmative action* be taken to make equal opportunity available to all who, directly or indirectly, are employed by the nation."

According to Hobart Taylor Jr., an African American attorney and Johnson adviser, the phrase "affirmative action" developed because the young lawyer liked its alliteration, in contrast to "positive action," wording he rejected. The choice was crucial, for it found its way into Executive Order 10925, which President Kennedy announced on March 6, 1961. In addition to establishing officially the Committee on Equal Employment Opportunity as a presidential commission, the order required the government to "consider and recommend affirmative steps which should be taken by executive departments and agencies to realize more fully the national policy of nondiscrimination." In addition to promoting equal opportunity in the federal government service, the executive order required that most federal contracts with business contain the following language: "The contractor will not discriminate against any employee or applicant for employment because of race, creed, color, or national origin. The contractor will take affirmative action to ensure that applicants are employed, and that employees are treated during employment without regard to their race, creed, color, or national origin. Such action shall include, but not be limited to, the following: employment, upgrading, demotion, or transfer; recruitment or recruitment advertising; layoff or termination; rates of pay or other forms of compensation; and selection for training, including apprenticeship." Scholars Terry Anderson and

Irving Bernstein have both observed that the Kennedy executive order constitutes the first time the language "affirmative action" appeared with reference to race in federal antidiscrimination policy. JFK named John G. Field executive director of the CEEO. Field brought a wealth of civil rights experience to the commission, including service on the Mayor's Interracial Committee in Detroit, the city where he had spent his youth.

In response to a press inquiry about whether Kennedy would introduce civil rights legislation to Congress during his first year in office, JFK was straightforward and realistic about his policy strategy. "When I believe that we can usefully move ahead in the field of [civil rights] legislation, I will recommend it to the Congress. . . . When I feel there is a necessity for a congressional action, *with a chance of getting that congressional action*, then I will recommend it to the Congress." Of course, as noted previously, Kennedy knew that he would get no positive congressional action on a genuinely potent civil rights bill because of the effective veto held by senior Democratic senators from the South. So, much to the consternation and anger of civil rights leaders, JFK initially did nothing in the legislative arena to expand equal opportunity for minorities. A 2006 book about Kennedy's civil rights record, by British journalist Nick Bryant, is entitled *The Bystander*, to symbolize what the author argues is JFK's "unresponsiveness" to the pleas of black Americans.

Nevertheless, the CEEO moved forward, with John Field at the helm, using all of the government authority at his disposal to expand opportunities for Negroes. He established a comprehensive data-gathering system on contractors' workforces and a compliance review procedure that conducted work site inspections. Private industry, either because of complaints brought against it or because it embraced the positive public relations of equal opportunity, signed on to Vice President Johnson's Plans for Progress. Lockheed Aircraft Corporation, against which the NAACP had lodged a complaint because of egregious segregation at its Georgia plant and which had a billion-dollar defense contract with the federal government, pledged to "aggressively seek out" qualified black candidates for employment. The pledge included alerting college placement offices about the new hiring policy, reviewing current black employees' records for possible promotion, and recruiting Negroes into the company's apprentice program. Within one year the Southern Region Council, a liberal civil rights policy organization, reported that Lockheed was fulfilling its pledge. Yet progress among other large corporations was sporadic and inconsistent. The CEEO extended its purview to labor unions, which had traditionally discriminated against minorities in membership. Through its programs, the committee at the very least began to focus the public consciousness on equal employment opportunity, though at the time the concept applied only to blacks. Moreover, the concept of affirmative action in the early 1960s did not include special preference or numerical quotas for hiring African Americans.

The painfully slow progress in employment, and the Kennedy administration's lack of initiative on the legislative front, only reminded blacks, especially in the Jim Crow South, how much farther the civil rights movement needed to go. President Kennedy and the whole nation were confronted by increasingly frequent and sometimes bloody demonstrations in the Deep South to integrate private accommodations (movie houses, restaurants, department stores, hotels/motels), as well as public transportation and higher education. The frightful images of white police using truncheons, fire hoses, and German shepherd dogs to attack peaceful protesters, including young blacks, all played out in the media, especially on television. When Alabama governor George Wallace barred the entry of the first two Negro students to the University of Alabama, Kennedy activated National Guard troops and Wallace finally gave way. Kennedy's similar action in Mississippi the previous year had forced the University of Mississippi to accept its first black student. In both instances, the president executed federal court orders to integrate the public universities at issue.

By the summer of 1963, JFK recognized that his administration's foot-dragging on civil rights legislation must end. In the wake of the University of Alabama's forced integration, President Kennedy made a nationally televised speech on June 11, 1963, in which he announced: "Next week I shall ask the Congress of the United States to act, to make a commitment it has not fully made in this century to the proposition that race has no place in American life or law." He proclaimed the nation's racial problem "a moral issue . . . as old as the Scriptures and as clear as the American Constitution."

After two and a half years of bowing to the political realities of congressional power, President Kennedy finally confronted the civil rights issue head-on. After months of equivocal language, he spoke bluntly:

> The heart of the question is whether all Americans are to be afforded equal rights and equal opportunities, whether we are going to treat our fellow Americans as we want to be treated. If an American, because his skin is dark, cannot eat lunch in a restaurant open to the public, if he cannot send his children to the best public school available, if he cannot vote for the public officials who represent him, if, in short, he cannot enjoy the full and free life which all of us want, then who among us would be content to have the color of his skin changed and stand in his place? Who among us would then be content with the counsels of patience and delay?

One week later, the president asked Congress to pass a broad civil rights bill, including provisions for desegregating public facilities, ending job discrimination, and empowering the U.S. attorney general to initiate school desegregation suits for those unable to do so themselves. A few days later the heads of eighteen trade unions declared their intention to stop racial discrimination in their organizations. Knowing the path through the Congress would be strewn with obstacles, civil rights leaders threatened a mass march on Washington if Kennedy's bill encountered a Senate filibuster. One southern senator, Allen Ellender (D-LA), accused blacks of "attempting to use their color to camouflage their lack of capability . . . when they cannot qualify to do a job they contend that they are being discriminated against because of their color."

In the meantime, JFK returned to his previous strategy of issuing executive orders on civil rights. He promulgated Executive Order 11114, which declared that it was the "policy of the United States to encourage by affirmative action the elimination of discrimination" in employment. The new order expanded the policy from federal contracts with private employers to any grants, loans, or other financial assistance to state and local governments. Additionally, employers with government contracts would have to open their records to the federal government, which could then determine compliance with the new policy. If a company was not in compliance, the government could rescind the contract and declare the business ineligible for future ones.

A journalist requested more specific information from Kennedy, regarding his civil rights policy in employment. The reporter asked if the president agreed with "some Negro leaders who are saying that like the Jews persecuted by the Nazis the Negro is entitled to some kind of special dispensation for the pain of second-class citizenship over these many decades and generations. What is your view of that in general, and what is your view in particular on the specific point that they are recommending of job quotas by race?" JFK responded that "the Negro community" generally did not advocate compensation for their race, particularly in education. "What I think they would like to see," JFK explained, "is their children well educated so that they could hold jobs and have their children accepted and have themselves accepted as equal members of the community." He admitted that the past could not be undone and that it

> is going to be with us for a good many years in uneducated men and women who lost their chance for a decent education. We have to do the best we can now. That is what we are trying to do. I don't think quotas are a very good idea. I think it is a mistake to begin to assign quotas on the basis of religion, or race, or color, or nationality. I think we'd get into a good deal of trouble. . . . On the other hand, I do think that we ought to make an effort to give a fair chance to everyone who is qualified — not through a quota, but just look over the employment rolls, look over our areas where we are hiring people and at least make sure we are giving everyone a fair chance. But not hard and fast quotas. We are too mixed, this society of ours, to begin to divide ourselves on the basis of race or color.

Just one week later, Kennedy's gradualist policy confronted the sense of urgency among civil rights advocates. On August 28, 1963, some 200,000 people (black and white) converged on the nation's capital for the March on Washington for Jobs and Freedom, which culminated with Dr. Martin Luther King Jr.'s historic oration on the steps of the dramatic Lincoln Memorial. His theme, which would become his epitaph, declared, "I have a dream." It was a dream, King asserted, that was "deeply rooted in the American dream. I have a dream that one day this nation will rise up and live out the true meaning of its creed: 'We hold these truths to be self-evident that all men are created equal.'" He told the throng that he looked forward to the day when his four young children would be judged not "by the color of their skin but by the content of their character." His stunning climax, uttered in the stirring cadences of a southern black preacher, roused the crowd as he proclaimed, "When we allow freedom to ring . . . we will be able to speed up the day when all of God's children, black men and white men, Jews and Gentiles, Protestants and Catholics, will be able to join hands and sing in the words of the old Negro spiritual, 'Free at last! Free at last! Thank God Almighty, we are free at last!'"

President Kennedy was genuinely impressed by King's oratorical skills, and JFK met with King, along with the march's other leaders, in the Oval Office later that day. At least the president's commitment to color-blind policy jibed with the demonstration's theme. JFK was also relieved over the peaceful outcome of the momentous event (after having amassed an unprecedented law enforcement and military presence in and around the nation's capital), but he continued to express his concerns about congressional opposition to the civil rights bill. His assessment was accurate, but he would not live to follow the ultimate course of the legislation. In the wake of Kennedy's assassination in Dallas on November 22, 1963, the new president, Lyndon Johnson, addressed the Congress with a fervent pledge to pursue the slain chief executive's policies, especially on civil rights: "No memorial or oration or eulogy could more eloquently honor President Kennedy's memory than the earliest possible passage of the civil rights bill for which he fought so long. We have talked long enough about equal rights in this country. We have talked for one hundred years or more. It is time now to write the next chapter and write it in the books of law."

An even more comprehensive bill, now supported by the Johnson administration, passed the House of Representatives relatively easily (290:130), but an eighty-two-day filibuster by southern senators delayed the bill's ultimate passage (73:27) through the upper house. A proud Lyndon Johnson, surrounded by the bill's supporters, including a still grieving Robert Kennedy, signed the 1964 Civil Rights Act into law at a ceremony in the Capitol on July 2. The act provided for, among other things, the extension of the Civil Rights Commission's tenure; the proscription of employment discrimination on the basis of race, color, sex (a last-minute addition), religion, or national origin; the prohibition of racial discrimination by voting registrars; judicial procedure to desegregate state and local government facilities; the exclusion of federal funding for public or private programs that discriminated on the basis of race, color, or national origin; and the proscription of race, color, or national origin discrimination in public accommodations that are linked to interstate commerce.

As black protests continued, with more brutal reactions from southern law enforcement, President Johnson submitted a bill to Congress that would finally end the unconstitutional effort of those who would deny blacks the right to vote in this country. Congress enacted the Voting Rights Act of 1965 and provided the legal mechanisms for overturning all legal roadblocks to black exercise of the franchise.

During congressional debates over the 1964 Civil Rights Act, opponents argued that Title VII of the bill, addressing equal employment opportunity, would inevitably lead to racial preferences and quotas in hiring. Senator Hubert Humphrey (D-MN), who managed the bill on the Senate floor, responded that "contrary to some opponents of this title, there is nothing in it that will give any power to the [proposed Equal Employment Opportunity] Commission or any court to require hiring, firing, or promotion of employees in order to meet a racial 'quota' or to achieve a certain racial balance." At one point in the debate, Humphrey offered to eat the pages of the bill if someone could point to the section requiring quotas! He described the quota question as a "bugaboo" and responded that "the very opposite is true. Title VII prohibits discrimination. In effect, it says that race, religion, and national origin are not to be used as the basis for hiring and firing. Title VII is designed to encourage hiring on the basis of ability and qualifications, not race or religion." Yet, ultimately, the title's section providing remedies for discrimination authorized judges to use "such affirmative action as may be appropriate," though quota hiring was not listed as a legal remedy. Indeed, Title VII stated, "Nothing contained in this title shall be interpreted to require any employer to grant preferential treatment to any individual or to any group" based on their "race, color, religion, sex, or national origin."

The victories represented by the Civil Rights Act of 1964 and the Voting Rights Act of 1965 were by no means the end of the movement to ensure full participation in American society for minorities and women. The summers of 1965 and 1966 witnessed more racial violence, especially in the streets of America's large cities with populous black ghettos, where deadly and destructive rioting occurred. President Johnson revealed his worries to a group of black bishops in 1966: "We have entered a new phase. . . . What if the cry for freedom becomes the sound of a brick cracking through a store window, turning over an automobile in the street, or the sound of a mob? If that sound should drown out the voices of reason, frustration will replace progress and all of our best work will be undone."

The Johnson administration, through its War on Poverty and other Great Society programs, was committed to economic advancement, particularly for the poorest of Americans. Assistant Secretary of Labor Daniel Patrick Moynihan had produced a report, "The Negro Family: The Case for National Action," detailing the adverse effects from years of poverty on blacks, especially young African Americans. Moynihan contributed to a 1965 speech delivered by President Johnson at the historically black Howard University in Washington, D.C. The speech would launch a new philosophical phase in the history of affirmative action. LBJ observed that "in far too many ways Negroes have been . . . deprived of freedom, crippled by hatred, the doors of opportunity closed to hope." Although the president expressed pride at the legislative progress made in establishing the legal framework for equal opportunity in employment, education, and voting, he declared that "freedom is not enough. You do not wipe away the scars of a century by saying":

> "Now you are free to go where you want, and do as you desire." . . . You do not take a person who for years has been hobbled by chains and liberate him, bring him up to the starting line of a race and then say, "You are free to compete with all the others," and still justly believe you have been completely fair. All our citizens must have the ability to walk through the gates. This is the next and more profound stage of the battle for civil rights. We seek not just freedom but opportunity. We seek not just legal equity but human ability, not just equality as a right and a theory but equality as a fact and equality as a result.

Johnson elaborated his theme: "Men and women of all races are born with the same range of abilities. But ability is not just the product of birth. Ability is stretched or stunted by the family that you live with, and the neighborhood you live in — by the school you go to and the poverty or the richness of your surroundings." He admitted that blacks would "have to rely mostly upon [their] own efforts," but he asserted that "endless years of hatred and hopelessness" meant that they "just cannot do it alone." Through his Great Society programs, Johnson intended to offer the government help that African Americans needed to overcome "the root causes of poverty." Later he again emphasized that blacks would have to "shoulder the responsibilities" in taking advantage of the new employment opportunities opened to them by Title VII, yet, in his Howard University speech, he had clearly opened what would become an unending debate over the distinctions between "equality of opportunity" and "equality of *result*."

The 1964 Civil Rights Act's Equal Employment Opportunity Commission began to define the kind of additional help minorities should expect from private business along the lines of "affirmative action," which would mean "aggressive recruitment" and training of minorities. "We must go out looking for potential employees," the EEOC instructed private businesses. "Let them know they are now welcome in places where doors were once closed . . . and give them special training so that they may qualify." In the wake of a deadly race riot in the Watts neighborhood of Los Angeles in 1965, President Johnson issued another executive order, 11246, which took additional steps to enforce equal opportunity in employment. It established the Office of Federal Contract Compliance (OFCC) and ordered federal contractors to take "reasonable efforts within a reasonable time" to comply with federal requirements of "affirmative action" in recruitment and employment to ensure that applicants and employees were treated "without regard to their race, creed, color, or national origin." The language was the same as President Kennedy's 1961 order, but the Johnson administration had ratcheted up the pressure on employers by focusing on "compliance." When that became the focus, measurement entered the picture. By what criteria could the government determine that contractors were *not* treating employees equally? An easy statistical measure, advocated by some civil rights leaders, would compare the percentage of minorities on a contractor's payroll with the percentage in the local population. Yet, if employers hired workers on the basis of their race, color, creed, or national origin to meet a population percentage, the company would be in direct violation of

Title VII's proscription on the use of such factors in employment. The dilemma within the dilemma had arrived: how could the United States end its historical racism through color-blind policies that, in effect, prompted color-conscious programs?

Professor John David Skrentny, in a sociological study of affirmative action, argues that this conflict between color-blind and color-conscious policies arose from the initial emphasis on the former by civil rights advocates. As Skrentny explains in *The Ironies of Affirmative Action*, "The problem was that anything beyond color blindness had a strange, taboolike quality. Advocacy of racial preference was one of those 'third rails' of American politics: Touch it and you die. In other words, advocate racial preference and lose your legitimacy as a serious player in American politics." The taboo had led Senator Humphrey to label quotas and racial balancing in employment "bugaboos" in floor debates over the 1964 Civil Rights Act. Yet, "the irony," argues Skrentny, "is that despite the enthusiasm for equal treatment and merit, we live in a society rife with exceptions to difference blindness, with exceptions to the abstract individual model as the base of the color blindness that dominated Congress in 1964." Farmers, senior citizens, and disaster victims are a few such groups who routinely receive special treatment from the government. This context provided one element that made the move toward race-based affirmative action less dangerous for policymakers.

In 1967 President Johnson performed a highly symbolic and color-conscious act in the civil rights movement by nominating the first African American to the nation's highest court. Thurgood Marshall, a veteran leader of successful civil rights litigation, including *Brown v. Board of Education*, which he argued at the Supreme Court, had been appointed by President Kennedy to the U.S. Second Circuit Court of Appeals in 1961. When Justice Tom Clark announced his retirement from the Supreme Court after his son Ramsey became attorney general in the Johnson cabinet, LBJ seized the opportunity to make history. On June 13, 1967, Johnson named Marshall to the nation's highest court, declaring: "He is the best qualified by training and by very valuable service to the country. I believe it is the right thing to do, the right time to do it, and the right man and the right place."

The last year of Johnson's presidency, 1968, proved a nightmare for him and the nation. The escalating war in Vietnam, and the massive draft of young men into the military, launched a vehement protest among the nation's youth. Shortly after antiwar candidate Senator Eugene McCarthy (D-MN) polled 42 percent of the vote in the New Hampshire primary, LBJ announced he would not run for a second term. This turn of events convinced Senator Robert Kennedy (D-NY) that he, too, should enter the presidential race, as an antiwar, pro–civil rights candidate. Kennedy had served as his brother's attorney general and played a key role in the 1964 civil rights legislation. Always a Johnson foe, RFK had resigned from the cabinet in 1964 and successfully ran for a Senate seat from the Empire State. While campaigning for the presidency in Indianapolis, Indiana, on April 4, 1968, Senator Kennedy received word that Martin Luther King Jr. had been murdered in Memphis, Tennessee, where he was leading a sanitation workers' strike. Kennedy announced the devastating news to a mostly black audience and calmed them with a plea to maintain Dr. King's commitment to nonviolence. Indianapolis was the only major U.S. city that did not erupt in violent rioting by blacks in the aftermath of King's assassination. Just two months later, Robert Kennedy was assassinated in Los Angeles as he left a campaign rally celebrating his California presidential primary victory.

By the end of the Johnson administration in 1969, the Labor Department had issued an unprecedented regulation requiring new contractors (businesses or labor unions) with the federal government to develop affirmative action plans with "specific goals and timetables" for hiring and promoting minorities. The governmental movement toward such numerical measures was already so relentless that even the Republican administration, led by Richard Nixon, who succeeded Johnson, promulgated a policy that required federal contractors and unions in the building trades to establish specific goals, targets, and timetables for hiring and promoting minorities. The new policy was labeled the Philadelphia Plan, for the "City of Brotherly Love," where the construction trade was 99 percent white, despite passage of the 1964 Civil Rights Act five years earlier and the fact that 30 percent of the city's population was black.

The Johnson and Nixon administrations hoped that this new version of affirmative action, using government contract funds to integrate the construction industry, would correct the inequity of white contractors and unions gladly accepting taxpayers' money, via federal contracts, but excluding blacks from employment. Thus, blacks were shut out of government largesse funded by their own tax money. The OFCC plan demanded that construction businesses and unions make "a good faith effort" to meet their personnel goals, which were based on moving closer to the percentage of minorities in the workforce at the job's location. Nixon and his attorney general, John Mitchell, argued that goals were not rigid quotas. Supporters of the program used the distinction (some would say without a difference) to maintain that it did not violate Title VII. Flexible goals were simply a lawful means to a lawful end of equal opportunity, maintained the Nixon administration. By 1970 it had expanded the Philadelphia Plan to cover *all* businesses that wanted contracts with the federal government; such contractors represented at least a quarter of the nation's labor force.

Skrentny argues that, ironically, it was white political and business elites who led the charge for affirmative action, even when public opinion and some civil rights leaders opposed abandoning the color-blind model. In the wake of race riots in the 1960s, Skrentny asserts, elites "followed a logic of crisis management, seeking to maintain order and control through affirmative action, one of the few means legitimate in the context of the Cold War and the rise of a global audience concerned with human rights." John Kennedy's call in 1960 for an end to racial discrimination against *individuals* as a means to distinguish the United States from enslaved Communist nations by 1970 had evolved into a concept of affirmative action that focused on taking racial *groups* into account when hiring and promoting. Instead of assessing the individual merit of an employment applicant, affirmative action now meant viewing how a minority employee could boost the percentage of blacks in a company or union in order to reflect the proportion of blacks in the workforce.

The U.S. Supreme Court confirmed this results-oriented measurement of racial group employment statistics in the 1971 case of *Griggs v. Duke Power Co.* The North Carolina company had a long record of racial discrimination in hiring, promotion, and pay prior to the passage of the 1964 Civil Rights Act. After the act's Title VII barred such discrimination in employment, Duke Power imposed requirements (a high school diploma and passage of two aptitude exams) for new hires and transfers within the company. With only 12 percent of black males in North Carolina having graduated from secondary school, and their poor performance on the company's tests, black representation in Duke Power's workforce remained low, especially in higher-paying positions. In the first high court interpretation of Title VII, the justices ruled unanimously in *Griggs* that ostensibly neutral hiring and personnel requirements (diplomas and test scores) are illegal if they perpetuate the effects of previous discrimination, thus continuing a "disparate impact" on a racial group protected by Title VII.

Given America's racially entwined history, it was inevitable that electoral politics in the 1970s would respond to the affirmative action movement. The South, which had been solidly Democratic for decades in reaction to its Civil War defeat at the hands of Lincoln's Republican Party, swung over to the GOP camp in the 1960s. In the wake of his signing the 1964 Civil Rights Act, President Johnson was so unpopular in the South that he sent his genteel wife, Lady Bird, to campaign for him in the southern states during the 1964 presidential campaign. Southern whites continued to abandon the Democratic Party in droves, however, as blacks swelled the Democratic ranks through their newly found franchise after passage of the 1965 Voting Rights Act. Nixon, eager to capture the states of the old Confederacy, began to appeal to the "silent majority," including southern whites distressed over the Black Power movement and what they perceived as special preferences given to African Americans. White male labor unionists in the so-called Rust Belt (northeastern and midwestern states), where American industry was struggling, resented affirmative action to hire minorities. Republican Ronald Reagan, who captured the White House in 1980, even turned the "hard hats" (many of whom were ethnic Catholics who had been part of FDR's New Deal coalition) into what were labeled "Reagan Democrats" during his two-term presidency. Nixon had attracted white male voters in the 1972 presidential election by forsaking affirmative action, condemning it for using quotas and ignoring hiring and promotion based on merit. By 1977 a Gallup poll indicated that not one demographic group, including minorities, supported affirmative action, expressed in the polling question as "preferential treatment in getting jobs and places in college" for women and minorities as a way to compensate "for past discrimination." The Reagan administration continued this popular anti-quota theme through the 1980s and immediately dismantled

Democratic president Jimmy Carter's affirmative action programs to place more minorities and women on the lower federal courts.

Yet the Nixon administration, regardless of Nixon's campaign rhetoric, did *not* abandon affirmative action. In fact, the federal government expanded it to university contracts, including contracts for research, requiring institutions of higher learning to establish plans for equal opportunity in employment. This move enraged Jewish academics who had been subject to quota systems in academe that limited the number of their coreligionists in the student body and on faculties. One Jewish political scientist, who had escaped from Nazi Germany in 1937, was told by his department chair at an Ivy League university that he could not promote the young, and demonstrably meritorious, professor because "we've already promoted a Jew this year." A number of Jewish neoconservatives, those who had been liberal Democrats and even Marxists, led the scholarly charge against racial preferences. Indeed, the academic setting would provide a proving ground for affirmative action in the federal judicial system. Tocqueville's adage that eventually every American political issue becomes a judicial one applied to affirmative action by the 1970s.

CHAPTER 2

Bakke to the Future
Affirmative Action Precedents

The first affirmative action case in education that the U.S. Supreme Court considered began at the University of Washington Law School, which had denied admission to Marco DeFunis, a white male, despite the fact that his entrance exam scores were higher than those of some minorities the law school admitted. DeFunis brought suit in a Washington trial court, arguing that the law school's admissions committee violated his Fourteenth Amendment guarantee of equal protection by using different criteria and procedures for nonminority applicants. The trial court ruled in his favor and ordered his admittance to the law school. On appeal, the Washington Supreme Court overturned the trial court's judgment, holding that the law school's policy was constitutional. By the time DeFunis's appeal made its way to the nation's highest tribunal for consideration, he was in his third and final year at the University of Washington. Because of that fact, the high court ruled in 1974 that the case was moot and refused to decide the constitutional question posed by DeFunis's appeal. Who could blame the five justices who voted to decline the appeal for wanting to buy more time to decide one of the twentieth century's most vexatious constitutional questions? They knew that soon enough the issue would again confront them.

Indeed it would. Just four years later the U.S. Supreme Court issued its first substantive ruling on affirmative action — in another case that arrived from academe and also involved a professional school. The University of California at Davis Medical School, founded in 1968, had no intention of discriminating against minorities. Yet its first class of 50 students had no blacks, Mexican Americans, or American Indians. Over the next two years, the faculty developed an affirmative action plan that, starting in 1971, doubled the size of the entering class (to 100) and set aside 16 of the positions for "disadvantaged" applicants to be chosen by a special admissions committee. In practice, "disadvantaged" meant minorities. Students accepted under the special program for the reserved 16 seats had lower grade point averages and Medical College Admissions Test (MCAT) scores than those students who competed for the 84 remaining positions in the entering class. In 1973 the average GPA of the "disadvantaged" admitted students was 2.88, in contrast to 3.49 for the other accepted students. The former group had an average MCAT ranking in the thirty-fifth percentile, whereas the latter group averaged in the eighty-third percentile.

Allan Bakke, a white male, applied to the UC-Davis Medical School in 1973 and 1974; each time the school rejected him, as did the other eleven schools to which he applied. Some of the schools that rejected him said he was too old. Bakke was thirty-three years of age when he first applied to medical school. Despite having earned an undergraduate degree from the University of Minnesota in mechanical engineering (with just under an A average), serving as a marine captain in Vietnam, receiving a master's degree in engineering from Stanford University, and working as an aerospace engineer at NASA, Bakke decided in midcareer that he really wanted to be a doctor. He took biology and chemistry courses required for medical school admission while he continued to work full-time and volunteered in a hospital emergency room. His overall GPA was 3.51, and his MCAT score placed him in the ninetieth percentile. Not only were his statistics significantly higher than those of the minority students accepted under the special program, but he even outscored the average GPA and MCAT rank of the students accepted via the regular admissions process.

Bakke believed that the affirmative action program at UC-Davis had blocked his admittance to the medical school, which was his first choice because of its proximity to his home. He wrote a letter to the chair of the admissions committee, arguing his conviction that "a significant fraction of medical school applicants [at UCD] is judged by a separate criteria [sic]. I am referring to quotas, open or covert, for racial minorities. I realize the rationale for these quotas is that they attempt to atone for past racial discrimination, but insisting on a new racial bias in favor of minorities is not a just situation." With that, the white male struggle against "reverse discrimination" commenced.

Bakke's first stop was a California state trial court where his lawyer contended that UCD unlawfully discriminated against him on the basis of his race when it prevented him from competing for the sixteen reserved seats and by operating a two-track admissions system. According to Bakke's position, the medical school's action violated the U.S. Constitution's Fourteenth Amendment's equal protection clause, a similar provision in the California constitution, and the 1964 Civil Rights Act's Title VI, which provides: "No person in the United States shall, on the ground of race, color, or national origin, be excluded from participation in, be denied the benefits of, or be subjected to discrimination under any program or activity receiving Federal financial assistance." The California trial court ruled that the medical school's admissions program violated the U.S. Constitution by giving preference to minority students; the California Supreme Court affirmed and ordered Bakke's admission. Without admitting him, the University of California at Davis, afraid that all its affirmative action programs would be invalidated, appealed the California Supreme Court's decision to the U.S. Supreme Court. The high tribunal accepted the case, *Regents of the University of California v. Bakke*, and heard a two-hour oral argument on it in October 1977.

The lawyers for the university, led by the venerable Archibald Cox, asserted that the classifications used in the medical school's affirmative action program, and its quota of accepting at least sixteen minority applicants, were legal because they were meant to be inclusive rather than exclusive. The special admissions criteria for minorities were to remedy the effects of societal discrimination. UCD also offered a quartet of reasons to justify the affirmative action plan: (1) to improve medical education by including diverse students from different segments of society; (2) to diminish separation of minorities from the American mainstream by including them in the medical profession; (3) to provide role models for minority children by proving that the medical profession was open to them; and (4) to improve health care in communities traditionally underserved by the medical profession. Moreover, if universities could use factors other than merit as demonstrated by grades and test scores, including geographic origin and athletic prowess, why couldn't racial classifications be applied?

Allan Bakke's lawyer, Reynold Colvin, emphasized that the Constitution was color-blind, and that quotas based on minority status were therefore unconstitutional, even if they were to help previously excluded racial and ethnic groups. He argued: "The Equal Protection

Clause [of the Fourteenth Amendment] does not expand and contract depending upon the purpose behind racial discrimination." Additionally, how far could UCD go in setting aside medical school seats for minorities? Could half of the 100 positions be reserved for minorities? Could all 100? And why should white applicants be penalized for their race?

Solicitor General Wade McCree presented the United States' position, backing UCD, at oral argument. He noted that Congress and the executive branch had allowed (indeed required) race to be considered in such programs as hiring and promotion by government contractors, loans for minority-owned businesses, and special scholarships for minorities. He assured the nine justices that such affirmative action efforts were temporary, but necessary, to combat the ravages of historical discrimination and achieve full racial equality. In interpreting the Fourteenth Amendment, the solicitor general returned to President Johnson's affirmative action metaphor from the 1966 speech at Howard University: "The Fourteenth Amendment should not only require equality of treatment, but should also permit persons who were held back to be brought up to the starting line where the opportunity for equality will be meaningful." Even if accepted minority applicants had lower GPAs and MCAT scores, the solicitor general asserted that they would have already demonstrated their ability to overcome the hardship of societal discrimination.

After seven months of reviewing the case record and an unprecedented number of amici curiae briefs (58) submitted by 150 interested parties, the Court finally handed down its decision in late June 1978. Its final product encompassed seven different opinions that covered 154 pages. In effect, the justices were split 4:4:1. On each issue raised by the case, the vote was 5:4, with centrist Justice Lewis F. Powell Jr. casting the swing vote between the liberals in this case (Justices William Brennan, Thurgood Marshall, Byron White, and Harry Blackmun) and the conservatives (Justices Stewart, Rehnquist, and Stevens and Chief Justice Warren Burger).

Justice Powell's controlling opinion applied "strict scrutiny" to the UC-Davis Medical School's program. On a sliding scale of equal protection clause analysis, which the Supreme Court developed in the twentieth century, the justices apply strict scrutiny to a contested government policy when it classifies based on race, ethnicity, or alienage or involves voting or interstate travel. In this highest category of judicial examination, the public entity using the "suspect classifications" or impacting "fundamental rights" must prove a "compelling state interest" and demonstrate a "narrow tailoring" of the policy and an "exact fit" between the classifications and the state interest. Using strict scrutiny, Powell ruled for himself and the four conservatives that UCD's rigid quota of sixteen seats for minority students was invalid for creating an unconstitutional broadly tailored, two-track admissions process on the basis of race and ethnicity. The quota resulted in a simple mathematical inequality; minorities could compete for all 100 seats in the entering medical school class, but whites could vie for only the remaining 84, after the 16 quota seats were filled with minorities.

Nevertheless, Powell, the courtly Virginian who had led the Richmond school board during the tumult of desegregation, argued that "the interest of diversity is compelling in the context of a university's admission programs [at the undergraduate, graduate, and professional levels]." Moreover, a narrowly tailored plan for admitting minorities could pass constitutional muster. Powell cited Harvard's admissions plan as a constitutional example in which the university used race and ethnicity as a "plus" (along with other personal attributes like "geographic origin or a life spent on a farm") for its undergraduate admissions decisions but did not segregate a minority applicant from comparison with other applicants or use quotas for admitting minorities. Harvard had provided its plan to the Court in an amicus brief, and Powell appended the plan to his opinion.

The four liberal justices in *Bakke*, led by Justice Brennan, argued that the Fourteenth Amendment allowed a university to establish a voluntary, race-conscious program that might include numerically based racial preferences to remedy the effects of past discrimination. On the opposite end of the spectrum, the four conservative justices in the dispute, led by Justice Stevens, maintained that Title VI unequivocally invalidated UCD's preferential admissions program for minorities. With Solomonic skill, Powell found a middle ground between these two poles. Affirmative action plans were unconstitutional if they used rigid quotas based on race/ethnicity. Therefore, Bakke won that part of his argument, and the Court ordered his admittance to the UCD medical school. He ultimately graduated, became an anesthesiologist, and returned to his native Minnesota to practice his dream profession. But affirmative action programs that used race or ethnicity as a "plus" factor (among others), did *not* use quotas, and did *not* utilize separate processes for admissions decisions were valid under Powell's judgment.

Although there was something for each side of the affirmative action debate to support in Powell's decision, like all compromises, it contained something for both positions to oppose. The affirmative action dilemma within the dilemma had taken on yet another complex facet. To create campus diversity, universities could take race into consideration to benefit minorities — but only certain kinds of consideration: pluses, yes; quotas, no. Because the "diversity as compelling state interest" assertion and the "plus" factor of Powell's opinion were not joined by the four other justices who signed on to his judgment, however, those segments were not considered precedential by some observers. It would be left to a future Court, the one that tackled the University of Michigan cases twenty-five years later, to determine the legal weight of Powell's reasoning in those two parts of his opinion.

Justice Powell's compromise seemingly molded public opinion in its favor. A 1979 Harris poll revealed that 79 percent of those surveyed approved of affirmative action (in contrast to the 1977 Gallup poll) because "after years of discrimination it is only fair to set up special programs to make sure that women and minorities are given every chance to have equal opportunities in employment and education" — "as long as there are no rigid quotas."

The U.S. Supreme Court, however, did not sustain Powell's approach to affirmative action — one that eschews strict numerical quotas — in two *employment* cases that came before the tribunal in the two years after *Bakke*. The 1979 case of *United Steelworkers of America v. Weber* arose when yet another white male, Brian Weber, argued that he had been the victim of unconstitutional reverse discrimination. Kaiser Aluminum and Chemical Corporation and the United Steelworkers of America union entered into what they termed a "voluntary" and "temporary" affirmative action plan to try to boost the number of higher-paid black craftsmen at the Kaiser plant in Gramercy, Louisiana. At least half of the thirteen on-the-job training positions were reserved for blacks. Weber, who was passed over for one of the coveted training jobs, filed suit in federal district court, claiming a violation of Title VII of the 1964 Civil Rights Act. As noted earlier, Title VII explicitly bans racial discrimination in employment and categorically denies that the title requires racial preferences be used to correct "an imbalance which may exist." Moreover, debates on the Senate floor in 1964 also made crystal clear that Title VII in no way was intended to result in racial preferences or quotas in employment decisions. Brian Weber might well have thought he had both the law and its legislative history on his side. In fact, the lower federal courts agreed and decided in Weber's favor that the challenged affirmative action plan was a violation of Title VII.

Yet neither Weber nor the lower tribunals reckoned on Justice William J. Brennan Jr.'s legal interpretation once the case arrived at the nation's highest court. With only seven justices sitting in the case (Powell and Stevens did not participate), Brennan produced a stunning 5:2 holding for the United Steelworkers' affirmative action plan. Joined by Justices Marshall, White, Stewart, and Blackmun, he conceded that the two courts below had indeed read the *letter* of the law correctly. But Title VII's *spirit* compelled a different result. If the 1964 Congress's concern had been, as Brennan put it, for "the plight of the Negro in our economy," then it would be "ironic indeed" if Title VII would be used to prohibit "all voluntary private, race-conscious efforts to abolish traditional patterns" of discrimination.

Justice Rehnquist's angry dissent accused the Brennan majority of countering the explicit language and intent of the 1964 Civil Rights Act, which was to require racial equality. "With today's holding," Rehnquist fumed, "the Court introduces . . . a tolerance for the very evil that the law was intended to eradicate, without offering even a clue as to what the limits on that tolerance may be. . . . The Court has sown the wind. Later courts will face the impossible task of reaping the whirlwind."

Despite Rehnquist's grim prediction, a majority of the justices were not persuaded by his argument in the next affirmative action case to come before them. In 1980 the U.S. Supreme Court faced its third such challenge in as many years. A provision of the Public Works Employment Act of 1977 (PWEA) required that 10 percent of the federal funds expended for local public works projects must be used to procure services or supplies from minority business enterprises (MBEs), defined in the statute as companies in which blacks, Hispanics, Orientals, American Indians, Eskimos, or Aleuts controlled at least a 50 percent interest. In *Fullilove v. Klutznick*, associations of construction contractors and subcontractors challenged the 10 percent set-aside provision as invalid under the equal protection component of the Fifth Amendment's Due Process Clause and Title VI of the 1964 Civil Rights Act, proscribing racial discrimination in any program receiving federal financial assistance. The contractors had to raise their constitutional question under the Fifth Amendment because the *federal* government had established the program at issue; the Fourteenth Amendment applies only to *state* or *local* governments and their entities.

A six-justice majority affirmed the federal court of appeals ruling that the set-aside provision did *not* violate the Fifth Amendment or Title VII. As in *Bakke*, the Court was badly fractured, producing six opinions. No opinion garnered a majority, but Chief Justice Burger's plurality opinion, joined by Justices White and Powell, announced the Court's judgment. He argued that the PWEA's objective was to ensure that the letting of federal government contracts for public works projects would not result in perpetuating discrimination that had historically impaired or foreclosed access by minority businesses to public funds. The PWEA had appropriated $4 billion for public works projects. Burger declared that such an objective was within the spending power of Congress (art. I, § 8, cl. 1). As to the means Congress employed (the 10 percent set-aside) to meet its objective, the chief justice validated the provision's "narrowly tailored" and "temporary" use of racial and ethnic criteria. (In fact, the policy became permanent in 1987 and added "women" to the list of "minority business enterprises" for which set-asides would apply.)

Justice Stewart, who had joined the majority in *Weber* to uphold the affirmative action plan, but had been on the other side in *Bakke*, voted against the government's set-aside program in *Fullilove*. In his dissent, he opined that the MBE provision, on its face, denied equal protection of the law by barring one class of business owners from the opportunity to partake of a government benefit on the basis of the owners' racial and ethnic attributes. Stewart repeated Justice John Marshall Harlan I's famous 1896 dissent in *Plessy v. Ferguson:* "Our Constitution is color-blind, and neither knows nor tolerates classes among its citizens." Justice John Paul Stevens also wrote a blistering dissent, criticizing the 10 percent set-aside as a "slapdash" law that failed to distinguish different degrees of injury sustained by the various minorities at issue. "Racial classifications," Stevens asserted, "are simply too pernicious to permit any but the most exact connection between justification and classification," which is the criterion required under strict scrutiny.

In the private sector, affirmative action goals and timetables, as the CEO of Merck explained it, had become "part of our culture and corporate procedures." Ninety-five percent of 120 large corporation CEOs agreed with the "use of numerical objectives to track the progress of women and minorities" in their companies. The corporate world had embraced diversity for its positive effects on all aspects of business. In addition, companies did not want to face employment discrimination lawsuits, and so they adopted affirmative means of increasing the numbers of minorities and women in their workforces.

Yet, with the anti–affirmative action Reagan administration firmly entrenched, and a recession tightening government budgets in the early 1980s, the judicial landscape surrounding race and employment began to shift. In 1984 the Supreme Court faced a new set of facts in hiring practices. This case, *Firefighters Local Union #1784 v. Stotts*, sprang from a 1980 court-approved affirmative action plan for the firefighters of Memphis, Tennessee. It required that at least 50 percent of all new employees be black until at least 40 percent of the department was African American. Prior to the affirmative action plan, Memphis had increased the number of its black firefighters from 4 percent to 11.5 percent of the department. When a budget crisis occurred in 1981, the city announced that it would follow a traditional "last-hired-first-fired" policy negotiated with the firefighters' union. The policy laid off black firefighters who had less seniority than their white counterparts. A federal district court denied the city's right to fire the new black firefighters, and, as a result, three more senior whites lost their jobs to three recently hired blacks. Both the city of Memphis and the firefighters' union appealed the case to the U.S. Supreme Court.

This time the white males won. Coincidentally, it was Justice *White* who wrote the opinion for the 6:3 Court, ruling that Title VII of the 1964 Civil Rights Act clearly "protects bona fide seniority systems," unless they are intentionally discriminatory or minorities can prove that they were the victims of individual employment discrimination. Where seniority was at issue, Justice White abandoned the pro–affirmative action position he had held in *Bakke, Weber,* and *Fullilove.* Predictably, Justices Brennan and Marshall, joined by Justice Blackmun, were in dissent, voting to moot the case because Memphis had canceled the layoff orders.

Seniority would again be the issue in the Court's next affirmative action case, *Wygant v. Jackson Board of Education,* a 1986 decision involving the Jackson, Michigan, school district's plan to lay off white teachers with seniority over black teachers, in order to preserve hiring gains for the latter. Once more, the justices were badly split, issuing six separate opinions in their 5:4 decision holding the Jackson plan unconstitutional as a violation of the Fourteenth Amendment's equal protection clause. Again, it fell to Justice Powell to draw the fine judicial lines. He argued that giving preference to "minority role models" to compensate for past societal discrimination did not constitute a "compelling state interest" to justify laying off white teachers with seniority. A *hiring* plan that preferred minorities might, however, pass constitutional muster, Powell suggested.

The Court's most junior justice, Sandra Day O'Connor, who had joined the Court in 1981 as its first female member, contributed an ironic concurring opinion in *Wygant.* She rejected the Reagan administration's contention that affirmative action could only be used to remedy discrimination against individual victims. "A carefully constructed affirmative action plan . . . need not be limited to the remedying of specific instances of identified discrimination," O'Connor wrote in her concurrence. The irony of her opinion lay in the fact that she was countering the very administration that had placed her on the bench. An additional paradox in her presence on the Court arose from the proclamations that President Ronald Reagan made against affirmative action, which he then, in turn, used to appoint the nation's first woman justice of the U.S. Supreme Court. He did so to fulfill a pledge he made in the 1980 presidential campaign when polls showed Reagan's rate of support among women to be lower than among male voters. Of course, O'Connor was not unaware of the factors that led to her appointment. After Justice Antonin Scalia launched into a tirade against affirmative action at one of the Court's private conferences in 1987, the only woman on the bench responded, "Well, Nino [Scalia's nickname], how do you think I got my job?"

In a tribute to her colleague Thurgood Marshall, Justice O'Connor admitted that "like most of [her] counterparts who grew up in the Southwest in the 1930s and 1940s [she] had not been personally exposed to racial tensions before *Brown* [*v. Board of Education*]. . . . [She] had no personal sense . . . of being a minority in a society that cared primarily for the majority." She wrote privately to Justice Powell during their exchanges on *Wygant*, however, to say, "I am inclined to think there is a legitimate state interest in promoting racial diversity in public school facilities."

In two more affirmative action cases decided by the Supreme Court in 1986, *Firefighters v. Cleveland* and *Sheet Metal Workers v. EEOC*, narrow majorities upheld Cleveland's promotion of one minority for every white firefighter promoted and a federal court's order requiring a New York sheet metal workers' union to meet a specific minority goal of 29.23 percent. Led by Justice Brennan, in direct opposition to the Reagan administration's stance, the Court asserted that the 1964 Civil Rights Act's Title VII did not apply remedies solely to actual victims of unlawful discrimination. Rather, quotas could be used to bolster minority group representation in workforces.

Justice Brennan also prevailed during the Supreme Court's next term in the 1987 decision *United States v. Paradise*, which upheld strict racial promotion quotas to overcome "long-term, open and pervasive discrimination." In 1983 and 1984, a U.S. district court judge in Alabama had ordered the state to promote one black state trooper for each white state trooper until Alabama could develop an affirmative action plan acceptable to the judge. Even Justice Powell, who would announce his retirement at the end of the Court's term in 1987, approved of the rigid quota system at issue in *Paradise*. He distinguished his position from the one he advocated, against quotas, in *Bakke* by contending that the Alabama quota for black state troopers imposed by the lower federal court judge was "short in duration" and "likely to be relatively diffuse" in its impact on "innocent white workers." Moreover, he cited evidence that Alabama "had engaged in persistent violation of constitutional rights and repeatedly failed to carry out court orders."

Court-ordered quotas were relatively rare, contrary to Republican Party attacks, which indicated that "activist" judges frequently imposed numerical hiring and promotion requirements on employers.

Yet, when no black employees appeared in the workforces of Cleveland's firefighters, Alabama's state troopers, or New York's sheet metal unions a full twenty years after Title VII of the 1964 Civil Rights Act outlawed racial discrimination, federal courts turned to quotas as a remedy for such egregious contempt for the law.

Justice O'Connor took a different view, penning the lead dissent in *Paradise*. She maintained that the federal judge should have ordered a remedial plan "that was narrowly tailored to accomplish [the] purpose" of eradicating the effects of Alabama's "egregious history of discrimination." O'Connor added that no evidence existed to justify "such an extreme quota" in order to eradicate the effects of Alabama's delay in developing a nondiscriminatory hiring program. She suggested that fining the state would have resulted in no diminution of the rights of white state trooper applicants. A shift in the Court's personnel before the 1986–1987 term produced a new lineup joining O'Connor's dissent. When Chief Justice Warren Burger announced his retirement in the summer of 1986, President Reagan shrewdly promoted Justice Rehnquist to chief justice and named Judge Antonin Scalia, of the U.S. Court of Appeals in Washington, to replace him. In so doing, Reagan now had a firm and reliable conservative in the chief's chair and an equally staunch conservative as the newest associate justice.

One month after *Paradise*, yet another affirmative action decision, this one with a gender twist, came down from the high tribunal. *Johnson v. Transportation Agency, Santa Clara County* validated the California agency's job promotion preferences for women. Paul Johnson, a white male, had worked for the Transportation Agency in Santa Clara for thirteen years and had scored two points higher than the successful applicant, Diane Joyce, for the position of road dispatcher — a job no women had ever held. By a vote of 6:3, the Brennan-led majority ruled that, even without any evidence that a particular employer had discriminated against women or minorities, that same employer could use race and *gender* preferences in hiring and promotions in order to bring its workforce into line with the local population or labor market. Brennan contended: "Given the obvious imbalance in the skilled craft division and given the agency's commitment to eliminating such imbalances . . . it was appropriate to consider as one fact the sex of Mrs. Joyce in making its decision." Once again, Brennan saw no impediment from Title VII, asserting that its purpose was to eliminate the effects of employment discrimination. He garnered the votes of Justices Marshall, Blackmun, Powell, Stevens, and O'Connor. The Court's only female justice was uneasy with the breadth of Brennan's conclusion, however. In a separate concurring opinion, O'Connor viewed Santa Clara's voluntary affirmative action plan as "ill-defined," especially in light of "limitations imposed by the Constitution and the provisions of Title VII." Yet she agreed with the majority's reading of the Court's affirmative action precedents.

Constitutional historian Mel Urofsky has observed: "One of Justice Brennan's concerns in his majority opinion in Johnson was keeping O'Connor with him, a struggle he eventually lost. He tweaked his draft opinion as much as he could to get her and Powell to stay on board; he got Powell, but not O'Connor. This is an important case in trying to read the tea leaves regarding O'Connor and affirmative action." She was willing to allow affirmative action to compensate for past discrimination, and perhaps for other compelling reasons, but it had to be carefully defined, narrowly tailored, and limited in duration.

Justice Scalia, taking the lead as a harsh opponent of affirmative action, wrote a blunt and blistering dissent in which he criticized the *Johnson* decision as "effectively requir[ing] employers, public as well as private, to engage in intentional discrimination on the basis of race or sex. . . . A statute [Title VII] designed to establish a color-blind and gender-blind work place has thus been converted into a powerful engine of racism and sexism." In an obvious slap at his liberal colleagues, Brennan, Marshall, and Blackmun, Scalia concluded that white males, like Mr. Johnson, "predominantly unknown, unaffluent, unorganized — suffer this injustice at the hands of a court fond of thinking itself the champion of the politically impotent."

Justice Powell's retirement from the Court at the end of its term in 1987 unleashed a long and intense fight over replacing his "swing vote" on the high bench. President Reagan eagerly nominated Judge Robert Bork of the U.S. Court of Appeals in Washington, a well-known conservative in the mold of the Reagan Revolution then under way. A former law professor, Bork had written extensively on constitutional law, revealing his staunch views opposed to the liberal activism of the Supreme Court since the 1950s. The Senate, which had swung to the Democratic column in the 1986 midterm elections, countered the Reagan administration's attempt to tip the balance on the nation's high court. Senator Edward Kennedy (D-MA) unleashed a bombastic attack against the nominee on the Senate floor. Liberal interest groups labored tirelessly for Bork's defeat. Following hearings before the Senate Judiciary Committee, in which an arrogant and pedantic Bork did not advance his cause, his nomination went down to defeat in the full Senate 42:58. After another failed nomination, that of Judge Douglas Ginsburg, also of the D.C. Circuit, whose name Reagan had to withdraw after the press reported that the nominee had smoked marijuana with his Harvard Law School students while a professor there, the president chose Judge Anthony Kennedy of the U.S. Ninth Circuit Court of Appeals to replace Justice Powell. The Californian was considered a moderate conservative, and his skillful performance before the Senate Judiciary Committee helped to assure his unanimous confirmation by the full Senate.

Justice Kennedy joined the Court in the middle of its 1987–1988 term; by the tribunal's next session, he was already making his presence felt in affirmative action cases by voting on the opposite side from his predecessor Justice Powell. In early 1989 Kennedy voted with a 6:3 majority, led by Justice O'Connor, invalidating in the case *City of Richmond v. J. A. Croson Co.* a local set-aside law in Virginia's capital that channeled 30 percent of public-works funds to minority-owned construction companies. O'Connor observed, "The 30 percent quota cannot in any realistic sense be tied to any injury suffered by anyone," including the Spanish-speaking, Oriental, Indian, Eskimo, or Aleutian groups cited in the ordinance, along with blacks. She added pointedly, "It may well be that Richmond has never had an Aleut or Eskimo citizen." O'Connor concluded that "an amorphous claim that there has been past discrimination in a particular industry cannot justify the use of an unyielding racial quota." The city's affirmative action policy failed all her criteria under strict judicial scrutiny. It was neither carefully defined nor narrowly tailored to remedy specific past discrimination, nor was it of limited duration.

At the end of the term in June 1989, a quintet of employment cases also reversed, or chipped away, elements of the Court's previous jurisprudence, with O'Connor in the majority. (She was diagnosed with breast cancer at the beginning of the 1988–1989 term, and, although she missed not one day on the bench after surgery or chemotherapy, she did not write the key opinions in the five employment cases.) The *Wards Cove Packing Co. v. Atonio* decision ruled 5:4 that a statistical disparity between an employer's workforce and the community's racial composition did not prove discrimination. Overturning the 1971 precedent (*Griggs v. Duke Power Co.*), *Wards Cove* shifted the burden of proving discriminatory effects of employment policies from employers to employees.

In another 5:4 ruling (*Martin v. Wilks*), the Supreme Court determined that white workers, alleging reverse discrimination from court-approved affirmative action settlements (known as consent decrees), could challenge them even if they took no part in the original litigation. A third five-justice majority ruled in *Lorance v. AT&T Technologies* that lawsuits claiming that seniority systems are discriminatory must be filed within 300 days of their adoption. A 5:4 judgment by the high court in *Jett v. Dallas Independent School District* limited damage suits against state and local government for racial discrimination to the Civil Rights Act of 1871. Finally, Justice Kennedy wrote for a unanimous Supreme Court in *Patterson v. McLean Credit Union* that the Civil Rights Act of 1866 could not be used for claims of on-the-job discrimination in the private sector, though it could still be used for such claims at the initial hiring stage.

Just when it appeared that the high tribunal had turned firmly, if by narrow majorities, against affirmative action, it approved in *Metro Broadcasting, Inc. v. Federal Communications Commission* (1990) a two-pronged policy promoting minority ownership of the airwaves. During the Carter administration, the FCC promulgated a policy that favored minority-owned broadcasting companies in bids for new licenses and created a limited category of existing radio and television broadcast stations that could be transferred only to minority-controlled firms. Once more Justice Brennan, by then eighty-four years of age, proved why he was fond of telling his new law clerks each term that the most important word at the Court was *five*, because that many votes could carry the day in any case. He had persuaded Justice White to join the majority. Brennan's 5:4 majority opinion in *Metro* asserted "that benign race conscious measures mandated by Congress — even if those measures are not 'remedial' in the sense of being designed to compensate victims of past governmental or societal discrimination — are constitutionally permissible."

O'Connor was perturbed over Brennan's use of "intermediate," rather than strict, judicial scrutiny, in the FCC decision, which she thought should have been controlled by her majority opinion in the Richmond set-aside case. She saw the federal government policy favoring minorities in broadcast licensing as stereotyping how racial or ethnic groups act and think. Under strict judicial scrutiny, which she imposed in *Croson*, such stigmatizing was certainly not a compelling state interest.

The FCC decision would be Brennan's swan song to the Court, where he had served since Eisenhower appointed him in 1956. Later in the summer of 1990, Justice Brennan suffered a mild stroke, and his physician encouraged him to step down from the bench. President George H. W. Bush nominated Judge David Souter, newly appointed judge on the First U.S. Circuit Court of Appeals, who Bush thought was a moderate conservative.

Congress responded swiftly to the 1989 quintet of employment decisions in which the Supreme Court reached conservative outcomes, including shifting the burden in employment discrimination cases from the employer to the employee. The legislation amended Title VII of the 1964 Civil Rights Act to allow, in addition to racial and ethnic minorities, religious minorities, the disabled, and women to bring suit against their employers for discrimination or sexual harassment, and to collect back pay and punitive damages if the jury found in their favor. After vigorous debates, particularly over the quota issue, Congress passed the Civil Rights Act of 1991. President George H. W. Bush then signed it into law, when polls clearly showed that businesses continued to support affirmative action goals for hiring and promotion of minorities and women in order to create diverse workforces. The Supreme Court decided 8:1 in 1993, however, that the new legislation did not apply to cases pending when Congress passed it.

Despite ongoing support for affirmative action in the corporate world, historian Terry Anderson argues that the anti-quota rhetoric of the Reagan-Bush era began to erode public support for affirmative action in general. Starting in the mid-1980s, polls showed that less than 25 percent of white respondents supported racial preferences for college admissions, and even fewer whites condoned such preferences in employment.

As the Supreme Court ended its 1990–1991 term in June, Justice Thurgood Marshall, Justice Brennan's jurisprudential soul mate and the tribunal's only racial minority, also succumbed to ill health and announced his retirement. President Bush faced a quandary: African Americans saw the Marshall position as the "black seat" on the high court, in the tradition of seats previously reserved for geographic constituencies, Catholics, and Jews. Yet Bush had voiced his opposition to racial quotas in employment and education, so he could hardly nominate a justice solely because of his or her race. In addition, he had riled the conservative wing of his party by failing to continue the Reagan legacy in many policy areas; therefore, he could ill afford to widen the chasm by nominating a politically moderate, let alone a liberal, minority.

Finding a qualified conservative African American lawyer, however, was somewhat problematic. On the other hand, conservatives had been grooming Clarence Thomas for this opportunity. A liberal until early adulthood, Thomas had come to despise affirmative action. Such programs had aided his admission to Yale Law School, but he realized that race-conscious plans could stigmatize their recipients. Neither white students nor blacks with more elite backgrounds accepted him at Yale. After law school, he had hoped to return to his native Georgia, whence he had risen from abject childhood poverty, but major law firms in the state rebuffed him. He therefore had spent most of his career in public service, with Senator John Danforth (R-MO) as his mentor and advocate. Thomas had worked in the Civil Rights Division of the U.S. Department of Education and had headed the Equal Employment Opportunity Commission, where he had made public statements against racial preferences in employment. He had served briefly on the U.S. Court of Appeals in Washington when Bush selected him to succeed Thurgood Marshall.

Civil rights groups portrayed varied reactions to the Thomas nomination. The NAACP's board was nearly unanimous in its 49:1 vote against Thomas's appointment; they accused him of being oblivious to institutional racism in his opposition to affirmative action and welfare policies. The National Bar Association (an organization for black attorneys) narrowly opposed the Thomas nomination. The National Urban League decided to express its neutrality on the appointment, and the National Council of Black Lawyers, a liberal interest group, announced its opposition. Only the Southern Christian Leadership Conference, among the major civil rights organizations, supported him.

After an undistinguished hearing before the Senate Judiciary Committee, during which Thomas refused to be drawn into lengthy discussions of his conservative record and writings, the committee tied 7:7 in its vote on the nominee, and his name headed to the full Senate without the committee's endorsement. Before the Senate's vote, however, journalists leaked a sensational story about an FBI report that the Judiciary Committee had received in which University of Oklahoma law professor Anita Hill accused Thomas of sexually harassing her when she worked with him at the EEOC. The committee summoned Hill, an African American graduate of Yale Law School, who described in shocking detail before the all-male committee the nature of the alleged sexual harassment in front of a transfixed, national television audience. The nominee was recalled to respond to the charges, which he denied absolutely with an obvious contempt for the process that he described as "a high-tech lynching for uppity blacks," evoking the fatal end that many black men met in the South before antilynching laws went into effect. Despite the improbable spectacle, Thomas was confirmed by the Senate 52:43, the closest Supreme Court confirmation vote of the twentieth century.

By the mid-1990s, the Supreme Court's contribution to affirmative action cases that continued to simmer in the lower federal courts consisted of "deciding not to decide," which is its prerogative not to accept cases on appeal. In so doing, it had let stand courts of appeals rulings in employment cases that had invalidated a quota for promotion of black firefighters in Birmingham, Alabama, and that had awarded a white engineer $425,000 in damages for being passed over for a promotion.

Racial preferences in higher education also were percolating through the courts of appeals. Would the U.S. Supreme Court accept a case on appeal that might revisit the *Bakke* precedent, which was almost two decades old? The Fourth Circuit declared unconstitutional a University of Maryland scholarship designated for blacks only. In a lawsuit filed by the Center for Individual Rights (CIR), a conservative public interest law firm, the Fifth Circuit invalidated a University of Texas Law School affirmative action policy that gave special admissions preferences to minorities, and the Eleventh Circuit did the same for a University of Georgia affirmative action plan for admitting minorities. The Supreme Court denied review in the Maryland and Texas cases; Georgia decided not to appeal. Twelve years of Reagan-Bush appointments, in which they replaced more than half the federal judiciary with primarily conservative judges, was having an impact on civil rights law.

Texas governor George W. Bush substituted the so-called 10 percent plan for the repudiated affirmative action programs in the state university system. It offered the top 10 percent of graduates from every Texas high school a position in the public university of their choosing. After two years, black and Hispanic enrollment had reached or exceeded the levels under the previous racial preferences programs in most of the public universities. The University of Texas also discovered that, under the new plan, it accepted students from low-income rural and urban schools, where UT had not had much success in recruiting.

The University of Texas Law School, however, struggled after the Fifth Circuit ruling struck down its race-based admissions policy. A "10 percent" scheme is unworkable beyond the undergraduate realm, and applications to the law school from blacks plummeted 42 percent in the year after the court decision.

In other states, public universities were rethinking affirmative action, not as a result of adverse court decisions but because of grassroots efforts to abolish racial preferences. By the mid-1990s, a *Newsweek* poll reported that more than three-quarters of white respondents opposed racial preferences in college admissions. Even minorities were not extremely supportive of such preferences; one poll indicated that only 50 percent approved of them. Ward Connerly, a black University of California regent, successfully led a 1996 voter referendum movement for Proposition 209, which declared that California "shall not discriminate against, or grant preferential treatment to, any individual or group on the basis of race, sex, color, ethnicity, or national origin in the operation of public employment, public education, or public contracting."

Initially, a federal district court judge enjoined state officials from implementing the new policy, concluding that it might "close the narrow but significant window" that permits governmental race- and gender-conscious affirmative action programs. Yet the Ninth Circuit overturned the lower tribunal in deference to the democratic process: "A system which permits one judge to block with the stroke of a pen what 4,736,180 state residents voted to enact as law tests the integrity of our constitutional democracy."

UCLA and the University of California at Berkeley Law Schools suffered the same fate as their Texas counterpart, experiencing severe drops in black and Hispanic admittees. Without using racial preferences, UCLA accepted only 21 black students, an 80 percent drop from the previous year and the lowest number of African American applicants offered admission since the early 1970s. Within two years of Proposition 209's passage, however, the undergraduate institutions in the Golden State reported a rebound in admissions for blacks, Hispanics, and Native Americans. California offered the top 4 percent of graduates from every high school in the state admission to one of the public universities, though not at any particular campus.

In Virginia, public universities began to reassess their admissions policies in the wake of threats from the Center for Equal Opportunity (CEO), a conservative think tank, and the Center for Individual Rights. The CEO released a report accusing the University of Virginia, the College of William and Mary, James Madison University, and Longwood College of giving strong preferences to black applicants over whites. The think tank cited statistics it had gathered and analyzed, which, it maintained, showed that black applicants to U.Va. were forty-five times more likely to be accepted over white candidates with the same SAT scores and class rank. Meanwhile, the CIR placed ads in fifteen college newspapers (including U.Va., William and Mary, and James Madison) across the country, with the declaration, "Nearly every elite college in America violates the law." It then asked students, "Does yours?" A checklist for answering the question was included in the ad. The CIR also sent handbooks to university trustees alerting them that they might be sued over illegal admissions policies at their schools. As political pundit Chris Matthews likes to say, "Let's play hardball!"

U.Va.'s board of visitors (its trustees) got the message. They immediately formed a committee to study the university's admissions policy to see if it violated federal law and whether they could be held liable if it did so. A few months later, after the study was completed, the board told the admissions office that the school's procedures for accepting minorities could probably not pass judicial muster. Dean of admissions Jack Blackburn admitted, "Race has been a factor here [in admissions decisions]. . . . With the precedents we've been seeing in these recent court cases, we're being urged to find other ways to do it." Yet he did not declare the end of racial preferences. Eventually, U.Va. president John Casteen ordered the elimination of the point-based admissions systems for minorities. A directive from the Virginia attorney general's office eventually warned public universities in the commonwealth that they could not use racial preferences to remedy past discrimination against minority students, which the U.S. Department of Education declared no longer an issue. But, according to the state directive, universities might have a legitimate interest in achieving diversity on their campuses. The Center for Equal Opportunity was not placated and argued that the affirmative action policies could still be challenged in court, and the CEO issued another report, this time on Virginia's public law schools, asserting that U.Va. and William and Mary Law Schools overwhelmingly favored less qualified blacks over whites in admissions.

Newsweek concluded from dwindling public support that affirmative action policy was "tearing at the Democratic party." When Bill Clinton, the Democratic governor of Arkansas, defeated incumbent George H. W. Bush for the presidency in 1992, he did so by running to the center on many issues. As a southerner who came of age in the 1960s, Clinton arguably cared most passionately about civil rights policy. In fashioning his "New Democrat" victory, however, he separated himself from the radical elements of minority politics. Ultimately, he decided that the nation should "mend," not "end," affirmative action. In his two appointments to the nation's highest court, in 1993 and 1994, Clinton chose moderate liberals Ruth Bader Ginsburg and Stephen Breyer, both of whom had more than a decade's experience on the U.S. courts of appeals. The president introduced Ginsburg as the Thurgood Marshall of the women's rights movement for her landmark work as head of the ACLU's Women's Rights Project, during which she won five of six cases for gender equity before the U.S. Supreme Court.

With four new justices in place by the 1994–1995 term, the high court once again accepted an affirmative action case on review after a several-year hiatus. In *Adarand Constructors, Inc. v. Peña,* a case challenging federal set-aside programs for minority business enterprises,

Justice O'Connor wrote for the 5:4 majority that such racial classifications could survive strict scrutiny only if the government (federal, state, or local) could prove a compelling state interest for them and narrowly tailor them to meet a goal of compensating for a specific instance of discrimination. She declared that a general policy of "racial diversity" in this context could not meet the compelling test. Her opinion also explicitly overturned the *Metro Broadcasting* precedent and declared *Fullilove* to be no longer controlling. The Court remanded the case to the Tenth Circuit Court of Appeals to apply the new precedent. The most conservative members of the high bench joined O'Connor's majority but wrote concurrences to indicate their view that *all* government racial preferences were unconstitutional. Chief Justice Rehnquist and Justice Kennedy rounded out the five-person majority. Justice Stevens wrote the lead dissent, joined by Justices Souter, Ginsburg, and Breyer, in which he urged adherence to precedent, including *Fullilove;* distinction between federal set-aside programs (justifiable) and state set-aside mandates (unjustifiable); and recognition of "invidious" discrimination in the workplace, in contrast to efforts at merely promoting "diversity." But Justice O'Connor's majority opinion foreshadowed the key role she would play in the landmark affirmative action cases from the University of Michigan that the U.S. Supreme Court would decide in 2003.

By the dawn of the twenty-first century, all three branches of the federal government had contributed to a body of affirmative action principles in business and education. As summarized by constitutional scholar Louis Fisher, they included requiring contractors who receive government funds to establish specific goals for hiring minorities, mandating race-conscious hiring quotas for recalcitrant employers who refuse to follow court orders to diversify, allowing race or gender among other factors in university admissions or employment decisions, sanctioning voluntary race-conscious employment policies in the private sector, establishing set-asides for minority contractors, and allowing less latitude for affirmative action in layoffs as opposed to hiring. When determining the constitutionality of affirmative action policies, the Supreme Court had settled on a standard of strict judicial scrutiny, necessitating that the programs be narrowly tailored to meet a compelling governmental interest. Exactly how would the Court apply these principles to higher education twenty-five years after *Bakke?*

CHAPTER 3

Admission Denied
The University of Michigan Rejects
Jennifer Gratz and Barbara Grutter

After the U.S. Supreme Court refused to hear an appeal from the Ninth
Circuit's decision upholding Ward Connerly's Proposition 209 in California, Clint Bolick of the conservative Institute for Justice remarked,
"The Court's [action] is a further repudiation of the arguments made
by the Clinton administration and its allies." Nevertheless, opinion polls
demonstrated that a plurality of the American public actually supported
the principle behind President Clinton's proposal to revise, not abolish, affirmative action. A *New York Times*/CBS poll reported in late 1997
that 43 percent of respondents answered "change them" when asked
"what is the best thing to do with affirmative action programs giving
preference to some minorities." Respondents who did not call for
reforming such programs were evenly split on what to do with them;
25 percent said they should be abolished, while 24 percent answered
"leave them as they are." Thus, two-thirds of those polled did not favor
abolishing affirmative action. In the same survey, a majority of whites
(59 percent) and blacks (82 percent) favored "special education programs to assist minorities in competing for college admissions." Perhaps support of these programs followed logically from the belief
revealed in the poll among whites (81 percent) and blacks (67 percent)
that "as a result of affirmative action, less-qualified people are hired and
promoted and admitted to college" "at least some of the time." Democratic Party pollster Geoff Garin, who had analyzed voter data on race
for the Ford Foundation, explained white ambivalence over affirmative
action this way: "On an intellectual level, plenty of white voters feel we
ought to have a color-blind society. But then they come to the view that
we don't have a color-blind society today, and they don't want to turn
the clock back."

Duplicating the successful strategy of liberal public litigation organizations, particularly in civil rights, the Center for Individual Rights (CIR) searched for individual litigants they could support in court cases. These litigants would constitute the tactical challenges to affirmative action programs in higher education. The CIR, founded in 1989 by Michael McDonald, an attorney who had worked in the Reagan administration, and Michael Greve, a conservative scholar, had an annual budget of nearly $2 million by 2000 thanks to conservative and libertarian foundations (including Richard Mellon Scaife's) that provide most of its funding. Its mission includes getting "government out of the business of classifying citizens by race." The center advertises that it "aggressively litigate[s] and publicize[s] a handful of carefully selected cases that advance the right[s] of individuals." It "provides free legal representation to deserving clients who cannot otherwise afford or obtain legal counsel." The *National Journal* commented, "CIR has been especially effective, carefully selecting both its battles and the circuits they fight them in, with an eye to victory."

Flush from its 1994–1996 win against affirmative action in the Texas Law School case (*Hopwood v. Texas*), the CIR turned to Michigan for its next skirmish against racial/ethnic preferences. A host of reasons made Michigan the perfect political and social landscape for waging war on affirmative action. Its major metropolitan area, Wayne County (home of the state's largest city, Detroit), was racially polarized, with more than 40 percent black residents, mostly concentrated within the urban boundaries, surrounded by predominantly white suburbs. White flight from Detroit had accelerated after the July 1967 race riot that left at least forty-three dead and property damage totaling close to $100 million. The riot also exposed a rift in Detroit's African American population between traditional NAACP integrationists and radical Black Nationalist separatists. Class lines were clearly drawn among the urban poor, suburban working-class, and high-income enclaves outside the city. In turn, political cleavages ran along these racial and social faults: Democrats drew support from the black urban poor, whereas Republicans had garnered votes from the white suburban blue-collar workers and white-collar professionals. In stark contrast to the latter stood the state's flagship institution of higher learning — the University of Michigan in Ann Arbor, less than fifty miles from Detroit, and a hotbed of liberalism.

With such a potentially volatile amalgam of race, class, and politics, it is not surprising that the Detroit area witnessed one of the most turbulent busing cases from the 1970s. *Bradley v. Millikan*, decided by the U.S. Supreme Court in 1974, "changed the course of school desegregation in the United States," according to Wayne State historian David Riddle's superb study of the case. In 1971 the NAACP branch in Detroit brought suit against the Detroit Board of Education in U.S. District Court claiming a litany of unconstitutional actions perpetrated by the board against black teachers and children. Blacks constituted 65 percent of the total student population. The NAACP alleged that the school board allocated funds for building and maintenance disproportionately to white schools, bused African American students beyond white schools to black schools, kept separate seniority lists for white and black teachers, and rarely assigned African American teachers to white schools.

After a forty-one-day trial, Judge Stephen J. Roth ruled in favor of the NAACP's contention that the Detroit school board had engaged in de jure (by deliberate policy/law) segregation. Judge Roth spent nine months fashioning a remedy for the plaintiffs. He ordered cross-district busing of 780,000 white and black students. The plan included 220,000 students from Detroit and primarily white students from fifty-two school districts surrounding the city. Roth's remedial order was the broadest busing plan ever imposed by a federal judge, and it ignited a firestorm of antibusing protests in the white suburbs caught up in the scheme. Ground zero for the backlash was Warren, Michigan, population 180,000 and the third-largest city in the state. A suburb of Detroit, it contained six school districts. As in many of the suburbs around Detroit, Warren's populace relied on the auto industry for well-paying, blue-collar jobs that funded an escape from the decay of urban life. Most of the escapees, however, were white. Despite the fact that blacks held one-third of the auto factory jobs in Warren, only a few African Americans lived in the town. Realtors guided blacks to other areas, and African Americans who became Warren homeowners often were victims of harassment and even violent attacks. In 1970 the U.S. Department of Housing and Urban Development ordered Warren to comply with the 1964 Civil Rights Act and the 1968 Open Housing Act in order to be eligible for a federal housing grant. The city's residents voted to retract the grant application rather than create a nondiscriminatory housing market.

Even before Judge Roth issued his cross-district busing order, the *Macomb Daily* (a newspaper published in Macomb County, Michigan) quoted one resident's prediction: "It will take an army to enforce that kind of a ruling if the court was foolish enough to try and force integration on suburban school districts." Rank-and-file members of the powerful United Auto Workers union expressed their hostility over busing to the UAW's Community Action Program. The most common sentiment was "I lived in Detroit. I came out to the suburbs for good schools. I paid my taxes. . . . Taking my kids from neighborhood schools that I fought so hard to get and why I built a house out here, taking and moving them back to all the dangers in Detroit [was unfair]." The complaints would often end with a final vitriolic attack on Judge Roth. Macomb County, which had supported Lyndon Johnson's 1964 presidential candidacy with 74 percent of the residents' votes, was rapidly tipping toward the right wing of the American political spectrum. One of the antibusing movement's leaders added a McCarthy era message to the debate when he declared, "If they are successful in forcing school integration through forced busing, next they'll send your kids to special Marxist-communist learning schools."

As Warren's busing crisis heated up, nearby Pontiac, Michigan, was undergoing its own school integration firestorm. Located less than fifty miles from Detroit, Pontiac was another company town — home to the General Motors Fisher Body factory, which had attracted black and Appalachian white workers. The city's school board had frequently redrawn school boundaries in order to maintain racial segregation. When black U.S. district court judge Damon Keith found the Pontiac school board guilty of de jure segregation, in a lawsuit brought by the NAACP, he issued a busing order for 8,000 of the district's 24,000 students to commence in fall 1971. Busing opponents invited Alabama's infamous segregationist governor, George Wallace, to speak at a rally. The Ku Klux Klan bombed empty school buses just before the school year was to begin, and 500 busing protesters shut down the Fisher plant a few weeks later.

Residents of Warren worried that such strife was a dress rehearsal for what could erupt in their city after Judge Roth issued his busing order. They made a strategic decision to avoid violent reactions if at all possible. The war of words continued, however, with antibusing leaders declaring at rallies of angry parents, "The legislators don't have the backbone to stand up and be counted. . . . They are trying to . . . force [the white community] to accept what we don't want. Let's face it — we're getting government of the minority against the majority." A Macomb County commissioner agreed, saying, "This country is supposed to be based on majority rule, but a minority of ten percent is dictating to us, the majority. We are being discriminated against." A Warren city councilman tried a more constructive argument: "If there's enough money to bus kids, then I say we put that money into the deprived areas to bring about equality. Give them new buildings and good teachers."

Leaders of the Catholic Church and the UAW tried to assert a calming influence on the flammable situation. The autoworkers' union had a history of educating the rank and file on integration dating to World War II. Yet union leaders admitted that their success in creating more open minds in the workplace regarding employment equality was not replicated in urging union members to support racial equity closer to home in their neighborhoods and schools. The Catholic cardinal who led the archdiocese of Detroit ordered priests in the Warren diocese not to use busing as a means of attracting white students to Catholic schools. As a result, he received the following illiterate missive: "Dear Cardinal, If you think we are going to send our white children to the Black schools in Detroit where Dopers, Rapers, Purse Snatchers, etc., the schools is full of them. And send black Hudlums to suburban schools that dont make sense. First of all you and your priests, nuns, etc. should go among Black Hudlums and . . . [p]reach to them Gospel 10 Commandment etc in Detroit and all over U.S. for that matter teach them there is god and god laws. Befor we mixed our white children with Black."

Inevitably, this social upheaval influenced Michigan politics. Along with the Vietnam War, the busing crisis fragmented the state's Democratic Party. As historian David Riddle has observed,

> Both issues split the party's leaders from its rank and file. The antiwar Democrats moved the party leaders to the left, while the issue of busing moved the rank and file the other way. On the issue of busing, Democratic party leaders tried to address racial integration

in ways that reached out to the party's black constituents without alienating the suburban white working class. This led state party leaders to adopt a wishy-washy endorsement of busing, a position that pleased no one and angered conservative suburban Democrats. Thus the efforts of Democratic party leaders to shore up a working coalition between urban blacks and suburban and outstate whites only contributed to the great sense of mutual distrust between the suburbs and the city of Detroit. . . . As anti-busing sentiments intensified, state party leaders lost their influence over Macomb County Democrats.

The Democrats' loss constituted a gain for conservatives. George Wallace, who had garnered more than 13 percent of the electoral votes as a third-party candidate in the 1968 presidential election, spoke to cheering throngs in Warren during the 1972 Michigan primary. (Ultimately, he was relegated to the sidelines when an assassination attempt in Maryland later that year left him a paraplegic.) The 1972 Democratic presidential nominee, liberal South Dakota senator George McGovern, could get no traction in Michigan, as he struggled to defeat incumbent Richard Nixon, who endorsed the Republican platform plank against busing. During the 1972 campaign, President Nixon instructed his adviser John Ehrlichman, "Lead on the busing issue on a state and local basis. . . . Hit busing hard in Michigan." Warren's mayor declared himself a "Democrat for Nixon" in the fall of 1972. Although Nixon had lost Michigan to Democratic vice president Hubert Humphrey in 1968, he carried it, along with all the other states, save Massachusetts (and the District of Columbia), in his landslide 1972 reelection victory.

Meanwhile, the Detroit busing case percolated through the federal judiciary. In 1973, the Sixth Circuit Court of Appeals, which includes Michigan in its jurisdiction, affirmed Judge Roth's finding of de jure segregation in the Detroit schools, as well as his cross-district busing order. Not surprisingly, the Sixth Circuit's decision was appealed to the U.S. Supreme Court. Just before its decision in his Detroit busing case, Judge Roth died at age fifty-four of heart disease, undoubtedly exacerbated by the intense stress of his most famous litigation. At the end of the Court's term in July 1974, the justices ruled 5:4 that, although Detroit had engaged in de jure segregation, Judge Roth's cross-district busing order exceeded his constitutional remedial power, absent proof of unlawful segregation in the suburban school districts. Countering Chief Justice Warren Burger's opinion for the narrow majority, Justice William O. Douglas's dissent accused the ruling of taking "a giant step backward" toward separate and unequal facilities for blacks in American society.

As a deluge of busing cases from around the country poured into the nation's high court, Judge Roth's successor, Judge Robert DeMascio, drew up a plan calling for busing within the Detroit school system and ordered Michigan to pay $70 million toward the cost of creating better education programs within the city. Responses to his orders were predictable: more white families fled the urban boundaries (Detroit became the most segregated metropolitan area in the United States), and the state appealed the funding order all the way to the Supreme Court. Ironically, the whole busing phenomenon, which was intended to integrate the schools, resulted in more racial segregation, more racial tension, and "mutual estrangement of the white and black people of southeastern Michigan," as David Riddle has concluded. He notes that even suburban whites who had never lived in Detroit embraced a "victimization/exodus myth [that] became part of the suburban identity." As Governor Otto Kerner (D-IL) wrote in his commission's report on the race riots that swept over 150 American cities in the mid-1960s, "Our nation is moving toward two societies, one black, one white — separate and unequal. Discrimination and segregation have long permeated much of American life; they now threaten the future of every American."

Less than a decade after the busing litigation, another Michigan race case made its way to the U.S. Supreme Court. As noted in chapter 2, it arose in the city of Jackson, located on Interstate 94, less than fifty miles from the outskirts of Detroit and just beyond Ann Arbor. In 1972, as a result of racial tension in the community, the Jackson school district (which itself had not engaged in discrimination) negotiated a collective-bargaining agreement with the teachers' union, stipulating that, when layoffs were necessary, the percentage of black teachers let go could not exceed their employment percentage. Because black teachers were the most recently hired in the district, the affirmative action plan inevitably meant that white teachers with more seniority were dismissed ahead of their black counterparts with less seniority. After the Jackson school district implemented the plan in the face of 1976–1977 and 1981–1982 budget cuts, Wendy Wygant and other dismissed white colleagues with more seniority than black teachers who kept their jobs brought suit in federal district court claiming that Jackson had violated their Fourteenth Amendment equal protection rights, along with Title VII of the 1964 Civil Rights Act. The U.S. District Court's ruling in *Wygant v. Jackson Board of Education* dismissed the white teachers' claims, arguing that black educators provided the necessary "role models for minority students" in the classroom. The U.S. Sixth Circuit Court of Appeals affirmed the lower court ruling; Wygant and her aggrieved colleagues appealed to the U.S. Supreme Court.

After hearing oral argument in the case, the nine justices met in their traditional conference to vote on the decision. Interestingly, in light of the case's seniority issue, the justices always vote in order of seniority. In the *Wygant* vote, as in many affirmative action cases, the justices were split four to four, and Justice O'Connor, who was still the most junior justice in 1985, could cast the last and tie-breaking vote. Chief Justice Burger and Justices White, Powell, and Rehnquist viewed the Jackson affirmative action plan as implementing an unconstitutional racial preference. Justices Brennan, Marshall, Blackmun, and Stevens were on the other side; they saw the plan as a constitutional effort to address societal discrimination and create role models for minority students. At the conference, O'Connor suggested remanding (returning) the case to the district court for an additional hearing that would allow the school board to prove that its plan was necessary to remedy historical discrimination in the district.

Supreme Court reporter Joan Biskupic's 2005 biography of Sandra Day O'Connor details the fascinating dynamic of how the justices crafted a majority decision in *Wygant*. Even though Justice O'Connor's remand vote was tentative and did not tip the balance to either side in the case, Chief Justice Burger assigned the writing of what he hoped would become a majority opinion to Justice Powell. Burger's decision was uncharacteristically wise. Justice Powell had crafted the compromise in *Bakke*, and he had developed a close, mutually admiring, working relationship and warm friendship with the first female justice. Ever the diplomat, Powell wrote to O'Connor, "It is obvious that I need your vote rather badly. I therefore would welcome any suggestions you may care to make [on the draft majority opinion]."

Ultimately, O'Connor cast her vote with Powell to strike down the Jackson plan. Powell's opinion rejected the school board's argument that general societal discrimination alone could justify racial preferences for blacks in layoffs. In Fourteenth Amendment analysis jargon, the school board did not present a "compelling state interest" for using race in layoff decisions. Powell, a former head of the Richmond, Virginia, school board, noted that the "role model" justification for Jackson's layoff policy also did not constitute a narrowly tailored remedy required by the Fourteenth Amendment's strict scrutiny analysis. Powell reasoned, "Carried to its logical extreme, the idea that black students are better off with black teachers could lead to the very system that Court rejected in [*Brown v. Board of Education* over twenty years earlier]." O'Connor's concurring opinion, however, suggested that a specific instance of past discrimination (as opposed to the general societal variety) was not the only compelling reason for affirmative action.

Despite the Court's invalidation of the Jackson affirmative action plan for teacher layoffs, nearby Macomb County residents continued to resent the impact of racial preferences. President Ronald Reagan's anti–affirmative action stance resonated with the county's white, working-class residents, 67 percent of whom voted for Reagan's reelection in 1984. "Reagan Democrats," they were now called, indicating their new allegiance to the conservative president and their previous support for the more liberal party. Democratic Party pollster Stanley Greenberg traced the Macomb County defection from his party's column to unemployment in the Rust Belt and racial issues such as busing and affirmative action. The Reagan Democrats viewed their former party as catering to blacks and other minorities, along with women. When the pollsters asked them, "Who do you think gets the raw deal?" men responded, "We do. The middle-class white guy. The working middle class." They viewed affirmative action as thwarting their own success and an explanation for their decreased status in society.

A relative few miles from the Michigan busing and employment cases' locales was the site of what would become two landmark Supreme Court affirmative action decisions, each involving the University of Michigan. Founded in 1817, the school constituted the state's flagship university. Its former provost, Nancy Cantor, has noted, as "a great public research university, [it was] home to a long and storied history of political activism. Nestled near Detroit's Big

Three [automaker] factories in the middle of America, it also commanded the attention of neighbors east and west. . . . The university's history has been extraordinarily rich in dialogues on diversity. . . . Michigan had much scholarly firepower, cultivated during more than fifty years of eminence in social science research, and diversity was ingrained as a primary value."

Michigan's first black students (two men from Detroit) enrolled in 1868. Controversy surrounded the first female admitted in 1870, but she set a precedent for the first black woman who enrolled eight years later. The university's third president, James B. Angell, spoke on the topic "The Higher Education: A Plea for Making It Accessible" at the 1879 commencement. In 1887, *Harper's Weekly* described "the broad and liberal spirit in which [the university] does its work. Women are admitted to all departments on equal terms with men; the doors of the University are open to all applicants who are properly qualified, from whatever part of the world they may come." Cantor observes that "Michigan had a scholarly tradition of research on group dynamics that grew out of the anti-Semitism of the 1930, 1940s, and 1950s. It was dedicated over many years to understanding intergroup relations, conflict, and community."

Nevertheless, as the twentieth century progressed, the Michigan campus usually had fewer than 20 minority students at any one time. They were passively accepted, with no direct intervention from the university to attract more. Just before World War II, only 1 percent of the student population was black, and they suffered financial problems, particularly because student jobs typically went to their white colleagues. African American students also reported that they were treated differently and had few social opportunities. In 1954 the student population included 200 black students. As recently as the early 1960s, the University of Michigan used photographs from student applications to segregate roommates according to race and gender, and fraternities were also segregated. By 1966 the 32,000 students at the university included 400 African Americans, just a little more than 4 percent of enrollment.

The University of Michigan, like most large campuses, experienced student unrest in the late 1960s and early 1970s. From February to April 1970, student protests for civil rights and against the Vietnam War rocked the campus. Students refused to attend classes and encouraged their professors to join the protests. The Black Action

Movement (BAM) formed its own demonstrations, demanding that the university increase African American enrollment to 10 percent by 1973. The university initially rejected the demand, accepted it after a student strike, and then abandoned it. The black student goal still had not been reached by 1975, and BAM II, as the protest was called, launched more demonstrations. Finally, in 1976, the 10 percent figure of black enrollment was reached. It then stagnated during the next decade. A university study in 1980 revealed that 85 percent of black students polled reported that they experienced severe racial isolation and discrimination from their fellow students. The mid-1980s brought student protests against South African apartheid, which prompted more demonstrations against the slow pace of black enrollment. BAM III led a blockade of the Michigan Student Union and sit-ins at the administration building.

After racist incidents roiled the campus in the late 1980s, student and faculty activists proposed, and the university accepted, "speech codes" to punish racist or sexist expression. Another response to the campus tensions came from UM's new president, James Duderstadt. In early 1990 he announced the "Michigan Mandate," which had already hired seventy-six minority faculty through affirmative action and would continue to attract more minorities and women to the faculty, staff, and undergraduate program. The university admitted that "prejudice, bigotry, discrimination and even racism" existed on the Michigan campus. President Duderstadt required each department to report statistics on its racial, ethnic, and gender makeup. "Our university," the president contended, "has the moral imperative to address the underrepresentation of racial and ethnic groups. . . . The insights and erudition of hitherto excluded groups can enrich our scholarly enterprise; indeed, it seems apparent that we cannot sustain the distinction of our university in the pluralistic world that is our future without the diversity that sustains excellence." UM created more scholarships and fellowships for black and Hispanic students, established a multi-million-dollar Afro-American center, and allocated $27 million for various minority-student programs. Earl Lewis, Michigan graduate school dean, has written that "the fundamental principle of the mandate was that the university should become a leader in creating a multicultural community that could serve as a model for society as well as for higher education."

Clearly, Michigan was trying to make up for society's failures at integration. In the early 1990s, surveys of entering freshmen revealed that about 90 percent of white students, and 50 percent of black, grew up in racially homogeneous neighborhoods and attended racially segregated high schools. Asian American and Hispanic students at Michigan, however, reported that they had considerable experience with whites in their primarily white neighborhoods and schools. Because two-thirds of the university's undergraduates hail from Michigan, where residential segregation of whites and blacks is well documented, their college experience is the first opportunity they have to cross racial barriers and interact with a more diverse peer group.

Former Michigan psychology and women's studies professor Patricia Gurin's research concluded, "For most of Michigan's students, its residence halls are the most diverse environments they have ever encountered. Students live with each other over an extended time. Rooming with a student from a different racial/ethnic background, though sometimes a genuine challenge for these previously racially segregated students, is potentially a very positive experience." Yet polling data, as well as anecdotal evidence, indicate that strains remained on the campus. In the early 1990s just over 25 percent of the white students surveyed responded that there was "quite a bit" or "a great deal" of "interracial tension on [the Michigan] campus." A decade later, as the affirmative action litigation reached its climax, black students reported to the *Washington Post* that racial tensions at the University of Michigan had increased. Many of them wanted to attend the prestigious school, which the *Post* referred to as "the Harvard of the Midwest," but one African American student lamented that racial slurs on the campus "affect[ed] her personally." The sophomore explained: "I am personally offended. One of the reasons I chose to come to UM is their boastful reputation on diversity. But I have to make a choice between socializing with black people or socializing with white people, because this campus is extremely segregated." Cultural stereotypes abounded, with one black student being called upon by her white colleagues to copy rap CDs for them. "I've never owned a rap CD in my life," the indignant woman, a Detroit resident and graduate of an elite technical school in the city, reported. Another told the *Post*, "There was this overwhelming feeling that I didn't belong [at Michigan]. I feel so isolated. I call my friend at Spelman [a historically black women's college in Atlanta] and say I want to transfer." The Michigan student had not followed through on her wish, however, knowing how valuable a degree from UM is. Besides, she noted that her father would not allow her to transfer.

By 1997 the University of Michigan minority enrollment had reached 25 percent. Yet the proportion of black students had actually dropped, from 10 percent two decades earlier, to 8 percent, or a little more than half of the 14 percent in the state of Michigan's population (12 percent nationwide). Hispanics constituted about 6 percent of the student body, twice as much as their rate in the state's census (but less than the almost 12 percent in the United States); and Asians represented approximately 10 percent of enrollment, ten times their proportion in Michigan (three times the 3.6 percent in the nation). If the university wanted general diversity in its student body, it had succeeded; if it wanted to replicate the racial/ethnic makeup of the state's population or the nation's, it had failed. Whites constituted 83 percent of the state but only three-quarters of the University of Michigan student body. White Michigan parents began to resent the rejection of their children from the state's premier institution of higher learning.

Even more frustrating to whites was the public release of the undergraduate affirmative action program. After reading an article in the *Journal of Blacks in Higher Education*, which reported that selective universities accepted blacks at higher rates than whites, UM philosophy professor Carl Cohen became suspicious about the details of his own school's admissions policies. In 1996 he obtained the previously confidential admissions policy under a Freedom of Information Act (FOIA) request. He then realized that the very kind of policy he had criticized in his book *Naked Racial Preference: The Case against Affirmative Action* (1995) was being used by his beloved university, where he had happily taught for forty years. The book agues that "racial preference is dynamite." Cohen recalls that when he received the material under his FOIA request, he realized that "some of it was shockingly blatant racial discrimination," which he believes "is a flagrant violation of the principles laid down in the law of the land." He forwarded a report on his analysis of the UM affirmative action policy to the university's president but received no response. Likewise, the board of regents ignored his findings. Cohen, a former president of the state chapter of the American Civil Liberties Union and onetime board member of his county's Democratic Party, knew some of the regents to be "good people," with whom he had worked on partisan causes. But he understood that they were "obviously uncomfortable" with the affirmative action controversy. So Cohen's complaints fell on deaf ears among the university's administrators; only when the press publicized the story did it receive attention. "[Cohen] really started the ball rolling," remembered Curt Levey, the CIR's director of legal and public affairs. "It is fair to say that this [litigation] would not have happened without him." Cohen's efforts against affirmative action earned him the "racist" label from student demonstrators, but he still viewed UM as "a wonderful place with wonderful people . . . [who] know that my energy is devoted to the university."

Marked "Confidential — Internal Use Only," the affirmative action plan for Michigan undergraduate admissions, which Cohen received as a result of his FOIA request in 1996, consisted of tables or grids on which the university's Office of Undergraduate Admissions (OUA) counselors would plot applicants' scores. In 1995 and 1996 the scores consisted of grade point average combined with what the counselors labeled "SCUGA" factors: the quality of the applicant's high school (S), strength of his or her high school curriculum (C), any unusual circumstances in the applicant's life (U), his or her geographic residence (G), and any alumni relationships the applicant might have (A). The OUA plotted these scores, which it called "GPA 2," on four different grids in 1995: (1) in-state, nonminority applicants; (2) out-of-state, nonminority applicants; (3) in-state, minority applicants; and (4) out-of-state, minority applicants. In 1996 the OUA collapsed the four grids into two — one for in-state applicants and one for out-of-state applicants. Along one axis GPA 2 scores were listed; along the other were plotted SAT/ACT scores. Each cell in the two tables contained different courses of action for minority applicants and nonminority applicants whose scores placed them in that cell. Lower standards were applied to the preferred minority applicants (African American, Hispanic, and Native American). For example, nonminority applicants with GPAs of 3.2 to 3.3 and SAT scorers of 1010 to 1080 (out of 1600), or ACT scores of 22 to 23 (out of 36), were sent rejection letters. Preferred minority candidates with the same credentials were accepted. After examining the material, Professor Cohen concluded that "the evidence is overwhelming and the conclusion indisputable" that "preference by race is given systematically at the University of Michigan to applicants for admission."

The university's public relations office denied the charge. Lisa Baker, vice president for university relations, responded, "There is no question that we are committed to diversifying our campus to reflect the diversity of our society and enrich the educational experience for all here. We have therefore recruited more students and faculty of color. But there are a number of factors that go into admissions decisions. Race is only one." In so stating, Baker clearly was trying to fall under the permissible form of affirmative action spelled out in Justice Powell's *Bakke* opinion, namely, that race could be used as a "plus" factor, among others, in admissions decisions. In 1997 the university revised the "U" category in the SCUGA factors to include underrepresented minority status, socioeconomic disadvantage, attendance at a high school with a predominantly underrepresented minority population, or underrepresentation in the unit to which the candidate was applying.

After the results of Professor Cohen's FOIA request became widely known, the Michigan House of Representatives' Constitution Committee asked him to testify about his findings. As Cohen recalled nearly a decade later, "The upshot [in the legislature] was anger (not at me!) on the part of some Michigan legislators, who greatly resented the fact that the university had misled them." Four Republicans were particularly inspired to pursue the issue. One of them, state representative Deborah Whyman, phoned the Center for Individual Rights to alert the conservative law firm. Whyman appeared on talk radio in the state and did other media interviews to spread the word in an effort to drum up potential plaintiffs. In addition to the state of Michigan's checkered history involving race, the University of Michigan's other characteristics also drew the interest of the CIR. The university is among a handful of highly selective public institutions of higher education, where it would be obvious if the admissions office was using a two-track system with higher standards for white students. In addition, the excessively high number of applications filed each year at Michigan (more than 20,000 to all schools on the campus), with about 13,000 accepted for only approximately 5,300 spaces in the entering class, meant that admission officers were likely to use numerical criteria for deciding quickly. (Most colleges and universities accept many more applicants than positions available in the first-year class in order to account for the fact that not all admitted students will accept the offer. Admissions officers refer to the actual student enrollment as the "yield" from accepted applicants.) In addition, because Michigan is a public institution, it is subject to the Freedom of Information Act. All the elements of a "perfect storm" lawsuit were falling into place for the CIR. It only needed the perfect plaintiff to lead a class action.

Jennifer Gratz was a disappointed white applicant whom the University of Michigan had rejected. Her parents discovered a newspaper article about a movement building against UM, and their daughter immediately wanted to sign up for any cause that might vindicate her. She contacted Representative Whyman's office and reported the facts of her case. Initially, Gratz thought she might simply stuff envelopes for a letter-writing campaign. Whyman sent 200 names to the CIR in Washington, which winnowed the list to a half dozen or so. After an interview with CIR lawyers in Detroit, she became the lead plaintiff in the undergraduate case *Gratz v. Bollinger* (the latter was the university's president). She was joined in the suit by Patrick Hamacher, another unsuccessful white applicant with credentials similar to those of his coplaintiff.

Gratz had grown up in Southgate, a working-class suburb of Detroit, about forty-five minutes from Ann Arbor. Her father, a police sergeant, and her mother, a secretary, did not have college degrees, but they were avid University of Michigan football fans. Their daughter's dream was to attend UM and major in forensic medicine; she believed that her high school record would make her a competitive admissions candidate. A graduate of Southgate Anderson High School, which was 94 percent white, Jennifer had accumulated a GPA of 3.8 and had been an active participant in the student council, National Honor Society, science club, spirit club, and cheerleading. She had also been selected homecoming queen and served as a math tutor. Her high school did not offer Advanced Placement courses, but she took three honors classes. On the ACT, she scored a 25 out of 36.

Jennifer was so certain that Michigan would accept her in 1995 that she applied to no other schools. Her first disappointment came when UM wait-listed her. Unbeknownst to her at the time, her GPA and test scores placed her directly in the "postpone decision" cell of the majority applicant grid. If she had been in the preferred minority grid, however, she would have been accepted without hesitation. In April of her senior year, Jennifer received the devastating word of her rejection by UM. Through her tears of disappointment, she asked her parents about suing the university. She later recalled, "My parents said we probably could but we didn't have the resources." She then submitted a late application to Notre Dame, which also denied her admission. The University of Michigan at Dearborn, however, accepted her into its honors program. She reluctantly attended the school, where she majored in math, made the dean's list, and graduated in 1999. Jennifer later said of her experience at Dearborn's commuter campus, "It wasn't college."

In October 1997 the Center for Individual Rights filed suit in the U.S. District Court for the Eastern District of Michigan in Detroit on Gratz's and Hamacher's behalf. (Hamacher had slightly higher test scores and a slightly lower GPA than Jennifer; UM had rejected his application in 1996.) CIR's president, Terence J. Pell, a former civil rights official in the Reagan Education Department, declared to the *New York Times*, "The racial preference policies at Michigan are more explicit and widespread than they were at Texas [where the federal courts had invalidated the law school's affirmative action plan in the 1996 *Hopwood* case]. They [UM] have an admissions grid with very different results whether you are black or white, effectively a dual admissions policy. This is a pretty extreme example but it is something which is going on at a lot of other schools."

With Gratz's lawsuit under way, the University of Michigan's undergraduate program abandoned its admissions grid system in 1998 and replaced it with a 150-point "selection index." Admissions officers assigned applicants points based on various factors, including test scores, "legacy" status, geographic origin, athletic ability, socioeconomic level, and race/ethnicity. The more points an applicant accumulated, the higher the chance of admission. Applicants from racial and ethnic groups considered "underrepresented" at Michigan (African Americans, Latinos, and Native Americans) were assigned 20 points. Scholarship athletes and students who were economically disadvantaged also received an automatic 20-point bonus. (Applicants could receive only one 20-point bonus award, however, even if they qualified in two or three categories.) Geographic origin earned 6 points, the child of an alumnus 4 points, and an "outstanding" admissions essay 3 points.

At approximately the same time the Gratz litigation was simmering, Barbara Grutter, age forty-three and the mother of two children, applied to the University of Michigan Law School. Her 1997 application included a GPA of 3.8 and an LSAT score of 161 (out of 165, or 86th percentile). Like Jennifer Gratz's undergraduate application, Barbara's candidacy was placed on the waiting list. Ultimately, the law school rejected her. She blamed the law school's affirmative action plan for her rejection. "I think that I was discriminated against in the admissions process, very specifically because I believe they have different criteria based on race," Grutter declared in a 2001 PBS interview. She commented, "We have always conscientiously taught our children that discrimination is wrong, morally wrong and illegal. . . . Is what I'm teaching them a platitude, or is it real?" "I certainly saw my share of sexist behavior" in the early part of her career as a health care consultant, Barbara remembered. "I never dreamed that twenty years later . . . I'd find myself discriminated against now on the basis of race. . . . I went through real struggle about whether to proceed with this [litigation] but came to the conclusion that it was the right thing to do," she reported. The Center for Individual Rights also filed her lawsuit, *Grutter v. Bollinger*, along with Gratz's.

The University of Michigan Law School first addressed its dearth of black students in the midst of the modern civil rights movement. When law applications rose around the country in the mid-1960s, many schools tightened their admissions standards. As a result, UM Law School could not find a single black applicant to meet its requirements between 1963 and 1966. Consequently, not one black student was enrolled as the clamor for civil rights increased across the nation. UM law faculty requested that the admission office actively recruit African American candidates and, if necessary, accept likely successful students even if they fell below the school's usual standards.

By the time Barbara Grutter submitted her application in 1997, Michigan Law School was known nationwide as a highly ranked and highly selective institution. Its first-year class typically enrolls no more than 350 students out of approximately 5,000 applicants annually. Like most elite law schools, it relied for admissions decisions on an index score, consisting of an applicant's undergraduate GPA and LSAT score. The admissions committee would also consider the applicant's under-graduate records, personal essay, and letters of recommendation. After 1992, however, it gave special preference particularly, but not solely, to the same three underrepresented minorities as the undergraduate school (African Americans, Hispanics, and Native Americans).

The law school's admissions statistics indicated that a white or Asian applicant with an LSAT score of 164 to 166 and a GPA of 3.25 to 3.49 had a 22 percent chance of admission, but a preferred minority candidate would have a 100 percent chance of acceptance. No more than one-tenth of majority applicants with LSAT scores below 164 could expect to gain admission, whereas four-fifths of the preferred minorities usually received acceptances down to an LSAT score of 155 (or the 55th percentile). To justify these divergent acceptance rates for white or Asians and preferred minorities, the Michigan Law School cited the fact that "in 2000, there were only 26 African-American applicants *nationwide* with at least a 3.5 GPA and a 165 on the LSAT compared to 3,173 whites and Asian-Americans." Michigan also argued that, although the number of minorities in each first-year class differed over the years, in the fall of 2000 only 4 percent of admitted students would have been minorities without the affirmative action program. That year, with the racial preferences in place, 14 percent of the incoming class were minorities.

The University of Michigan Law School had drafted its most recent affirmative action plan during the 1991–1992 academic year. Jeffrey Lehman, former dean of the UM Law School, recalls his par-ticipation on the committee that created the plan, which the full fac-ulty adopted in 1992. "Part of our mandate was to produce a policy that was lawful under the guidelines established by Justice Powell [in *Bakke*]. We sought to develop a policy that would incorporate this pedagogic vision of diversity into a general philosophy of admissions that accurately captured our own definition of ourselves as an institu-tion and linked our admissions process to our more general efforts to become the kind of law school we aspired to be. And we attempted to devise a system that would carry that philosophy forward into the daily work of an admissions office."

The plan specifically described its commitment to racial and ethnic diversity: "This is a commitment . . . with special reference to the

inclusion of students from groups which have been historically discriminated against, like African Americans, Hispanics, and Native
Americans, who without this commitment might not be represented
in our student body in meaningful numbers. These students are particularly likely to have experiences and perspectives of special importance to our mission." The policy asserted that the law school had
"made special efforts to increase the numbers of such students" over
the previous two decades. Moreover, the presence of minorities,
according to the plan, had "made the University of Michigan Law
School a better law school than it could possibly have been otherwise."
It then used the term "critical mass" to describe the number of minority students UM had attracted for "their ability to make unique contributions to the character of the Law School."

While still dean of the law school in 1999, Jeffrey Lehman posited
that "if we did not consider race, we would not be an integrated and
diverse school. Racial integration does not happen by acci-
dent. . . . Maybe some day white children and black children will really
grow up together, in the same neighborhoods, on the same blocks, at
the same schools. . . . But that day is not here. . . . Racial integration
. . . only happens when people act affirmatively to bring it about." UM
could cite survey data from the University of Michigan and Harvard
law schools, reporting that diversity had increased students' "ability
to work more effectively and/or get along better with members of
other races." At Harvard 68 percent, and at Michigan 48 percent, of
students reported such a positive outcome from diversity on their respective campuses. For Barbara Grutter, however, diversity did not
produce a salutary result.

All lawsuits begin with a set of circumstances and outcomes that
aggrieved parties wish to contest in court. With two complex and controversial affirmative action policies at issue, one involving the undergraduate program at the University of Michigan, the other addressing
the UM Law School, the alliterative pair of Gratz and Grutter, with
the powerful CIR behind them, were off to court — and their place
in history.

CHAPTER 4

"Can We Sue?"

Gratz and Grutter Go to Court

Although Jennifer Gratz's parents wanted to answer "yes" to her tear-ful question about suing the University of Michigan after its rejection of her application in 1995, they knew they did not have the resources to undertake such an expensive venture. When the Center for Indi-vidual Rights chose her and Patrick Hamacher, another disappointed Michigan applicant, to be the lead plaintiffs in its class-action lawsuit against the university, the resource obstacle was moot. The CIR would fund the suit. The class, as certified by the district court, consisted of "those individuals who applied for and were not granted admission to the College of Literature, Science, and the Arts [CLSA] of the Uni-versity of Michigan for all academic years from 1995 forward and who are members of those racial or ethnic groups, including Caucasian, that defendants [the university] treated less favorably on the basis of race in considering their application for admission." On October 14, 1997, the CIR filed suit for Gratz and Hamacher, as well as "all others sim-ilarly situated," in the U.S. District Court for the Eastern District of Michigan, Southern Division, in Detroit, claiming that the university had violated Title VI of the Civil Rights Act and the equal protection clause of the Fourteenth Amendment by considering race as a factor in admissions decisions. The next year, as the case made its way through the trial court, Michigan dropped the grid system for admis-sions decisions and substituted the 150-point "selection index."

In preparing the lawsuit, the CIR, which typically works with lawyers outside the organization, developed a clear division of labor among the team of attorneys. Michael McDonald, then president of the center, asked a good friend from law school, Kirk Kolbo, of the Minneapolis firm Maslon, Edelman, Borman, and Brand, to assist in the case. "Mike couldn't find a law firm in Michigan to take on an insti-tution as large and influential as the University of Michigan," Kolbo recalled. "Apparently, he thought that Minnesota was just a cab ride away." Kolbo praised the "great relationship" he had with the CIR, and he especially singled out the center's general counsel, David Rosman, as a "brilliant" strategist and brief writer. Leading up to the trial, Kolbo performed most of the deposition work. Terry Pell, who later became the CIR's president, was responsible for media communications.

In both *Gratz* and *Grutter*, the plaintiffs' key strategy was to emphasize as clearly as possible "the extent to which race was considered in the [admissions] process." According to Kolbo, "the very explicit double standards" for minority and nonminority applicants to the Michigan undergraduate college made the racial preference argument an easy one in *Gratz*. In the law school case, however, even Kolbo had to admit that the "extent of discrimination was not as explicit." Therefore, the plaintiffs' lawyers focused on gathering as many depositions as possible, along with expert analysis of the UM Law School admissions data, to prove the unconstitutional use of racial preferences.

On November 16, 2000, the district court heard oral argument in *Gratz v. Bollinger* before U.S. district court judge Patrick J. Duggan, a Reagan appointee. Documents and testimony before the court described the University of Michigan as a selective public institution, to which many more students applied than could be accepted. In 1997, for example, the College of Literature, Science, and the Arts (one of several UM undergraduate schools and the one to which Gratz had applied) accepted only 3,958 students out of 13,500 applicants — an acceptance rate of 29.3 percent. UM's explicit admissions policy was to construct a first-year class with diverse races, ethnicities, cultures, and socioeconomic backgrounds. The university described diversity as a key component of its mission because it "increase[s] the intellectual vitality of education, scholarship, service, and communal life." In order to create such diversity, the CLSA admittedly used race as a factor in its admissions decisions.

Within this context, both Gratz and Hamacher, who applied for undergraduate admission in 1995 and 1997, respectively, received letters from the university informing them that, although they were qualified, they were not at the level of students accepted in the first review and, therefore, action on their applications was postponed. Subsequently, each was rejected and enrolled in other institutions (Gratz at UM's Dearborn campus and Hamacher at Michigan State).

Judge Duggan issued the district court's decision on December 13, 2000. His discussion of the case's merits began with the standard of review for Fourteenth Amendment equal protection clause questions. (The ruling did not specifically address the plaintiffs' claim that the university's affirmative action program was also violative of Title VI.) He noted the U.S. Supreme Court's identification of the Fourteenth Amendment's "central mandate," which requires "racial neutrality in governmental decisionmaking." Quoting Justice Lewis Powell's opinion in *Bakke*, upon which he relied almost exclusively, Duggan asserted, "The basic principle is straight-forward: 'Racial and ethnic distinctions of any sort are inherently suspect and thus call for the most exacting judicial examination.'" At this highest level of "strict scrutiny," such distinctions or classifications based on race or ethnicity "are constitutional only if they are narrowly tailored measures that further compelling governmental interests," as the high court had noted most recently in its 1995 decision in *Adarand Constructors, Inc. v. Peña*, addressing set-asides for minority businesses in government contracts.

Under this standard of review, the district court had to determine whether the University of Michigan's use of race and ethnicity in CLSA admission decisions, to further its goal of diversity in the student body, constituted a compelling governmental interest and, if so, whether UM's admission procedures were narrowly tailored to meet such an interest of racial and ethnic diversity.

In turning to the first question, Judge Duggan had to discern whether U.S. Supreme Court precedent viewed diversity as a compelling interest. Here the plaintiffs (Gratz and Hamacher) and the defendants (University of Michigan) were at odds over how to interpret the high tribunal's ruling in *Bakke*, the justices' only decision on affirmative action in higher education prior to 2000. As described in chapter 2, the Supreme Court was split 4:4:1 in *Bakke*, with Justice Powell casting the deciding vote on each of the case's issues. The University of Michigan read Justice Powell's opinion, in which he had stated that "the interest of diversity is compelling in the context of a university's admission program," as controlling precedent. Gratz's attorney, however, argued that the diversity portion of Powell's judgment had not attracted four additional votes and thus had no precedential value.

On the diversity issue, Duggan sided with the university, arguing "that under *Bakke*, diversity constitutes a compelling governmental interest in the context of higher education justifying the use of race as one factor in the admissions process." The judge also ruled that "this Court is not convinced that recent Supreme Court precedent has established, as a matter of law, that the consideration of race in an attempt to attain the educational benefits that flow from a racially and ethnically diverse student body in the context of higher education can never constitute a compelling interest under strict scrutiny."

Duggan continued, "This Court is satisfied that, if presented with sufficient evidence regarding the educational benefits that flow from a diverse student body, there is nothing barring the Court from determining that such benefits are compelling under strict scrutiny analysis." He determined that UM had "presented this Court with solid evidence regarding the educational benefits that flow from a racially and ethnically diverse student body." Judge Duggan particularly cited Michigan psychology and women's studies professor Patricia Gurin's research demonstrating that "students learn better in a diverse educational environment, and they are better prepared to become active participants in our pluralistic, democratic society once they leave such a setting." In addition, Gurin concluded, with Duggan's approbation, that diversity in higher education helps to destroy "patterns of racial segregation and separation historically rooted in our national life." The judge especially noted that the Association of American Law Schools, the National Association of State Universities and Land Grant Colleges, and the Committee on Institutional Cooperation (an academic consortium including all of the major midwestern universities), representing more than 360 institutions of higher education, had joined an amicus brief supporting the University of Michigan's arguments in favor of diversity's positive outcomes for students. These universities also informed the court that a ruling against the University of Michigan "would significantly undermine their ability to provide the highest quality of academic experience and to prepare their students to effectively contribute to society after graduation."

The plaintiffs presented no evidence countering the benefits of diversity for both minority and nonminority students. Indeed, the plaintiffs' counsel at oral argument conceded that diversity in higher education is "good, important, and valuable." Nevertheless, Gratz's attorney asserted that, despite the benefits of diversity, it was a vague concept, as well as "limitless, timeless, and scopeless," and thus could not be deemed compelling. Judge Duggan also rejected the conservative National Association of Scholars' (NAS) viewpoint, filed in an amicus brief, that "intellectual diversity bears no obvious or necessary relationship to racial diversity." The NAS had attacked Gurin's research for not indicating the number of minority students necessary to achieve the reported results.

Judge Duggan concluded his compelling state interest analysis: "This Court is persuaded based upon the record before it, that a racially and ethnically diverse student body produces significant educational benefits such that diversity, in the context of higher education, constitutes a compelling governmental interest under strict scrutiny."

Having approved Michigan's affirmative action program for its compelling diversity goal, the district court then focused on the question of whether the admissions procedures at issue from 1995 to 2000 were narrowly tailored enough to survive the second element of strict scrutiny. Once again, Judge Duggan relied on Justice Powell's *Bakke* opinion, which had rejected the University of California at Davis Medical School's rigid quota (sixteen seats) for admitting "disadvantaged" (in practice, "Negro, Asian, or Chicano") students. Justice Powell, however, had cited approvingly Harvard's admissions policy of using race/ethnicity as a "plus," along with other factors (e.g., geographic origin or life experiences), to achieve diversity. Powell, following Harvard's amicus brief in *Bakke*, observed that affirmative action programs, in order to pass judicial scrutiny, must consider each applicant individually and not place students in different pools based on race/ethnicity.

Using Powell's analysis in *Bakke*, Duggan made short work of the University of Michigan CLSA affirmative action plan used in 1995–1997 when Gratz's and Hamacher's applications were considered and ultimately rejected. Because the grid systems used prior to 1999 separated minorities and nonminorities into different pools for consideration, and protected or reserved seats for underrepresented minorities, the policy "cross[ed] that thin line from the permissible to the impermissible," in Judge Duggan's opinion. "It is clear," he declared, "that the [C]LSA's system operated as the functional equivalent of a quota, and, therefore, ran afoul of Justice Powell's opinion in *Bakke*."

Yet the district court upheld the newer "selection index" put in place at UM after 1997. This revised affirmative action program allowed admissions officers to assign applicants points based on various factors, including GPA, test scores, "legacy" (relation to a Michigan alum) status, Michigan residence, geographic origin, extracurricular achievement, athletic ability, socioeconomic level, and race/ethnicity. The more points an applicant accumulated, the higher the odds of admission. Students from racial/ethnic groups deemed "underrepresented" at UM (African Americans, Hispanics, and Native Americans) were assigned 20 points, as were scholarship athletes and economically disadvantaged applicants. (Even if applicants fell into multiple 20-point categories, however, they could receive only one award of 20 points). The highest number of points were awarded for high school GPA (80 for a perfect 4.0), with a sliding scale of points for lower GPAs. Twelve points were the highest total for perfect SAT or ACT scores. A Michigan resident earned 10 points, while other geographic origins earned 6 points. Extracurricular achievement scored 5 extra points, and legacies added 4 points. An outstanding application essay garnered 3 points. Admissions officers followed these decision guidelines based on the point totals: 100 to 150, admit; 95 to 99, admit or postpone; 90 to 94, postpone or admit; 75 to 89, delay or postpone; 74 or below, delay or reject. Officers could also flag applications for further review. Plaintiffs argued that such flags were used primarily for minority applicants.

The University of Michigan persuaded the district court that the point-based procedure did not separate minorities and nonminorities into different pools, nor did it impose rigid quotas on admission of underrepresented minorities. Instead, UM argued successfully that the index system was exactly the same as Justice Powell's example of using race as a plus, or tipping point, for admissions decisions in order to create a diverse entering class of undergraduates. Duggan opined that "race or ethnic background is simply one element — to be weighed fairly against other elements — in the selection process." The judge was not dissuaded by the fact that race/ethnicity earned more points than most of the other criteria in the index, noting Justice Powell's conclusion that, when universities use race as a plus, they do not have to accord it the same weight as other admissions factors.

Summarizing his ruling in favor of the index system used by the university's CLSA after 1997, Duggan wrote, "The Court is satisfied that the [C]LSA's current admissions program, under which certain minority applicants receive a 'plus' on account of their race but are not insulated from all competition with other applicants, meets with the requirements set forth by Justice Powell in *Bakke* and is therefore constitutional."

A few months later, Duggan issued another ruling in the University of Michigan CLAS case. The Federal Rules of Civil Procedure allow third persons, not originally a party to the suit, but claiming an interest in the subject matter, to enter a case in order to protect their rights or interpose their claims. Such persons, who come into the case by right or permission of the court, are labeled "intervenors." Seventeen African American and Latino students, who had applied for, or intended to apply for, admission to UM, joined by Citizens for Affirmative Action's Preservation, an organization whose mission is to preserve opportunities in higher education for African American and Latino students in Michigan, became defendant-intervenors in *Gratz v. Bollinger* by permission of the Sixth Circuit U.S. Court of Appeals (after the district court had denied the minority students' petition to intervene). On February 26, 2001, Judge Duggan announced the district court's opinion on the intervenors' assertion that the CLSA's admissions programs "serve the uncontroverted compelling interest in remedying [UM's] past and current discrimination against minorities." In particular, the intervenors contended that the university's race-conscious admissions policies should be upheld because they served to "remedy the present effects of discrimination that it has caused or tolerated; remedy the negative racial climate that it has sustained or that has been caused by others on the campus; and, remedy or off-set the effects of any current discrimination in which it is engaged."

Citing U.S. Supreme Court cases that addressed gerrymandering of "majority-minority" voting districts, government contract set-asides for minorities, and race-based layoffs, Judge Duggan asserted that "racial classifications may be justified by a State's interest in remedying the effects of past or present 'identified' discrimination. To rise to the level of 'compelling,' however, such an interest must meet two conditions. 'First, the discrimination must be "identified discrimination" . . . with some specificity. . . . Second, the institution that makes the racial distinction must have had "a strong basis in evidence" to conclude that remedial action was necessary, "before it embarks on an affirmative-action program."'"

Because the intervenors had offered the district court no evidence that the state of Michigan ever segregated its higher education system or that the University of Michigan's admissions policies at issue were voluntary plans to integrate that system, Duggan ruled that the intervenors had to "present evidence of particular identified discrimination." The judge noted Justice O'Connor's conclusion in the local government contract set-aside case (*City of Richmond v. J. A. Croson Co.*) that "a generalized assertion of past discrimination in a particular industry or region is not adequate because 'it provides no guidance for a legislative body to determine the precise scope of the injury it seeks to remedy.'" Moreover, Justice Powell's decision striking down the Jackson, Michigan, school district's race-based layoff program (whereby white teachers with more seniority were let go before junior black colleagues during budget cutbacks) stated that "an effort to alleviate the effects of societal discrimination is not a compelling interest."

The intervenors, according to Judge Duggan, failed to demonstrate that the university's undergraduate admissions programs had any intention other than to create diverse classes. Moreover, there was no evidence that the admissions decisions had ever discriminated against minorities. In fact, their numbers on campus had trended upward even prior to when the affirmative action programs were put in place.

Although the intervenors provided credible evidence of racial tensions on the Michigan campus well into the 1990s, they could not demonstrate that the university had caused the tensions or even been a "passive participant" in allowing racial hostility to escalate. Judge Duggan cited the U.S. Supreme Court's acknowledgment in *Croson* that "the sorry history of both private and public discrimination in this country has contributed to a lack of opportunities for African Americans. This observation, however, by itself, is not sufficient to justify race-conscious measures." Therefore, Duggan dismissed the intervenors' contention because they had "failed to present sufficient evidence . . . in support of their claim that the [C]LSA's admissions programs in existence from 1995 through 1997 were a narrowly tailored means of achieving the compelling governmental interest of remedying the present effects of past discrimination." He specifically observed, however, that his ruling on the intervenors' claim had no effect on his previous ruling upholding the CLSA's post-1997 point-based affirmative action admissions policy, which he had found constitutional as a narrowly tailored means of achieving the compelling governmental interest of diversity.

The district court's split decision, invalidating the grid-based affirmative action program in place from 1995 to 1997, while upholding the point-index admissions policy used starting in 1998, gave each side one victory and one defeat. Not surprisingly, both parties in the litigation (Gratz/Hamacher and the University of Michigan) appealed Judge Duggan's ruling to the U.S. Court of Appeals for the Sixth Circuit, which includes the states of Michigan, Kentucky, Ohio, and Tennessee in its jurisdiction. On December 6, 2001, the Sixth Circuit heard oral argument in the appeal en banc, that is, the hearing included the full complement of judges from the circuit, as it can agree to do for especially important litigation, instead of the usual three-judge panel used in most cases. Circuit procedure usually requires a trio of judges to hear the case first, whereupon the losing party can petition the circuit to rehear the case en banc. In *Gratz* the CIR had petitioned for an *initial* hearing en banc.

On the same day, the Sixth Circuit also heard oral argument en banc in Barbara Grutter's case addressing the University of Michigan Law School's affirmative action policy in admissions. In December 1997 Grutter, the unsuccessful white applicant to UM Law School, had originally commenced her lawsuit, *Grutter v. Bollinger,* in the U.S. District Court for the Eastern District of Michigan, Southern Division, Detroit. After a procedural hearing three years later, the district court identified the issues for trial, which it heard over fifteen days in February 2001 before Judge Bernard A. Friedman, a Reagan appointee. The plaintiff had applied for admission to the law school in 1996, was placed on the waiting list, and ultimately rejected in 1997. Grutter alleged that the law school had denied her admission because it used race as a "predominant" factor, providing minority applicants (African Americans, Native Americans, Mexican Americans, and mainland Puerto Ricans, identified by the law school as deserving special attention in the admissions process) "a significantly greater chance of admission than students with similar credentials from disfavored racial groups." The law school responded that it had "a current intention to continue using race as a factor in admissions, as part of a broad array of qualifications and characteristics of which racial or ethnic origin is but a single though important element."

Like Gratz and Hamacher in the undergraduate case, Grutter claimed that the defendants violated the Fourteenth Amendment's equal protection clause and Title VI. On March 27, 2001, Judge Friedman issued the district court's opinion in *Grutter v. Bollinger.* He began by identifying three issues in the case: "1) the extent to which race is a factor in the law school's admissions decisions; 2) whether the law school's consideration of race in making admissions decisions constitutes a double standard in which minority and non-minority students are treated differently; and 3) whether the law school may take race into account to 'level the playing field' between minority and non-minority applicants."

Friedman summarized the law school's affirmative action admissions policy adopted by the faculty in 1992. "To admit a group of students who individually and collectively are among the most capable students applying to American law schools in a given year . . . with varying backgrounds and experiences who will respect and learn from each other," the law school used an index of applicants' LSAT scores and undergraduate GPAs, along with "soft" variables. These could include "the enthusiasm of recommenders, the level of the undergraduate institution, the quality of the applicant's essay, and . . . undergraduate course selection." The admissions committee also looked for applicants whose "perspective or experiences . . . will contribute to the diverse student body." The law school's policy stated, "The applicant may for example be a member of a minority group whose experiences are likely to be different from those of most students, may be likely to make a unique contribution to the bar, or may have had a successful career as a concert pianist or may speak five languages."

The policy also stated the law school's commitment to a particular type of diversity, that is, "racial and ethnic diversity with special reference to the inclusion of students from groups which have been historically discriminated against, like African Americans, Hispanics and Native Americans, who without this commitment may not be represented in our student body in meaningful numbers," which the school labeled a "critical mass." In addition to creating a diverse class to start law school each fall, the university also wanted to serve the public interest by training lawyers from groups that the faculty identified as historically underrepresented in the law profession.

At trial the director of Michigan Law School's admissions office

testified that only ten underrepresented minority students per entering class would be admitted if the decisions were based totally on
LSAT and GPA numbers. Under the affirmative action policy, at least
11 percent of each entering class since 1992 were African American,
Hispanic, or Native American. Jeffrey Lehman, dean of the law
school, stated that the extent to which race/ethnicity entered into
admissions decisions varied from one applicant to another. Sometimes
minority status played no role, whereas at other times it was "determinative." The dean contended that a critical mass of minority candidates could not be achieved without affirmative action because of
the disparity between minority and nonminority applicants' LSAT
and GPA statistics. Lehman also acknowledged that in 1995 all
African American applicants with an LSAT score of 159 to 160 and a
GPA of 3.00 were admitted, whereas only 1 of 54 Asian and 4 of 190
Caucasian applicants with these same qualification were admitted.

Professor Richard Lempert, who chaired the law school committee that drafted the 1992 admissions policy, told the district court that
racial diversity is an important part of "perspective" or "experiential"
diversity born of discrimination. A critical mass of minorities was necessary so that they did not feel that they were serving as spokespersons
for their race. Lempert asserted that the affirmative action program
was not intended as a remedy for past discrimination; race was considered in admissions only to the extent it was needed to achieve critical mass. He also indicated that groups such as Asians and Jews,
though they had suffered from past discrimination, were not included
in the law school's admissions policy because they were already admitted to the school in significant numbers. Lempert reported that critical mass figures of 11 to 17 percent (with a cap of 20 percent) for
underrepresented minorities were deleted from the final draft of the
admissions policy out of concern that they might be viewed as quotas. UM Law School's dean and admissions director both attested to
the fact that they monitored "daily admissions reports," which
classified applicants by race. The reports indicated the numbers of
minorities who applied, were accepted, and paid the enrollment
deposit, as well as the number placed on a waiting list.

In addition to such testimony from the defendants, revealing the extent to which race/ethnicity played a role in admissions, Judge Friedman was influenced by statistics that the plaintiff's side provided,

showing that the relative odds for acceptance of Native Americans, African Americans, and Latinos were many times greater than for similarly credentialed Caucasian applicants. This led Friedman to conclude, "Evidence shows that race is not, as the defendants have argued, merely one factor which is considered among many others in the admissions process. Rather, the evidence indisputably demonstrates that the law school places a very heavy emphasis on an applicant's race in deciding whether to accept or reject." Despite the law school's attempts to steer clear of illegal quotas, Friedman's opinion for the district court noted that the admissions and graduation data confirmed the school's consistent enrollment of African Americans, Native Americans, and Latinos in the 10 to 17 percent range, even though their LSAT scores and GPAs were considerably lower than Caucasian applicants. He also emphasized that there would be no need for the racially categorized "daily admissions report" "unless it were being used to ensure that the target percentage is achieved." In Friedman's words, "The court finds that the law school explicitly considers the race of applicants in order to enroll a critical mass of underrepresented minority students — that is, the law school wants 10 percent to 17 percent of each entering class to consist of African American, Native American, and Hispanic students."

Friedman's opinion then turned to the "central issue" in the case: "whether the Constitution permits the consideration of race in order to achieve racial diversity. In current constitutional parlance, the question is whether the achievement of racial diversity is a compelling state interest, and, if so, whether the law school's admission policy is narrowly tailored to serve that interest." He then collapsed the equal protection and Title VI claims into one, saying that the legal analysis for both was the same, with the starting point at the 1978 *Bakke* decision.

Although Judge Friedman noted that some courts had interpreted *Bakke* to embrace the diversity rationale for affirmative action in higher education as a compelling state interest (including his colleague Judge Duggan in the *Gratz* decision released three months previously), the *Grutter* ruling rejected Michigan's argument that *Bakke* had declared constitutional "a state's educational desire to assemble a racially diverse student body." Friedman dismissed the position taken by the university in both *Gratz* and *Grutter* that four other justices had joined Justice Powell's *Bakke* opinion declaring diversity a compelling state interest. "Further, in *post-Bakke* decisions," Friedman argued, "the Supreme Court has indicated quite clearly that it looks upon racial classifications with even more suspicion than was the case at the time *Bakke* was decided [in 1978]." He cited *Adarand* and *Croson* as "clearly indicat[ing] that racial classifications are unconstitutional unless they are intended to remedy carefully documented effects of past discrimination." Therefore, the district court concluded that diversity in university admissions was not a compelling interest if it was not a remedy for past discrimination.

Judge Friedman could have stopped at this point, simply striking down the University of Michigan Law School's affirmative action plan for its failure to meet the first criterion of equal protection clause analysis, namely, the compelling state interest requirement. Yet he moved to the next criterion, a narrow tailoring of the program at issue, and he concluded that the law school's policy failed that test, too. The defendants never defined the "critical mass" of minorities that they hoped to enroll in each first-year class. The court was not persuaded by the admissions office's apparent ability to "know it when they see it," regarding the number of minorities needed to go beyond mere tokenism. Moreover, Friedman observed that the law school had set no time limit on its use of race in admissions decision. In *Croson*, he noted, the Supreme Court had "been highly critical of racial classifications which are not strictly limited in duration." In addition, the district court found that the "critical mass" goal meant, in effect, that at least 10 percent of each entering class was reserved for minorities, which was "indistinguishable from a straight quota system," the kind Justice Powell struck down in *Bakke*. The lack of a "logical basis" for choosing the three minority groups singled out for preferred treatment also drew Judge Friedman's criticism.

The law school's inability to meet the standards of constitutional/ statutory review for its affirmative action program led the district court, via Judge Friedman's opinion, to conclude that the affirmative action policy violated the equal protection clause of the Fourteenth Amendment and Title VI of the 1964 Civil Rights Act.

As in the *Gratz* case, intervenors participated in the *Grutter* litigation and argued similarly that affirmative action programs in higher education are legal remedies for societal discrimination. The intervenors' witnesses presented thirty hours of testimony before the district court.

They included four minority students who testified about their experiences in higher education and professional schools. Gary Orfield, professor of education and social policy at Harvard and the nation's premier scholar of race's impact on American schools, provided massive amounts of data and expert testimony on affirmative action. Renowned civil rights historian John Hope Franklin, an African American, presented his own experiences with discrimination over the course of his education and career. He even recalled that, throughout his adulthood, white patrons at hotels where he stayed assumed he was part of the staff instead of a celebrated guest!

Yet Judge Friedman observed that no party in the *Grutter* litigation had "alleged, or offered any evidence to suggest, that the law school or the University of Michigan has committed any acts of discrimination against any minority group which might warrant a race-based remedy." Even if such evidence had been presented to the court, Friedman concluded that "the law school's use of race [could not] be justified on the alternative grounds urged by the intervenors — to 'level the playing field' between applicants of minority and non-minority races — because the remedying of societal discrimination, either past or present, has not been recognized as a compelling state interest."

Although Judge Friedman agreed with his colleague Judge Duggan on the U.S. District Court for the Eastern District of Michigan regarding this last point, they had come to diametrically opposed decisions on the affirmative action plans challenged in *Gratz* and *Grutter*. Duggan had upheld the "selection index" used by the undergraduate college at UM; Friedman had invalidated the racial preferences at issue in the Michigan Law School case.

The university appealed the district court's decision in *Grutter* to the Sixth Circuit, which now had appeals before it in both the undergraduate and law school litigations. The polarizing effect of affirmative action issues, as evidenced in *Bakke* and the two divergent district court opinions in *Grutter* and *Gratz* almost a quarter century later, starkly revealed itself at the appeals court level. The Sixth Circuit U.S. Court of Appeals is one of the most ideologically contentious of the federal appellate tribunals. Nominations to the circuit have been especially conflictual because it is closely divided between liberals and conservatives.

Barbara Grutter, like Gratz, requested an initial hearing by an en banc bench. At the time of Grutter's request, the Sixth Circuit had eleven judges. Five were conservative jurists, appointed by Republican presidents. If she could sway one more vote to her side, she would win at the appellate level by a vote of 6:5. Her request was granted, but not before two of the conservative judges took senior status, which removed them from the en banc panel. The controversy over the panel's composition even reached the U.S. Senate, where conservative staff members of the Judiciary Committee accused Elaine Jones, then head of the NAACP's Legal Defense and Educational Fund (LDF), of contacting Senator Edward Kennedy (D-MA) to encourage him to delay decisions on the Bush administration's nominees to the Sixth Circuit who might vote to overturn Judge Duggan's decision upholding the Michigan undergraduate affirmative action policy and vote to uphold Judge Friedman's ruling against the UM Law School's racial preferences. Conservative interest groups petitioned the Virginia Bar Association to disbar Jones for interfering in ongoing litigation. Shortly thereafter, she announced her retirement from the LDF.

On May 14, 2002, Chief Judge Boyce Martin Jr., a Jimmy Carter appointee, handed down the much-anticipated opinion of the Sixth Circuit's nine-judge en banc panel. With a razor-thin majority of 5:4, the appellate tribunal reversed the district court's judgment and upheld the University of Michigan Law School's affirmative action policy for admissions. The first line of Chief Judge Martin's opinion for the majority signaled that the court would find in favor of the university appellants. Martin wrote, "The Law School drafted its admissions policy to comply with the Supreme Court's opinion in *Bakke*." He also emphasized that the admissions officials evaluated each applicant individually and read each application in order to consider all its information in making the decisions on whether to admit. In following another requirement set out in *Bakke*, the law school, according to the appeals court, did not set aside or reserve seats for underrepresented minorities. The court accepted the law school's argument that the critical mass of such minorities was not a set number or percentage.

Martin then reviewed the district court's finding that the law school's admissions policy to produce diversity was neither a compelling state interest nor narrowly tailored. He began by rejecting Judge Friedman's view that Justice Powell's acceptance of diversity as a compelling state interest in *Bakke* was nonbinding and that the U.S. Supreme Court had only accepted remedying specific instances of discrimination as compelling. Intoned Martin for himself and his four colleagues, "Because Justice Powell's opinion is binding on this court . . . and because *Bakke* remains the law until the Supreme Court instructs otherwise, we reject the district court's conclusion and find that the law school has a compelling interest in achieving a diverse student body." (In validating diversity as a compelling reason for the affirmative action plan at issue, Martin did not address the intervenors' argument that it was a means to remedy past discrimination.)

The circuit's majority interpreted Justice Powell's position on diversity as binding precedent because it provided the narrowest rationale (narrower than Justice Brennan's rationale for affirmative action to remedy past societal discrimination) for the Supreme Court's judgment in the California-Davis case. In fact, Chief Judge Martin accused the lower court of overruling the Supreme Court's *Bakke* decision, which only the highest court in the land could do. That said, the appellate court declared Powell's interpretive standard as governing the outcome of the *Grutter* case. Simply stated, "Because this court is bound by Justice Powell's *Bakke* opinion, we find that the law school has a compelling state interest in achieving a diverse student body." Given that universities had been relying on *Bakke* since 1978 as a "how-to-do-it manual for the admission of minority applicants to professional schools," Martin refused to read the Supreme Court's 1995 decision in *Adarand* (allowing affirmative action in government contracts only to remedy documented effects of past discrimination) as an implicit overturning of Powell's judgment.

The appeals court then examined the narrow tailoring component of strict scrutiny, using Powell's requirements that affirmative action plans to promote the compelling state interest of diversity in higher education must not employ segregated, dual-track admissions systems or use quotas for underrepresented minorities, but could use race/ ethnicity as plus factors in admissions decisions à la the Harvard model. Martin repeated the first line of his opinion for the court that Michigan Law School had drafted its admission policy in 1992 to comply with *Bakke* and therefore closely followed the Harvard plan and did not impose quotas. The appellate court simply accepted at face value the Michigan witnesses' testimony, including the current and former admissions directors of the law school, who swore that they did not reserve or set aside seats for minorities and that they maintained a single admissions system, not a two-track procedure that separated minority and nonminority applicants. Martin's opinion determined that the law school's policy was "virtually indistinguishable from the Harvard plan Justice Powell approved in *Bakke*." The court did not view the critical mass for admitting underrepresented minorities as a quota because the law school had "no fixed goal or target."

The appellate tribunal then dismissed the remaining factors that Judge Friedman had used to invalidate the Michigan plan, including the lack of clarity in defining critical mass and its apparent open time frame, as well as the dearth of logic the district court had found in the university's selection of only three minority groups for favored treatment. Chief Judge Martin countered that if critical mass was more clearly defined as a definite percentage, it would then run afoul of the *Bakke* quota ban. Michigan's selection of African Americans, Hispanics, and Native Americans was similar to Harvard's identification of "blacks and Chicanos" in its affirmative action plan, and "some degree of deference must be accorded to the educational judgment of the [UM] Law School in its determination of which groups to target," concluded the appeals court. Addressing the open-ended element of the Michigan plan, Martin contended, that, "unlike a remedial interest, an interest in academic diversity does not have a self-contained stopping point. . . . The record indicates that the law school intends to consider race and ethnicity to achieve a diverse and robust student body only until it becomes possible to enroll a 'critical mass' of underrepresented minority students through race-neutral means."

Thus, by the narrowest of margins, the Sixth Circuit Court of Appeals reversed the U.S. District Court for the Eastern District of Michigan and overturned the trial court's order prohibiting the law school from considering race and ethnicity in its admissions decisions.

Judge Danny Boggs, a Reagan appointee, wrote the lead dissent from the Sixth Circuit's majority opinion. Its blunt opening line established the tone of the dissenters, as did the remarkable "Procedural Appendix," accusing Boyce Martin, the circuit's chief judge, of manipulating the outcome of the case by Machiavellian machinations that stacked the deck in his favor at the en banc hearing. Boggs tartly commenced the substantive portion of his opinion: "This case involves a straightforward instance of racial discrimination by a state institution." He believed that all elements of the Michigan Law School's affirmative action program "point[ed] to a denial of equal protection of the laws. I, therefore, dissent from our court's decision today finding this discrimination to be constitutional."

Quoting from his own inquiries at oral argument, Judge Boggs reported that he had asked the Michigan Law School's counsel, "If Barbara Grutter walked in to whoever the current Dean of the law school is and said, 'Dean, would you let me in if I were black?' wouldn't he have to say either 'Yes' or 'pretty darn almost certainly'?" The counsel agreed, but replied that "a black woman who had otherwise an application that looked like Barbara Grutter, *would be a different person.*" (Boggs emphasized the final phrase.) His opinion included a pithy observation on the Michigan counsel's response: "That answer puts starkly the policy of discrimination practiced throughout the ages."

Rather than using *Bakke* as a starting point for his dissenting analysis, Boggs went back to the framers of the Fourteenth Amendment, who "decided that our government should abstain from social engineering through explicit racial classifications." If government does use such classifications, they must withstand "strict scrutiny." Under the compelling state interest and narrow tailoring doctrines required by that level of judicial examination, Boggs simply concluded that the law school's admissions scheme could not pass constitutional muster. He could find no convincing evidence that diversity in professional education was compelling, and, even if it was, he judged the law school's plan not narrowly tailored to meet that interest. "Even a cursory glance at the Law School's admissions data reveals the staggering magnitude of the law school's racial preference. Its admissions officers have swapped tailor's shears for a chainsaw," Boggs derisively concluded.

The lead dissent also rejected the majority's interpretation of the various opinions in *Bakke*, with Boggs offering that the most guidance they provided was that the UC-Davis affirmative action plan was unconstitutional because of its strict quota and that some sort of racial preference may be constitutional. Even if more specificity could be gleaned from *Bakke* on permissible rationales for racial preferences in admissions, Boggs argued that they did not form any precedential core

of the case because Alan Bakke brought the litigation as the sole plaintiff, not as the lead party in a class action suit. Once the Supreme
Court struck down the plan that prevented his admission, and ordered
his acceptance to the Davis medical school, the rest of the court's
opinions were dicta, that is, not related to the main issue in the case
and therefore not binding on future courts.

With *Bakke*, and particularly Powell's arguments, diminished as the
controlling precedent in *Grutter*, Judge Boggs resurrected the district
court's reasoning that more recent Supreme Court cases, especially
Adarand, clearly mandated that "racial classifications are unconstitutional unless they are intended to remedy carefully documented effects
of past discrimination." The dissent observed that UM Law School
"declined to justify its policy as remedying past discrimination," and
"even if we give full force to Justice Powell's discussion of the 'virtues
of diversity,' the law school's program provides the linguistic term, but
not substance."

Even if diversity could be deemed compelling, Boggs saw no way
to interpret it as narrowly tailored. He was dismissive of the Harvard
model that Justice Powell relied on to exemplify constitutional narrow
tailoring. How could a vague plan, appended to an amicus brief, and
not even part of the factual record, become the basis of determining a
program's validity? Moreover, Boggs proclaimed, "I cannot believe that
a 'plus' of any size, no matter how large, would therefore be constitutional. I believe that the law school's preference is just too large to be
narrowly tailored." Moreover, the discrepancy in rates of acceptance
for underrepresented minorities with lower qualifications than majority
applicants proved to Boggs that the law school maintained a "two-
track," segregated admissions system. He focused on statistics indicating that race could take the chances of admission from near zero to
near 100 percent in the Michigan scheme. The data showing that the
law school admitted its target critical mass each year were evidence to
Boggs that the plan was "indistinguishable from a quota system."

As the dissent came to its inevitable conclusion, Judge Boggs dismissed the findings of Michigan professor Patricia Gurin, claiming
that her research submitted to the trial court "suffer[ed] from pro-
found empirical and methodological defects that lead me to doubt its
probative value." The alleged claim of diversity's salutary impact on
students rested solely on their subjective self-reporting.

Boggs acknowledged that race, ethnicity, religion, and other ancestral characteristics may still matter in American society, but "we cannot simply suspend the Equal Protection Clause until such factors no longer matter." He concluded the substantive portion of his lengthy dissent: "Michigan's plan does not seek diversity for education's sake. It seeks racial numbers for the sake of the comfort that those abstract numbers may bring. It does so at the expense of the real rights of real people to fair consideration. . . . Barbara Grutter . . . ended up outside a door that a government's use of racial considerations denied [her] a fair chance to enter. I therefore respectfully dissent from the court's legitimation of this unconstitutional policy."

Boggs's meticulous disagreement with the merits of the Sixth Circuit's majority opinion would have seemed more than adequate to express the dissent of four members of the en banc panel with Chief Judge Martin. The fact that Boggs felt the need to append a "procedural" dissent demonstrated the rift that the affirmative action controversy had opened in a federal appellate circuit that reached from the mid-South to the upper Midwest. Boggs accused his colleague Boyce Martin, chief judge of the Sixth Circuit, of violating the court's internal rules by placing himself on the three-judge panel that heard procedural motions in the *Grutter* case. More damning was Boggs's complaint that Martin held Grutter's petition for an en banc hearing for 150 days (considerably longer than usual) in order to prevent two judges from participating on the enlarged panel before they took senior status. Because these judges (Alan E. Norris, a Reagan appointee, and Richard F. Suhrheinrich, nominated by George H. W. Bush) were conservatives, they could well have tipped the balance in *Grutter* to the position affirming the district court's decision invalidating the Michigan Law School's admissions policy.

Even more stunning was the open warfare between the two sides on the Sixth Circuit over whether procedural differences should be aired publicly. In a concurring opinion, Boggs's colleague Judge Karen Nelson Moore accused the dissenters who supported the "Procedural Appendix" of perpetrating "grave harm not only to themselves, but to this court and even to the Nation as a whole." Although Judge Moore, a Clinton nominee, accepted the tradition of jurists disagreeing over "principle" in their published opinions, she vociferously countered Judge Boggs's effort to publicize "disagreements over the internal workings of the court," which, as Boggs himself conceded, "do not directly affect the legal principles discussed in this case." She accused her dissenting colleague of articulating an "unfounded assertion that the majority's decision . . . is the result of political maneuvering and manipulation. The baseless argument of the 'Procedural Appendix' is that the decisions of this court are not grounded in principle and reasoned argument, but in power, and that the judges of this court manipulate and ignore the rules in order to advance political agendas. . . . I am concerned that my dissenting colleagues' actions will severely undermine public confidence in this court." Judge Moore stated the truism that "because we judges are unelected and serve during good behavior, our only source of democratic legitimacy is the perception that we engage in principled decision-making. . . . The decisions of this court are not self-executing but instead must be carried into practice by other actors. They will do so only as long as they regard us as legitimate, as we possess neither the power of the purse nor the sword, but only judgment. . . . Our ability to perform these crucial tasks is imperiled when members of this court take it upon themselves to 'expose to public view' disagreements over procedure." She labeled the conduct of Judge Boggs, and those who joined his procedural dissent, as "nothing short of shameful. . . . [It] will irreparably damage the already strained working relationships among the judges of this court." After challenging his "inaccurate and misleading account of the procedural facts underlying" the *Grutter* appeal, Judge Moore concluded that "Judge Boggs's opinion marks a new low point in the history of the Sixth Circuit."

Judge Boggs specifically contested Judge Moore's conclusion, ending his dissent with the counterpunch, "Legitimacy protected only by our silence is fleeting. If any damage has been done to the court, it is the work of the actors, not the reporters." Judge Alice Batchelder, another George H. W. Bush appointee, who voted with the four dissenters, briefly put pen to paper to support

Judge Boggs's careful and scholarly dissent. I write separately to say that I concur in all of that dissent, including the exposition of the procedural history of the case. In her separate concurrence, Judge Moore expresses her belief that by revealing that history, Judge Boggs — and I, by concurring — undermine the legitimacy of the court and do harm to ourselves, this court, and the nation. I believe that exactly the opposite is true. Public confidence in this court or any other is premised on the certainty that the court follows the rules in every case, regardless of the question that a particular case presents. Unless we expose to public view our failures to follow the court's established procedures, our claim to legitimacy is illegitimate.

The appellate court's decision upholding the University of Michigan Law School's affirmative action plan in *Grutter* attracted predictable responses — none of which focused on the Sixth Circuit's extraordinarily public infighting over internal procedural matters. The university's interim president, B. Joseph White, hailed the ruling as "a very wise decision, both for the university and for all of higher education. There is broad recognition of the importance of a diverse student body and that diversity is obviously crucial for preparing students for our diverse democracy." Grutter's lawyers vowed to take the case to the nation's highest court. The CIR's president, Terence Pell, commented, "While UM may have eked out a 5:4 decision, the opinions themselves suggest little legal support for racially segregated admissions policies. I am confident the Supreme Court will correct this error." Pell and his CIR colleagues had also suffered another loss at the circuit level. In December 2000 the Ninth U.S. Circuit Court of Appeals had sided with the University of Washington Law School in upholding its affirmative action program under Powell's *Bakke* precedent. The so-called split in the circuits, however, with the Sixth and Ninth affirming racial preferences and the Fifth (in *Hopwood*) striking them down, made it more likely that the U.S. Supreme Court would accept the *Grutter* appeal to create uniformity in the law.

The woman at the vortex of the controversy, Barbara Grutter, tried to put a positive gloss on her loss at the circuit level: "I've anticipated from the beginning that this would have to go to the Supreme Court, and today's decision just takes us one step closer." The next step in Grutter's journey to the nation's highest tribunal came three months later, in August 2002, when her lawyers submitted a petition for a writ of certiorari asking the justices to accept *Grutter v. Bollinger* on appeal. "At the most fundamental level," the lawyers wrote, "the question [the case] raises is whether our nation's principles of equal protection and nondiscrimination mean the same thing for all races." Arguing that the high court should reverse the Sixth Circuit's ruling, the petition contended, "Enshrined as a compelling interest, diversity will instead give the nation its first permanent legal justification for racial classifications. That justification, despite the language or label applied, will be one that is indistinguishable from an interest in simple racial balancing." Grutter commented to the press at the time her petition was submitted that, if the University of Michigan Law School really took a broad view of diversity, it would have admitted her — a mid-career businesswoman and forty-three-year-old mother when she applied, whose experiences would have truly been different from those of her younger classmates. Instead, she concluded, "It was not a diversity issue, it was a race issue." UM's vice president and general counsel, Marvin Krislov, responded to Grutter's filing of a "cert" petition that "if the Supreme Court decides to hear this case, we believe that we will prevail, and that the court will reaffirm that colleges and universities may consider race to achieve the educational benefits of diversity."

The Sixth Circuit's fractious approach to the Michigan cases once again drew Congress's attention. Representative James Sensenbrenner Jr. (R-WI), chair of the House Judiciary Committee, contacted Chief Judge Martin shortly after release of the dueling opinions in *Grutter* to say that he was investigating the matter. Martin met with committee staffers and provided public documents explaining the circuit's procedures. Nothing came of the inquiry at that time.

In October 2002, attorneys for Gratz and Hamacher also petitioned the high court to issue a writ of certiorari. They did so under highly unusual circumstances. Without explanation, the Sixth Circuit had still not issued an opinion (despite hearing oral argument) on the appeal of the Michigan undergraduate case in which the district court had upheld the current point-based admissions policy. The students' lawyers reported that they could not wait any longer for the Sixth Circuit's ruling; nearly a year had passed since the appellate court had heard oral argument. Considering that the UM Law School litigation had already been appealed to the high bench, counsel for the rejected undergraduates argued in their petition that "the two cases considered together will present the court with a broader spectrum and more substantial record within which to consider the rule upon the common principles they involve." *Gratz v. Bollinger* "presents issues of fundamental national importance . . . and the resolution of these issues will almost certainly have effects that extend far beyond the parties to the case." Gratz's bitter question to her father, "Can we sue?" had come to this. She now had to hope that the U.S. Supreme Court would agree to hear her case without the usual step of having an appellate court decision before it. If it did, she would have to wish for better treatment outside the high court in Washington. After the Sixth Circuit's oral argument in her case, she had emerged from the federal courthouse in Cincinnati to be confronted by a protester who shouted at her, "Racist bitch!"

"All the Way to the Supreme Court"
Briefs for the Justices

On December 2, 2002, the U.S. Supreme Court granted the appeals of Gratz, Hamacher, and Grutter. The students rejected by the University of Michigan could take heart that their litigation was still alive and on its way to a hearing before the highest court in the land. The tribunal scheduled the oral argument for April 1, 2003, and the undergraduate and law school cases would each receive the standard one-hour allotment for presentations before, and questions from, the nine justices.

Solicitor General Ted Olson would be given time in each case to offer the United States government's argument. President George W. Bush's administration was temporarily divided over which position to take in the Michigan dispute. The Clinton administration had supported the university's affirmative action programs at the district court level. While governor of Texas, Bush had been pleased at the outcome of the *Hopwood* case, the Fifth Circuit U.S. Court of Appeals decision striking down racial preferences in admissions at the University of Texas Law School. In place of the university's similar policy for its undergraduate program, Governor Bush had implemented what he called "affirmative access," admitting the top 10 percent of students in each of Texas's high schools to the state university of their choice. As the Republican candidate for president in 2000, Bush had indicated his opposition to the use of quotas and racial/ethnic preferences in public education.

Bush's White House counsel and future attorney general, Alberto Gonzales, a Mexican American and proponent of affirmative action, along with Deputy Attorney General Larry Thompson, an African American, were reluctant to have the administration oppose programs favoring minorities at the same time that the Republican Party was attempting to expand support among them. Moreover, although opposition to "reverse discrimination" had been a mainstay of the party's attraction for white males, polling data showed that white women were more likely to support affirmative action. In addition, large corporations, including Microsoft and General Motors, were on the record as touting the benefits of diverse workforces. As Clint Bolick of the conservative Institute for Justice described the dilemma, "The issue of race is radioactive for this administration."

Clouding the GOP political picture even further at the time the Supreme Court announced it had granted certiorari in the Michigan cases was a firestorm around comments made by Senate majority leader Trent Lott (R-MS). At a 100th birthday party for onetime segregationist Senator Strom Thurmond (R-SC), Lott proclaimed that the country would have been better off if Thurmond's run for the presidency on the Dixiecrats' Jim Crow platform in 1948 had been successful. In an effort to salvage his leadership position, Lott announced that he supported affirmative action. (Shortly thereafter, the public pressure against him, spurred by bloggers and 24/7 media coverage, forced him to resign the majority leader position.) Conservatives worried that if Bush took a moderate position on the affirmative action cases, he would only encourage swing voter Justice Sandra Day O'Connor to issue one of her patented "split-the-difference" rulings (similar to Justice Powell's compromise in *Bakke*). They failed to realize that presidents have virtually no influence over how justices vote.

As the deadline neared for the Bush administration to submit a brief to the Supreme Court in the Michigan case by mid-January, officials announced that Bush would oppose the racial preferences used by the university in both its undergraduate and law programs. The president's press secretary revealed that Bush had been deeply involved in guiding the administration's position on the affirmative action litigation. On January 15, 2003, Bush made a seven-minute statement at the White House in which he declared both affirmative action policies employed by Michigan to be "divisive, unfair, and impossible to square with the Constitution." "At their core, the Michigan policies amount to a quota system that unfairly rewards or penalizes prospective students based solely on their race," Bush argued. In addition to the Lott debacle, the affirmative action debate in the administration was complicated by a desire to shore up its conservative base, long opposed to racial preferences, while trying to court Hispanics and African American voters for the president's 2004 reelection bid, which he hoped would provide a more definitive win for him than the virtual tie of election 2000. Ted Olson, who had successfully argued *Bush v. Gore* before the U.S. Supreme Court, which placed Bush in the White House, and was also the winning counsel in the *Hopwood* case, won the debate in the administration to make a strong argument *against* affirmative action in higher education. Curt Levey, director of legal affairs at the Center for Individual Rights, praised President Bush's statement as "very heartening." He came "as close to saying you can't use race as one can come without explicitly saying it," Levey observed.

Solicitor General Olson's friend-of-the-court briefs, stating the United States' position on behalf of the students denied admittance to Michigan, argued that the university's affirmative action policies relied unconstitutionally on race as a "decisive factor" in admissions decisions. His briefs emphasized alternative, race-neutral methods for achieving diversity, such as the percentage plans used by Texas, Florida, and California.

The petitioners (Gratz/Hamacher and Grutter) had to meet the same deadline (January 16) as the solicitor general for filing their "briefs on the merits" of the cases. According to the Court's rules, the merits briefs may not exceed fifty pages. After outlining the details of the undergraduate affirmative action policy used by the University of Michigan's College of Literature, Science, and the Arts, the *Gratz* brief drew a stark contrast between the federal government's argument in *Brown v. Board of Education* and UM's premise. The United States had declared in its 1954 *Brown* brief that "racial discriminations imposed by law, or having the sanction or support of government, inevitably tend to undermine the foundations of a society dedicated to freedom, justice, and equality." By contrast, Michigan assumed that "race is a defining characteristic of American life." Thus, the *Gratz* side argued that, even if the university's premise was accurate, it only emphasized the need for government to remain scrupulously nondiscriminatory in decisions regarding individuals. Moreover, Justice Powell's opinion in *Bakke* did *not* establish a Court precedent for viewing diversity in university admissions as a compelling state interest because he alone supported that view. The very concept of diversity is "simply too open-ended, ill-defined, and indefinite to constitute a compelling interest capable of supporting narrowly tailored means."

Therefore, the UM policy violated each prong of the Fourteenth Amendment's standard of review. In addition, the CLSA selection index that awarded 20 points to underrepresented minorities (African Americans, Hispanics, and Native Americans) constituted, in effect, a two-track system of consideration — one for preferred minorities and one for all other applicants (including Asian American minorities).

After delineating the facts of the Michigan Law School's affirmative action policy, as determined by the district court, the *Grutter* merits brief argued that the Supreme Court had recognized only "identified discrimination" as "sufficiently compelling to support narrowly tailored remedies." Justice Powell was the sole member of the *Bakke* court to accept diversity as a compelling state interest, the brief maintained, and the concept "is simply too indefinite, ill-defined, and lacking in objective, ascertainable standards to be fitted to narrowly tailored measures." The *Grutter* position, as presented to the Court in the brief, asserted that the law school's "critical mass" target for admitting underrepresented minorities (the same three groups that the undergraduate policy identified) was a "quota." "The point at which this 'critical mass' is reached can best be described as a matter for mystical and metaphysical inquiry," the brief sarcastically observed. It also described the preference granted to the favored minorities as a "dual" admissions system. Justice Powell was squarely on the record as opposing both quotas and two-track systems in university affirmative action plans. A review of the admissions statistics under the law school's affirmative action plan, Grutter's counsel contended, "demonstrate[d] that disadvantage on the basis of race works not only against Caucasian Americans, but also against other groups, including minority groups historically discriminated against, especially Asian Americans." The dean of the law school was even on the record as admitting "a willingness to admit minority students from generally lower academic qualifications [than] majority students."

Grutter's brief also cited *Brown* as a model for banning the use of race in providing education for Americans. The citation of such an icon in U.S. constitutional law was even more potent in light of the impending celebration of its fiftieth anniversary in 2004. The *Grutter* and *Gratz* briefs both used a strategy aimed at the Court's swing voter, Justice Sandra Day O'Connor, who was predicted to hold the determinative vote in these momentous cases. Each brief quoted her more than

{ *Chapter 5* }

any of the other previous or current members of the Court, with the exception of Justice Powell. They repeatedly cited her opinions in *Croson* and *Adarand*, in which she had focused on remedying identifiable discrimination as the only compelling state interest for using narrowly tailored racial or ethnic preferences in the employment context. The *Grutter* brief also equated the Michigan Law School's focus on diversity using just three racial/ethnic groups, based on the historical discrimination against them, with remedies for *societal* discrimination, which the Court had ruled previously did not rise to the level of a compelling state interest. "Mere evidence of some educational benefit," as portrayed in Michigan professor Patricia Gurin's research, did not raise diversity to the level of a compelling policy goal. "The preferences are both overinclusive and underinclusive, and hence there is no close 'fit' of means to end," as required under the narrow tailoring criterion.

The University of Michigan administrators representing the College of Literature, Science, and the Arts, as well as the law school, now had one month to submit to the Court their "briefs for respondents," which also could be no longer than fifty pages. Counsel for the respondents included the University of Michigan's general counsel, the law school's dean, and attorneys from law firms in Ann Arbor and Washington, D.C. In explaining the CLSA's admissions process, the brief focused on the University of Michigan's selectivity and its mission to create a diverse learning environment for its students. "Racial and ethnic diversity is a single, though crucial, element of the diversity the university seeks," but, the university contended, the predominant factor in admissions decisions was the high school GPA, which in the admissions 150-point "selection index" counted for up to 80 points. In contrast, membership in an underrepresented minority group (African Americans, Hispanics, or Native Americans) could win an applicant only 20 points. Admittedly, the racial and ethnic preferences could also earn an applicant's file a more "in-depth" review at the discretion of admissions counselors. UM argued that the results of this affirmative action policy had been "a student body of remarkable talent and diversity" that could not be achieved through race-neutral processes because "nationally and in the state of Michigan, average grades and test scores are lower for minority students."

UM rejected the purported race-neutral "percentage plan," being used in Texas, Florida, and California and supported by the Bush administration and the Gratz petitioners, because programs admitting the top 10 percent of graduates from each high school in order to diversify higher education "are premised on racial segregation in a state's elementary and secondary public school system." The university's brief observed that UM's undergraduate college is much more national in scope than most state schools, so that using the "10 percent" plan for Michigan high schools would not produce the selective enrollment traditionally accepted by the state's flagship institution. Other than the Detroit school system, which is overwhelmingly African American, Michigan's schools are primarily white. Hispanics and Native Americans do not constitute the majority of any school district in the state. These demographic realities made the percentage plans advocated by President Bush and the *Gratz* brief as a substitute for affirmative action ineffective for UM.

The university's brief in *Gratz* then turned to the heart of its legal argument: "In the twenty-five years since this Court's decision in *Regents of the University of California v. Bakke* virtually all of this nation's selective colleges and universities have embraced the educational value of a broadly diverse student body and have relied on *Bakke* in crafting admissions policies designed to obtain that diversity." Indeed, the U.S. Department of Education relied on *Bakke* as a guide in enforcing Title VI, according to the university's brief. In contrast to Gratz's argument that *Bakke* did *not* establish controlling precedent on the matter of diversity, the university asserted that "a majority of this Court held in *Bakke* that 'the state has a substantial interest that legitimately may be served by a properly devised admissions program involving the competitive consideration of race and ethnic origin.'" Clearly, the nub of the argument before the Court in 2003 was whether Justice Powell's 1978 judgment in *Bakke*, declaring diversity a compelling state interest, would control the outcome in the Michigan cases. The university countered Gratz's plea to set *Bakke* aside with a prediction that to do so "would have serious consequences for our national educational culture, leading, among other things, to a near-total absence of minority students in our nation's selective colleges and universities." Attempting to square its admissions procedures with the Harvard model of affirmative action that Justice Powell cited approbatively, UM declared unequivocally that it used no quotas or numerical targets for admitting or enrolling minority students and that every application received an individualized reading "according to a uniform set of standards." "Race is only one 'plus' factor among many" in the admissions process, concluded the university.

UM's legal brief for its undergraduate college tried an interesting tack in quoting Justice O'Connor, appealing to her pioneering status as the first female justice on the nation's highest court. In her concurring opinion from a 1994 jury case, O'Connor had stated, "We know that like race, gender matters. . . . [O]ne need not be a sexist to share the intuition that in certain cases a person's gender and resulting life experience will be relevant to his or her view of the case." Yet O'Connor once commented to a female interviewer who asked her about the impact of gender on her jurisprudence, "Each of us is the sum total and product of our experiences, but, when I walk across the threshold of this Court, I try to put that behind me."

Michigan refuted the Gratz position that to consider race and ethnicity in admissions results in stereotyping and stigmatizing of minority students. The research of former Harvard president Derek Bok and former Princeton president William Bowen of the Mellon Foundation found that "the overwhelming majority of African-American graduates of selective colleges and universities with race-sensitive admissions programs performed well and were very satisfied with their undergraduate educational experience." Such "concrete educational benefits generated by a diverse student body," the university maintained, "bears no resemblance to the generalized interest in remedying societal discrimination that has been rejected [by the Court] as 'amorphous.' " UM wrote that it looked forward to the day when race and ethnicity would not have to be a part of the admissions process to produce a diverse student body, but it did not speculate on when that day might arrive. Unlike Gratz, whose brief urged that race should never be decisive in an admissions decision, the university posited, "If race never made a difference in the outcome, it would not be a 'plus' factor in any meaningful sense," which would be "irreconcilable with *Bakke*."

The university concluded its Supreme Court brief in the undergraduate case: "The University of Michigan has a substantial interest in creating and maintaining a world-class, selective institution of higher learning, seeking to enroll a diverse array of the best students from within the State and beyond its borders. The University's current admissions system represents a careful and measured effort to tailor its admissions processes to its legitimate — indeed, unchallenged — educational objectives."

The University of Michigan Law School used the same team of attorneys to produce the respondents' brief in *Grutter* as the university utilized for the *Gratz* document. The only exception was that law school dean Jeffrey Lehman, who was one of the respondents in *Grutter*, therefore was not listed as a counsel in the law school case. UM had an advantage in the law school litigation that the undergraduate college did not enjoy; the law school had won at the court of appeals level, albeit with a closely divided and politically charged opinion. Though the undergraduate college had its most recent affirmative action policy upheld by the trial court, no appeals court opinion had been forthcoming prior to the oral argument at the U.S. Supreme Court. Thus, the law school brief began with a trio of "central realities" based on "historical facts" and "evidence" in the judicial record that supported the Sixth Circuit's opinion upholding the affirmative action program, which the brief asked the high court to affirm. First, academic selectivity and student diversity (including racial diversity) are crucial to the law school's mission. Second, the Michigan Law School's admissions policy was "virtually indistinguishable" from the Harvard plan approved by five justices in *Bakke*. Every applicant's dossier received an individual evaluation, and the Michigan process did not use quotas or set-asides. Third, no genuinely race-neutral scheme could yield meaningful diversity or students prepared to succeed at an elite law school. "There is accordingly no way for this Court to reverse the Sixth Circuit's decision without 'breaking . . . new ground,' " the university told the justices in its brief.

The law school also possessed another advantageous point in contrast to the undergraduate college. It could appeal to the justices' understanding of the legal profession and the need for a top law school to produce "leaders of the profession and of our nation." Those two points constituted a particularly resonant message for Justice O'Connor, who had led the way for women in the legal field and who is especially concerned with training civic leaders. Indeed, she came to the high court after a career in civic and political leadership, including her position as the first female majority leader of a state senate (in her native Arizona). By not assigning numerical points to race/ethnicity, the law school also distinguished itself from the undergraduate college's admissions index. In addition, racial and ethnic characteristics were not the only ones the law school considered in creating a diverse entering class each year.

The law school provided the justices with statistics indicating that color-blind admissions criteria would not yield a racially diverse student body. In 1997, when Grutter applied, only 67 minority applicants had LSAT scores above 163, the range from which more than 90 percent of the law students were admitted. Among the white and Asian American applicants, 1,236 had scores at that level. The record showed that to select a class of 400 based on grades and LSAT scores alone would yield 16 African American, Hispanic, and Native American students in the first-year law school class, as opposed to 58 students from those three "underrepresented" minority groups. Because the rate of these minority students enrolled varied from 13.5 percent to 20.1 percent over the history of the law school's affirmative action program, UM argued that no "fixed quota" was part of the policy. Despite the fact that the students from the three preferred minority groups had lower grades and scores than white and Asian American admittees, the law school contended that they were "superior to most applicants nationwide. They graduate, pass the bar exam, obtain judicial clerkships, and succeed in the practice of law at rates essentially indistinguishable from their white and Asian-American classmates."

The law school brief tackled the *Bakke* precedent head-on: "Twenty-five years ago, this Court resolved a bitter national controversy over the constitutionality of race-conscious admissions policies in its landmark decision in *Bakke*. The essential holding of *Bakke* is that quotas and set-asides are illegal, but that some attention may be paid to race in the context of a competitive review of the ways that each applicant will contribute to the overall diversity of the student body." The Sixth Circuit Court of Appeals held that the UM Law School's admissions policy was virtually the same as the one endorsed by a majority of the Supreme Court in 1978. Therefore, Grutter "cannot prevail unless the square holding of *Bakke* is overruled, expressly or sub silentio." The brief predicted dire consequences if the high tribunal were to overturn the *Bakke* precedent. Doing so, declared UM, "would force most of this nation's finest institutions to choose between dramatic resegregation and completely abandoning the demanding standards that have made American higher education the envy of the world." The brief labeled as "fantasy" the federal government's argument that Michigan could maintain a diverse law school by using color-blind procedures; to lower the standards across the board for all applicants would dilute its academic excellence. The school's mission would be destroyed by a stroke of the Court's pen invalidating affirmative action. Furthermore, if the Court decided that the kinds of affirmative action admissions goals used by Harvard and Michigan were now unconstitutional, then so too would be those upheld in employment cases like *Johnson*, in which the Brennan-led majority validated goals for promoting women in the Santa Clara County (California) Transportation Agency.

Another appeal to Justice O'Connor in the *Grutter* respondents' brief was slightly more subtle than directly quoting the swing justice. Instead, the law school invoked Justice Powell's similar role as a swing vote in *Bakke*, observing that he "forged a middle ground that constituted (and has ever since been relied on as) the holding of the case." The association of two judicial diplomats, who could often split the difference with colleagues in order to find a compromise holding in contentious cases, was particularly meaningful for O'Connor. The courtly Virginia gentleman, Powell, had befriended and mentored her when she arrived at the high tribunal as its first female member in 1981. He even loaned her one of his secretaries to help her sort through the mounds of unfamiliar paperwork. Powell and O'Connor were fond of teasing that they were the first two justices ever to dance together! When the elderly Powell informed his only female colleague that he was stepping down from the bench in 1987, she wrote to him, "Your announcement leaves me devastated. No one on the Court has been kinder than you. There is no one with whom I have felt as free to discuss our cases and how to resolve them than you. There is no one for whom I have greater respect and affection than you. In short, you are irreplaceable." A particularly moving photograph taken at Powell's funeral in 1998 pictures Justice O'Connor tenderly placing a flower on his coffin at the interment ceremony in Richmond, Virginia.

Another appeal to O'Connor's public-spiritedness was the data offered by the law school regarding the ramifications of overturning her mentor's *Bakke* holding. UM estimated that such a decision would cut the minority lawyers currently being trained by half or three-quarters, resulting in the near-complete absence of minority students from the schools that train most of our federal judges, prosecutors and law clerks (to say nothing of the new lawyers at our country's leading law firms). This is a chilling prospect. As our country becomes increasingly racially diverse, the public confidence in law enforcement and legal institutions so essential to the coherence and stability of our society will be difficult to maintain if the segments of the bench and bar currently filled by graduates of those institutions again become a preserve for white graduates, trained in isolation from the communities they will serve.

The law school's brief also noted the demographic fact that, within the span of current law students' careers, whites will become the *minority* in the United States. It then quoted Condoleezza Rice, who, while provost of Stanford University, had commented that diversity in the educational context could help students forge a peaceful and progressive future.

Finally, the law school brief addressed whether the plus factor it used for admissions decisions on minority applicants was properly tailored for achieving educational diversity. Because UM carefully engaged in "holistic" reviews of each candidate and considered all the ways that he or she could contribute to the diverse ambience of the law school, the brief argued that its procedure followed the narrow tailoring requirements of equal protection analysis. In other words, race was *not* the "predominant factor" in the admissions process.

A sign of the heated controversy surrounding the affirmative action debate now squarely before the Supreme Court was the deluge of nearly 100 amici curiae briefs that flooded the tribunal. Three-quarters of those briefs supported the University of Michigan. One of the most stunning was what came to be known as the "military brief." It included such well-known generals and admirals as Norman Schwarzkopf (commander of Allied forces in the first Gulf War); John Shalikashvili (former chairman of the Joint Chiefs of Staff); Anthony Zinni (former commander in chief of U.S. Central Command); Hugh Shelton (former chairman of the Joint Chiefs of Staff); Wesley Clark (former supreme allied commander in Europe); and William Crowe (former chairman of the Joint Chiefs of Staff). Two former superintendents of the U.S. Military Academy, the former superintendent of the U.S. Air Force Academy, the former commander of the U.S. Pacific Fleet, the former Marine Corps commandant, along with former secretary of defense William Cohen, were also among those who included their names on the military brief in support of affirmative action.

The brief began with a pithy argument:

> Based on decades of experience, amici have concluded that a highly qualified, racially diverse officer corps educated and trained to command our nation's racially diverse enlisted ranks is essential to the military's ability to fulfill its principal mission to provide national security. The primary sources for the nation's officer corps are the service academies and the ROTC, the latter comprised of students already admitted to participating colleges and universities. At present, the military cannot achieve an officer corps that is *both* highly qualified *and* racially diverse unless the service academies and the ROTC use limited race-conscious recruiting and admissions policies. Accordingly, these institutions rely on such policies, developed to comport with this Court's instruction in *Regents of the University of California v. Bakke.*

The military and civilian leaders cited an effective military and national security as constituting the compelling state interest of diversity in the officer corps. Stating the case in stark combat terms, the brief warned the Court, "The military cannot lose ground." As of 2003 the U.S. military was nearly 40 percent minority, including 21.7 percent African American, 9.6 percent Hispanic, 4 percent Asian American, and 1.2 percent Native American. The services had grown more diverse in their enlisted ranks during the 1960s and 1970s. The Vietnam War era draft contributed to diversity among noncommissioned personnel. Yet the dearth of minorities in the officer corps at that time contributed to "racial polarization, pervasive disciplinary problems, and racially motivated incidents in Vietnam and on posts around the world," according to the military brief. It described the pre–affirmative action armed forces as teetering "on the verge of self-destruction." In 1962 only 1.6 percent of all commissioned military officers were African American.

With race-conscious recruitment for ROTC programs and service academy admissions, however, the active duty officers had become much more diverse by 2003. Nineteen percent were minority; among them were 8.8 percent African American, 4 percent Hispanic, 3.2 percent Asian American, and 0.6 percent Native American. These officers had trained in racially diverse educational settings, which gives them experience to lead the increasingly diverse enlisted ranks.

A disparity still exists between the rates of African American officers (8.8 percent) and enlisted personnel (21.7 percent), so the brief argued for continued affirmative action in officer recruitment in order to fulfill the military's mission. One senior Pentagon official declared, "Doing affirmative action the right way is deadly serious for us — people's lives depend on it." Diversity in the armed services also bolsters public confidence in the military, the brief maintained.

No alternative to "limited race-conscious programs" exists to ensure ongoing diversity within the officer corps. Affirmative recruiting of minorities for the service preparatory academies, whose mission is to prepare minorities, women, enlisted personnel, and athletes, had been especially successful in procuring a diverse pool of qualified candidates for the prestigious service academies. These federally funded schools, one for each of the service academies, provide the single most significant source of minority candidates. For example, 20 to 40 percent of African American cadets at West Point were trained at the preparatory academy. One-third of the minority midshipmen at Annapolis come from the Naval Academy Preparatory School. The Air Force Preparatory School provides 30 to 50 percent of minority students at the academy in Colorado Springs.

The U.S. Military Academy at West Point develops goals for each class to determine "desired percentages of scholars, leaders, athletes, women, blacks, Hispanics, and other minorities." The military brief observed that the class of 2005 was one-quarter minority, with 8 percent African American and 6 percent Hispanic. The U.S. Naval Academy sets goals of commissioning at least 7 percent African Americans and 4 percent Hispanics in each class. The academy accepts slightly higher rates to allow for attrition. Likewise, the U.S. Air Force Academy developed affirmative recruiting measures to attract minorities, which by 2000 constituted 18 percent of enrolled students.

As of 2000, ROTC provided nearly one-half of active duty officers. As the brief noted, ROTC uses "aggressive race-conscious admissions programs." Each service urges its ROTC programs throughout the nation to meet the service's goals for recruiting minority officers. Junior ROTC, which operates in high schools, targets inner-city schools with high minority populations. The military also concentrates considerable resources on historically black colleges and universities to increase the number of scholarships for African American ROTC students. The military brief quoted the nation's most celebrated product of ROTC, General Colin Powell, who had stated, "In the military, we . . . used affirmative action to reach out to those who were qualified but who were often overlooked or ignored as a result of indifference or inertia." The brief concluded, "It requires only a small step from this analysis [of affirmative action in the military] to conclude that our country's other most selective institutions must remain both diverse and selective. Like our military security, our economic security and international competitiveness depend upon it. An alternative that does not preserve both diversity and selectivity is no alternative at all."

The reference to the United States' economic and global competitiveness constituted the theme of the amicus curiae brief submitted by General Motors. As it noted in the first sentence, GM "is a multi-national corporation headquartered in Detroit, Michigan." Indeed, the venerable company was located in the geographic heart of the *Gratz* and *Grutter* cases, and its brief noted that GM employs a large number of University of Michigan graduates. The company "provides significant financial assistance" to the university because UM trains so many of GM's employees. "The quality of the education these students receive profoundly affects the ability of General Motors, and indeed all major American corporations, to compete [in the global marketplace]," the brief asserted. It argued that the need to create racial and ethnic diversity in academic institutions was not only compelling but crucial to the future of American business and the nation's entire economy. In fact, General Motors had made diversity a "core business objective" in 1995, and it contended that diverse workforces, which are more creative and innovative, enhance a corporation's "bottom line."

The GM brief delineated the contributions that diverse education makes to the corporate world. The company's experience had proved that only a diverse workforce, which had "learned to work productively and creatively with individuals from a multitude of races and ethnic, religious, and cultural backgrounds, can maintain America's competitiveness in the increasingly diverse and interconnected world economy." Because workers in the twenty-first century confront cultural variations among customers, colleagues, employees, and global business partners, they must be prepared to meet these differences with sensitivity and creativity. GM warned the Supreme Court that "a ruling proscribing the consideration of race and ethnicity in admissions decisions likely would dramatically reduce diversity at our nation's top institutions and thereby deprive students who will become the core of our nation's business elite of the interracial and multicultural interactions in an academic setting that are so integral to their acquisition of cross-cultural skills." Thus, the arguments for the business world and military were strikingly similar: banning affirmative action in higher education would have severe repercussions for corporations and the armed forces.

General Motors focused on two "inevitable forces" to which the United States must respond in the twenty-first century. The interconnection of the global world economy and the increasing diversity of America's population demand a workforce that graduates from racially and ethnically diverse schools. The company cited a $1 billion deal with China, achieved because the Chinese purportedly appreciated GM's outreach to Asian American employees and their community, as illustrative of how diversity had contributed to success in the global economy. The brief also cited demographic projections showing that, by 2050, 47 percent of the American population will be African American, Hispanic, Asian American, or Native American.

In 2000 more than one-third of the new workers in America were minorities. Management studies showed that those companies that handle diversity effectively are successful in hiring and retaining the best employees. Similar to the military brief, GM argued that managers who cannot lead multiracial forces are doomed to fail:

In sum, the graduates whom businesses recruit from top academic institutions, such as the University of Michigan, to serve as managers and professionals will shape the corporate cultures and reputations for diversity of those businesses in the years to come. Graduates who lack sensitivity to perspectives influenced by race and ethnicity will be ill-equipped to meet the fundamental challenge of attracting, retaining, and managing the human capital that businesses need to survive. . . . Graduates from our nation's elite academic institutions who have been immersed in cross-cultural learning environments will be better prepared to meet it.

As GM's president and CEO, Jack Smith, put the case for diversity so succinctly, "Having people of different ethnic, racial, and social backgrounds in our corporation has not slowed our pursuit of excellence — it has accelerated it." His company's brief begged the justices, "For the sake of the nation's collective economic future, institutions of higher learning must be permitted to continue to achieve the diversity that enhances both the education of these individuals and the endeavors that they will undertake as graduates."

An additional amicus brief filed in favor of the University of Michigan included another segment of the corporate world, this one involving science and engineering. Two of America's largest industrial companies, DuPont and IBM, joined forces with MIT, Stanford, the National Academy of Sciences, the National Academy of Engineering, and the National Action Council for Minorities in Engineering, to argue for diverse student bodies in science and engineering, where minorities have traditionally been underrepresented. DuPont and IBM paralleled General Motors in asserting that diversity is one of their "greatest assets" — a "core value" for DuPont and a "strategic imperative" for IBM. They rely on colleges and universities to produce a diverse pool of scientists and engineers, and therefore the corporations support race- and ethnic-conscious admissions in selective private and public schools like MIT and Stanford. The brief also expressed concern about how science and engineering enrollments in other countries were outpacing those in the United States.

On the labor side of the business equation, the AFL-CIO weighed in for the University of Michigan in another friend-of-the-court brief. It described the labor organization as the largest in the United States, encompassing sixty-five national and international unions that represent more than 13 million members. The labor federation predicted that

virtually every graduate of the University of Michigan and its Law School, as well as graduates of comparable institutions of higher education, will leave academia and enter the workplace as an owner, manager supervisor, union officer, union member, and/or employee. . . . The experience of the AFL-CIO teaches that the unique opportunities to interact with people from other races and ethnic groups on a university campus — at the threshold of the workplace — that are fostered by the admissions policies at issue in this case, will have substantial, positive impact on students, making them better citizens in our democracy as well as more productive members of society. Specifically, the challenged policies will reduce employment discrimination.

Therefore, organized labor asserted that affirmative action in higher education fulfilled the compelling state interest of reducing employment discrimination.

The American Association of Law Schools (AALS), an organization representing 165 private and public law schools, predictably contributed an amicus brief supporting affirmative action in law school admissions already used by most of its members. The AALS contended that "the legitimacy of the American legal system depends on meaningful minority participation at every level." More specifically, about a dozen of the nation's most selective private and public law schools (including the University of Michigan) produce a notable share of Congress members and federal judges. Many black and Hispanic jurists have received degrees from these same law schools. Of the 138 African Americans who had served on the federal bench up to 2003, 18 had received law degrees from Howard University (virtually the only law school in the nation with large black enrollment prior to the late 1960s), 12 from Harvard, 10 from Yale, and 6 from Michigan. Twenty-seven of the 57 Hispanic federal judges up to 2003 had received their law credentials from top-twenty-five law schools; the University of Texas had produced the plurality (9) of Hispanic federal jurists. "Race-conscious admissions policies are necessary to achieve the paramount government objective of ensuring equal access to legal education, the legal profession, and the process of self-government," declared the AALS.

The latter point, in particular, was another contention that would appeal to Justice O'Connor. From her undergraduate days at Stanford University, where she took a law course whose professor advocated public service, O'Connor had been devoted to civic engagement. The private sector in law held few opportunities for women in the 1950s, when young Sandra Day graduated from Stanford Law School near the top of her class. William Rehnquist, her classmate and clearly a star among the graduates, accepted a prestigious Supreme Court clerkship with Justice Robert Jackson. Day, however, was told by a law firm that the only job it would offer her was that of a legal secretary. That rebuff launched her career in the public sector, which was more accommodating to women. As a senior justice on the U.S. Supreme Court, O'Connor annually attended a reception at the busiest time of the Court's term to welcome civics teachers from around the nation to the high tribunal. Each year she would tell the educators how inspired she was by her law professor at Stanford and urge them to promote democratic values to their students. As she was wont to say, "Democracy is not genetic; each generation has to be taught." When she retired from the bench in 2005, one of the first causes she embraced was civic education, agreeing to co-lead the ABA's new initiative on the subject, with former U.S. senator Bill Bradley. In 2006 she accepted the cochairmanship of the National Advisory Council of the Campaign for the Civic Mission of Schools and produced an editorial that advocated the necessity for schools to teach civic education as vigorously as math, science, and reading.

The AALS brief also quoted an article by O'Connor, subtitled "The Influence of a Raconteur," in which she described her colleague Thurgood Marshall's contributions to the Supreme Court through his unique life experiences. "At oral arguments and conference meetings, in opinions and dissents," O'Connor recalled, Marshall brought "a special perspective" to the high tribunal as its first and only black member from 1967 to 1991.

The brief on behalf of the UM Law School by the AALS distinguished between affirmative action programs for public undergraduate universities and law schools. The former might be able to achieve diversity by admitting the top 10 percent of the state's graduating high schoolers. But such a program would not be applicable to a law school, especially one like Michigan that was among the nation's top selective public law schools. "Moreover," the AALS asserted, "any rule this Court fashions under the Equal Protection Clause will apply, through Title VI, to nearly every private law school as well." On the issue of divining a central holding from *Bakke*, the law schools' brief concluded that "if ever there were a case in which a divided Court nonetheless produced a clear holding, it is *Bakke*, where it was crystal-clear that five justices disapproved of rigid quotas and (a different) five justices permitted race to be used as a plus factor in the selection of a diverse student body."

About these, and other amici briefs in support of the University of Michigan, constitutional historian Melvin Urofsky commented, "Never before, to the best of my knowledge, had corporate, educational, and military leaders all spoken out, practically in unison, in favor of diversity and affirmative action."

The one-quarter of the total amici briefs that sided with Grutter and/or Gratz were primarily submitted by conservative public interest groups. One particularly poignant brief was produced by the Asian American Legal Foundation (AALF), based in San Francisco and founded to protect and promote the civil rights of Asian Americans. The brief's opening statement was startling in its bluntness: "Despite the fact that Asian Americans are considered culturally 'different' from other Americans and have historically experienced — and continue to experience — overt racial and ethnic prejudice, diversity-based admission schemes are almost always used to exclude Asian Americans from educational institutions." The AALF was particularly concerned that if the Supreme Court upheld race-conscious treatment in order to achieve diversity at the University of Michigan, then the San Francisco school district would reimpose racial quotas in school assignment that the AALF had successfully fought in the federal courts. Because Chinese American students were the most numerous of the defined groups in the San Francisco school district, they often were denied their school preference because the district insisted on racial balance. For example, San Francisco's Lowell High School, one of the best high schools in California (and the alma mater of Supreme Court justice Stephen Breyer), capped the number of Chinese Americans who could attend in order to limit their percentage at Lowell. The AALF brief compared this limiting quota to the "admission ceiling" used against Jews at Harvard in the 1920s to prevent Jewish students from being "over-represented" in the student body. "Thus, like Jewish applicants to American universities in the past, Chinese-American applicants to Lowell throughout the 1980s and 1990s were being penalized for their ethnicity and success," until the AALF's litigation brought an end to the San Francisco district's racial quotas. The brief argued that *Bakke* did not support the nonremedial use of race because

Justice Powell's articulation of diversity as a compelling state interest was "dictum expressed only by Justice Powell. Also, Justice Powell failed to consider that the Harvard Plan, upon which he expressly based his dictum concerning a constitutional diversity-discretion plan, was originally designed to keep Jews out of Harvard College." Moreover, because no objective standard exists by which to measure racial diversity or limit it in scope or time, the University of Michigan's admissions programs cannot be narrowly tailored to meet the criterion of equal protection analysis. Without time limits, the UM admissions program would have to use racial classifications forever, according to the AALF.

The reference to the history of anti-Jewish quotas at Harvard in the AALF's brief raised the rationale for why the three major Jewish interest groups in America supported Alan Bakke with amici briefs in his 1978 case before the Supreme Court. Yet uniformity in that litigation disappeared among the American Jewish Committee, the American Jewish Congress, and the Anti-Defamation League (ADL) of B'nai B'rith in the Michigan cases. The 100,000-member American Jewish Committee decided to file a friend-of-the-court brief on behalf of the University of Michigan because it did not view its programs as quota-driven, as the California-Davis plan had been. Professor Alan Dershowitz, of Harvard Law School, who had assisted the committee in its pro-Bakke brief, further explained the change of heart over a quarter century. He recalled that fears of a new "Jewish quota" did not materialize after 1978. "We feared," Dershowitz said, "that our hard-earned right to be admitted on the merits would be taken away. The WASP quotient would hold constant, and the Jews and African Americans would be left to fight over the crumbs. What happened is that Jews have become the new WASPs. They are among the dominant groups on campus, in terms of numbers." He reported that, from his own experience in classrooms at Harvard, affirmative action was effective in successfully diversifying student enrollment.

The 50,000-member American Jewish Congress, however, was divided over how to approach the UM undergraduate and law school affirmative action schemes. Marc Stern, general counsel of the Congress, explained part of the internal tension within his organization. "Today there is an entire conservative apparatus challenging affirmative action, so some Jews say: 'Why do we need to be in the middle of it? Why do we need to alienate the black community [with whom they had been united in fighting segregation]?'" Ultimately, the Congress was not listed as filing an amicus brief in the Michigan cases. Abraham Foxman, national director of the ADL, reported that his organization believed diversity was a proper goal in education but that it "should be achieved in a racially neutral manner." The ADL eventually submitted a brief in support of neither party in the UM litigation.

The Center for Equal Opportunity, the Independent Women's Forum, and the American Civil Rights Institute combined to produce an amicus brief on behalf of Grutter and Gratz. One of the core missions of these three organizations is to research and advocate the abolition of racial, ethnic, religious, and gender discrimination by federal and state governments, as well as the private sector. The brief argued that the University of Michigan employed quotas, clearly unconstitutional under *Bakke*. Because universities were using discriminatory systems in the name of diversity a full twenty-five years after the California-Davis case, admissions offices could not be trusted to narrowly tailor their use of racial/ethnic preferences. Thus, argued the three interest groups, the Supreme Court should reject the diversity rationale for affirmative action and overturn the Sixth Circuit's decision in *Grutter* and the district court's ruling in *Gratz* upholding the revised undergraduate admissions policy. The brief dismissed the research, particularly of Professor Gurin, alleging that diversity is a compelling state interest. Even if such data were foolproof, the equal protection clause did not create a "social science exception" to its ban on racial or ethnic classifications.

The Center for Individual Freedom (CIF), an organization with a mission similar to that of the Center for Individual Rights, which brought the Michigan cases before the courts, "defends individual freedoms and rights guaranteed by the Constitution." In the affirmative action cases involving higher education, the CIF particularly supported "the constitutional guarantee of equal protection that affords an individual the right to compete for admissions to state institutions of higher education on equal footing irrespective of race or ethnicity." Its amicus brief for Gratz and Grutter began with Martin Luther King Jr.'s famous hope that his children would "not be judged by the color of their skin but by the content of their character." The CIF accused the University of Michigan of turning King's dream on its head in judging applicants by their race and ethnicity in violation of the Constitution's equal protection clause. The brief argued that student diversity could in no way be justified as a compelling state interest and only constituted "odious stereotyping" based on skin color. It proclaimed that the Court had never labeled diversity as compelling and never should. The CIF borrowed a portion of Justice Powell's opinion in *Bakke* for its own position, citing his statement that "the guarantee of equal protection cannot mean one thing when applied to one individual and something else when applied to a person of another color." Even if the Court accepted Powell's opinion in *Bakke* as controlling, the CIF believed his concept of diversity was much broader than Michigan's, which relied on "race and ethnicity to near exclusivity." Furthermore, UM's programs were not narrowly tailored, used two-track procedures for minorities and nonminorities, imposed quotas (disguised as "critical mass"), and offered no terminus for the preferences.

The voluminous written record in the two Michigan affirmative action cases was complete and in the justices' hands. Nearly 100 amici briefs, three opinions from two lower courts and three different judges, petitions for certiorari, petitioners' and respondents' briefs, and supporting documents presented the justices with all the facts and legal interpretations they would review before oral argument. Many justices receive a memo from one of their law clerks summarizing the case and perhaps suggesting questions for the justices to pose at the public argument. But once on the bench, the justices are on their own, and the debate is an unpredictable discourse played out before 300 spectators within the churchlike confines of the nation's highest court.

CHAPTER 6

"Jim Crow, Hell No!"

Oral Argument at the U.S. Supreme Court

Finally, April 1, 2003, the scheduled date for oral argument in the two Michigan appeals, arrived. Thousands of partisans from both sides of the UM cases chanted outside the Supreme Court building. In the university's camp, a group from the United Steelworkers of Indiana and Illinois hoisted a banner mocking the incumbent president's family connections. "Affirmative Action: Hey, it got Bush into Yale," read the sign. As the pro-diversity demonstrators headed toward the Lincoln Memorial, they passed by two white men dressed in business suits, holding a sign supporting Gratz and Grutter: "Affirmative action breeds incompetence." Meanwhile, spectators fortunate enough to obtain a seat were about to witness a historic conversation among the nine justices and advocates for both sides, including U.S. Solicitor General Ted Olson, who argued against affirmative action for the Bush White House.

In 2003 only two justices (William Rehnquist and John Paul Stevens) remained from the Supreme Court that had decided *Bakke* twenty-five years previously. Rehnquist, an associate justice in 1978, had been promoted to chief in 1986 by Ronald Reagan. Chief Justice Rehnquist was a consistent opponent of affirmative action for the entire quarter century since it first came before the Court. On the other hand, Justice Stevens had a mixed record on racial preferences. In *Bakke* he opposed them, but he sometimes supported preferences in the employment realm. Most recently, he had voted to uphold affirmative action for federal government contracts in the 1995 *Adarand* case. Justices Antonin Scalia and Clarence Thomas were on the record as being unequivocally opposed to affirmative action. They were convinced that race-based policies per se violated the equal protection clause. Although Justice Anthony Kennedy was a swing voter in some decisions, his votes in race cases were usually with the conservatives.

He was expected to side with Grutter and Gratz. Conversely, Justices David Souter, Ruth Bader Ginsburg, and Stephen Breyer were considered reliable votes for diversity policies. Thus, the justices seemed as evenly divided as they were in *Bakke*, with four justices supporting affirmative action and four opposing it. Most observers thought the fate of racial preferences in higher education was in the hands of the Court's other swing voter, Justice Sandra Day O'Connor. She, along with Ruth Bader Ginsburg and Clarence Thomas, were the only members of the Court to experience gender or racial discrimination. Ginsburg and Thomas ended up on opposite sides of the affirmative action debate. With which side would O'Connor cast her lot?

The first female Supreme Court justice had a nuanced record in race cases. In the 1986 *Wygant* case (invalidating a race-based layoff policy for Jackson, Michigan, teachers), her concurring opinion implied that an affirmative action plan, as long as it is "carefully constructed," could be used to remedy *general* societal discrimination. Yet in the 1990s, she wrote opinions for the Court arguing that racial preferences could pass constitutional muster only if they were "narrowly tailored" to remedy a *specific*, demonstrable instance of racial discrimination. Her application of this "strict scrutiny" criteria (the highest judicial standard in equal protection cases) to set-aside programs for minority contractors had the effect of invalidating such policies, first in *City of Richmond v. J. A. Croson Co.* (involving local set-asides) and then in *Adarand v. Peña* (addressing federal programs). Likewise, in race-based gerrymandering cases, such as *Shaw v. Reno* from 1993, she refused to write a sweeping opinion for the Court that would ban majority-minority redistricting per se, but she argued that such districts must satisfy a "compelling state interest." Once more, she applied the highest level of equal protection analysis, this time to invalidate bizarrely shaped congressional districts in North Carolina drawn solely on the basis of race.

Following long-standing tradition, the justices appeared from behind the Court's red velvet curtains at the stroke of 10:00 A.M., on April 1, 2003, as the marshal wielded her gavel and intoned, "The honorable, the chief justice, and the associate justices of the Supreme Court of the United States. Oyez! Oyez! Oyez! All persons having business before the honorable, the Supreme Court of the United States are admonished to draw near and give their attention, for the

Court is now sitting. God save the United States and this honorable Court!" With the utterly silent 300-seat courtroom packed to capacity, Chief Justice Rehnquist, who had served in the center seat for seventeen years, announced in his usual perfunctory monotone that did not betray the phenomenal controversy before him, "We'll hear argument now in No. 02-241, *Barbara Grutter v. Lee Bollinger.*"

Petitioner's counsel, Kirk Kolbo, an attorney from a Minneapolis law firm who had practiced civil litigation for almost two decades, stepped forward first, and the clock began to run on the thirty minutes his side had to present its argument for Barbara Grutter, who was seated in the courtroom, along with Jennifer Gratz. Solicitor General Ted Olson would take ten minutes of that time, as amicus curiae in support of the petitioner, to offer the federal government's position in favor of Grutter. Several years later, Kolbo recalled that he "just argued in a straightforward fashion our legal and factual points and let the Court do what it would, as we could only do." After the standard opening address to the justices, "Mr. Chief Justice and may it please the Court," Kolbo began by noting pointedly that "Barbara Grutter applied for admission to the University of Michigan Law School with a personal right guaranteed by the Constitution — that the application would be considered free from the taint of racial discrimination. The law school intentionally disregarded that right by discriminating against her on the basis of race as it does each year in the case of thousands of individuals who apply for admission." Because the U.S. population was an amalgamation of races and ethnicities, Kolbo argued, the government had "to honor its solemn obligation to treat all members of our society equally without preferring some individuals over others."

He managed to deliver four short paragraphs from his prepared remarks before, not surprisingly, Justice O'Connor launched the initial volley of questions. In her self-described manner of speaking "clearly and enunciating every word," she pounced on Kolbo's seemingly absolutist ban on the use of race: "The Court obviously has upheld the use of race in making selections or choices in certain contexts, for instance to remedy prior discrimination in other contexts. . . . [Y]ou are speaking in absolutes and it isn't quite that. I think we have given recognition to the use of race in a variety of settings." Kolbo conceded that fact documented in the Court's precedents.

Justice Kennedy, who often speaks publicly about the crucial role that lawyers play in American society, then suggested that law schools and the states that run them should have "a very legitimate concern" that minorities, particularly blacks and Hispanics, were underrepresented in "a profession which is designed to protect our rights and to promote progress." Grutter's attorney acknowledged the concern but asserted again that racial preferences were not the means to address the problem.

Citing the amicus brief submitted by retired military officers and civilian leaders, Justice Ginsburg raised a point that would become crucial to the outcome of the case. She wanted to know Kolbo's response to the former generals' and admirals' arguments that a diverse officer corps could be achieved only by using race as a plus. Kolbo tried to dodge the point, which was obviously not advantageous to his side, by noting that diversity in the armed services was not part of the official record in the case. Counsel at oral argument often try to sidestep the justices' disadvantageous positions or hypotheticals by responding that they do not apply to the case at hand. But Justice Ginsburg is nothing if not determined, so she merely told Kolbo to assume that the military brief's points were factual, that the nation's military academies would have "very few, if any," minorities if race was not used in admissions decisions. "Still you cannot use race?" Ginsburg, who had won five out of six cases she argued before the Supreme Court prior to her judicial career, demanded of Kolbo. Now on the spot, he answered starkly, "I believe race could not be used." Yet he continued to duck and weave by saying that the military brief represented only the views of those individuals who signed it, not the United States or the military academies. Justice Stevens and especially Justice Souter were growing impatient with what they perceived as obfuscation. They noted that the military brief had taken a position and quoted materials from the U.S. service academies regarding their use of racial preferences. Souter, with a note of frustration in his voice, challenged Kolbo: "Are you serious that you think there is a serious question about that? That we cannot take that [military] brief as a representation of fact?"

As the *Washington Post*'s Supreme Court correspondent Charles Lane reported the next day, "Unstated, but obvious, was the broader context: the current battle for a Muslim country's [Iraq's] liberation being waged by multiethnic U.S. Army and Marine platoons." Several years after the Michigan arguments, Kolbo agreed that the start of the Iraq war just two weeks before the Court heard the affirmative action cases made the questions on the military brief "all the more noteworthy at the time." Kolbo commented that he was not surprised by such questions, though their intensity from the liberal justices was unexpected. "I should have been better prepared for it," the counsel admitted.

Justice Scalia tried to help, resorting to another strategy that justices can use at oral argument, namely, bail out the side with which you are sympathetic. He gently nudged Kolbo toward the position that everyone accepted the fact the military academies were giving racial preferences, but urged him to think about whether there was another way to create a diverse officer corps. Nevertheless, Souter continued with his more adversarial line of questions about the service academies. He contended that, even if they recruited from economically disadvantaged groups, such a criterion would simply be a "surrogate for race," not a "race-neutral measure." Kolbo was not only losing ground on his argument for what constituted permissible criteria in admissions, he was watching precious minutes tick away in which to convey his arguments. Justice Kennedy offered a friendly question to get Kolbo back on point: "It's about the military brief that you didn't come here to argue about, but it will maybe help you get back to your case." "Sure," replied Kolbo, sounding relieved to be thrown a potential lifeline. Kennedy remarked that the military brief described the service academies' preparatory schools, which are 40 percent minorities. Could the government fund recruiting efforts to attract minorities to the schools? Kolbo saw no "constitutional objection" to Kennedy's hypothetical, and Grutter's counsel drew a line between "casting a wider net [in] recruiting," which he thought permissible, and the impermissible use of race in admissions decisions "at the point of competition."

Justice Breyer, the Court's most junior justice, though he had ascended the bench nine years earlier, began his participation in the oral argument with one of his patented professorial questions-cum-lectures. With several full paragraphs as a preface, the justice pressed Kolbo on the line between recruiting and admissions; the counsel held firm to his original distinction between the two. Breyer tried again to see if Kolbo might accept the "sound legal distinction" of using race as a plus for minorities previously "discriminated against." Kolbo stood his ground with the affirmation that "sound and reasonable, Your Honor, is not enough when it comes to race. It must be a compelling purpose."

After several more references to the military academy preparatory schools, the discussion veered into another significant affirmative action category — employment — when Justice Ginsburg specifically asked whether, under Kolbo's interpretation of the equal protection clause and applicable statutes, he thought racial preferences were invalid in employment. Counsel conceded that "there could be [racial preferences] . . . to remedy past identified discrimination, but not to exceed diversity." After several more inquiries, Kolbo asked the chief justice if he could reserve the balance of his time, which the petitioner's side is allowed to do for rebuttal of the respondent's arguments.

Now it was Solicitor General Ted Olson's turn to make the U.S. government's position as a friend of the court for Grutter. A skilled veteran of numerous arguments before the high bench, both as a counsel in private practice at the prominent law firm of Gibson, Dunn, and Crutcher and as the federal government's premier advocate, Olson, who was often mentioned as a possible nominee to the Court, has the perfect authoritative bass voice for oral advocacy. The sound of his words fills the cavernous courtroom, usually noted for its poor acoustics and anemic audio system. He opened with this pithy declaration: "The Michigan Law School admissions program fails every test this Court has articulated for evaluating governmental racial preference."

Justice Stevens, the Court's eldest member at nearly eighty-three years of age, interrupted with a deceptively, but characteristically, polite inquiry reflective of his midwestern mannerliness: "General Olson, just let me get a question out and you answer it at your convenience. I'd like you to comment on Carter Phillips's brief. What is your view of the strength of that argument?" Olson seemed momentarily thrown by Stevens's reference to the name of the counsel who contributed to the military brief. "Well, I'm not sure . . . ," he began. Stevens clarified his citation: "That's the one about the generals and about the military academies." His description sounded like the setup for a joke, but there was nothing funny to Olson about the fact that the former military leaders' pro–affirmative action amicus brief was again taking center stage at the Court.

Olson tried the Kolbo tack: "Our [the federal government's] position with respect to that is we respect the opinions of those individuals, but the position of the United States is that we do not accept the proposition that black soldiers will only fight for black officers." Ginsburg now rejoined the fray, pointing out that all the military academies have racial-preference programs for admissions. Olson was prepared this time with a retort that the Coast Guard Academy does not, by congressional prohibition, but he had to admit that the other academies use racial preferences in admissions. Ginsburg wanted to know if such programs were illegal. Paralleling the Kolbo strategy, Olson stated that the U.S. government had not examined that issue and had presented no brief on each of the academies.

Souter was not buying that approach from Olson any more than he had from Kolbo. He fired off a barrage of questions to the solicitor general aiming directly at how the academies could fill a "substantial number of minority slots," which the military brief said was necessary for an effective military, through the types of "race-neutral" recruiting programs advocated in the solicitor general's amicus brief. Olson simply stated that the government did not accept the opinion of the former military leaders that only racial preferences in admissions would result in diverse officers.

After some sparring between Breyer and Olson over the exact nature of the preferences granted minorities by UM Law School, O'Connor cut to the chase as the argument session approached the halfway point. Again in her best schoolteacher locution, she prodded, "General Olson, do you agree with the articulated proposal of Justice Powell in the *Bakke* case of using race as a plus factor as he saw the use of it? Do you disagree with that approach?" Finally, someone had acknowledged the proverbial "elephant" in the room. The precedent around which all the arguments had swirled was now on the table for public discussion before the justices.

Olson responded with the now-familiar position that Powell's opinion was the only one proposing that diversity was compelling. Before he could complete his thought, O'Connor interrupted, "I don't think it commanded a Court. I'm just asking if you agreed with that approach [of Powell in *Bakke*]." The solicitor general revealed that the government was "reluctant to say never" could Powell's approach be used, but Olson added that the UM Law School's use of race failed every test that Powell had proposed.

After a brief colloquy comparing race and gender, in which Justice Ginsburg, who was a pioneer in the gender equity movement, corrected her friend Justice Scalia's misinterpretation that the Court had not allowed the use of sex as a plus (it had in *Johnson v. Santa Clara County Transportation Agency*), Justice Stevens brought Olson back to *Bakke*. "General Olson, I'm not sure you answered Justice O'Connor's question," Stevens pointed out. "Do you agree with Justice Powell's suggestion that race could be used as a plus in something like the Harvard program?" "No," Olson replied, "the Harvard program wasn't examined according to any compelling governmental interest." Stevens persisted, "So your answer is no, you would not agree with that?" "We would not based on what we see in that opinion," Olson said.

Kennedy wanted to know whether diversity is "a permissible governmental goal." "If it's an end in and of itself," Olson offered, "obviously it's constitutionally objectionable." To Breyer's query whether Texas's 10 percent plan is constitutional because its motive is to promote diversity, Olson denied that diversity was the "stated motive"; rather, such plans in Texas, California, and Florida were intended to open higher education "to a broader selection." He also disagreed with Souter's premise that the percentage plans work only because the high schools from which they draw are segregated. The solicitor general labeled the schools "diverse," not segregated. With that, the chief justice called time on Olson's ten minutes before the Court.

The University of Michigan Law School now had a half hour to defend its affirmative action plan at the nation's highest tribunal. Counsel for UM, Maureen Mahoney, a partner at the prestigious Washington law firm of Latham and Watkins, had a distinct advantage. She had clerked for Rehnquist and was a familiar face at the Court, having served on its Judicial Fellows Commission. Her former boss began with requisite formality, "Ms. Mahoney, we'll hear from you." The justices were now more than warmed up, and she barely completed a short paragraph about how the solicitor general's brief acknowledged that diversity may be a compelling interest but contended that the law school could achieve it through race-neutral measures. She added that his argument ignored the record in this case.

Kennedy jumped in to disagree that the government's brief labeled diversity compelling, but Mahoney stood her ground that it did and contended that the U.S. Department of Education for the twenty-five years since *Bakke* had used diversity as the "governing standard" for schools. Her former boss then posed this hypothetical: after the *Bakke* decision, could the University of California at Davis Medical School have said it tried to create diversity without setting aside sixteen seats for minorities, which the Court had invalidated as an impermissible quota, but it was not successful, so now it would like to go back to the sixteen-seat set-aside? Mahoney referred to Powell's opinion that recommended the Harvard model as a way to create diversity without strict quotas. She then managed to describe the UM Law School plan as one without quotas, and she provided enrollment statistics to prove her point. Offers to minorities had ranged from 160 to 232 applicants with enrollment from 44 to 73 over an eight-year period. She termed the program "very flexible."

Whereas the Grutter counsel had to withstand an onslaught of questions from the Court's more liberal and centrist judges, the Michigan attorney's inquisitors were coming from the right side of the spectrum. Scalia pounced with a typically sharp stab at the law school's program. In a disapproving tone, he mocked Michigan's contention that racial diversity was a compelling interest, "compelling enough to warrant ignoring the Constitution's prohibition of discrimination on the basis of race." He had an easy answer: if Michigan would simply lower its standards, it could attract a diverse student body without violating the Constitution. It didn't have to be one of the top law schools in the country. To do so meant it had created its own racial imbalance and then asked permission to view diversity as a compelling state interest to rectify a problem it had generated by its desire to remain elite *and* diverse. Mahoney was respectful but firm, saying, "Your Honor, I don't think there's anything in this Court's cases that suggests that the law school has to make an election between academic excellence and racial diversity." Kennedy stepped in to bolster Scalia's stance, which he said was "designed to put to you the fact that this isn't a compelling interest, because it's a choice that the Michigan Law School has made to be like this." Mahoney stressed to Kennedy that "there is a compelling interest in having an institution that is both academically excellent and richly diverse because leaders need to be trained in institutions that are excellent, that are superior academically, but they also need to be trained with exposure to the viewpoints, to the perspectives, to the experiences of individuals from diverse backgrounds." Kennedy tried a different tack, observing, if the "critical mass" of minorities desired by the law school is "a disguised quota," "you lose [the case]." Mahoney was being painted into a corner on the quota issue, so she relied on the district court's opinion, which "did not make any factual findings that would support the conclusion that this is a disguised quota." Her response raised Kennedy's hackles regarding the justices' authority: "Is it beyond this Court's capacity to say that? It certainly at a minimum is a mixed question of law and fact. . . . I'm certainly at least open to the possibility that we can disagree with you." Mahoney elaborated, noting that, in order for the Supreme Court to find a forbidden quota in the law school's program, there would have to be evidence in the case record to support that conclusion. She did not believe that Michigan's aspirational goal of wanting 10 to 17 percent African Americans, Hispanics, and Native Americans in each class met the Court's definition of a quota as a "fixed number." In asking his former clerk to clarify one word in her statement to make sure he had heard it correctly, the seventy-eight-year-old chief slipped and referred to Mahoney by her first name — an unusual occurrence in the formal atmosphere of the high tribunal.

Now Mahoney received a helpful query from Ginsburg, which included the latter's view that Harvard's program, approved by Powell in *Bakke*, and the Michigan plan were "pretty close." The two plans were "exactly" the same in practice, Mahoney asserted, and she cited similar statistics for each. Harvard reported in an amicus brief that it had enrolled 8 to 9 percent African Americans over the past four years; Michigan Law School had enrolled 7 to 9 percent African Americans during the same period. She referred to the rates as a "stable range."

Scalia saw an opportunity to question the legitimacy of relying on the Harvard model from *Bakke*. He peppered Mahoney with an even dozen inquiries/comments on the nature of the Harvard plan, as well as quotas. Had *Bakke* held the Harvard program constitutional? Yes. If adopted by a public institution? Yes. Scalia wanted to know how either result was possible, since the Court had not even examined the details of Harvard's affirmative action program in *Bakke*. Mahoney noted that Justice Powell had appended the plan to his opinion in the case. Scalia then raised an ugly specter from Harvard's past, namely, its anti-Jewish quotas. He wanted to know if the Court had considered Harvard's original enrollment goals that attempted to reduce the number of Jewish students from New York, who "were getting into Harvard on the basis of merit alone." Michigan's attorney retorted that the Harvard plan approved by Justice Powell was much more recent than the anti-Jewish scheme from the early twentieth century. Scalia tried one more strike, pointing out that quotas at Harvard began in a fit of anti-Semitism. When Mahoney returned to her main point that the UM Law School "attempted to take race into account in a very modest limited fashion, no more than necessary to achieve the goal of trying to have sufficient numbers of minorities [so] that there can be an excellent educational experience for everyone," Scalia called "sufficient numbers" "a quota." "Your Honor, it is not a quota," counsel asserted. But her conservative adversary did not accept the distinction. To him, sufficient numbers connoted a "minimum," which was effectively a quota. Mahoney parried again, "Your Honor, there is not a minimum." She explained that a university can be aware of numbers without resorting to quotas, and she observed that the U.S. Department of Education interpreted *Bakke* as authorizing schools to set and pursue "numerical goals," as long they did not use set-asides or race as a sole criterion. With that observation, she provoked her mentor. Chief Justice Rehnquist dismissively declared, "Certainly they [the Department of Education] don't interpret the Constitution?" Mahoney agreed, but she did not lose the point, reminding the Court that she was only stating what *Bakke* had indeed decided.

None too soon more friendly fire came from Justice Souter, who suggested that what Justice Powell and those four justices who agreed with him had demarcated was a "zone" that schools could aim for in enrolling minorities, not a quota or set-aside. "Absolutely, Your Honor," Mahoney agreed. But Kennedy wanted to know how the Court could accept her argument that Michigan Law School's plan was not quota driven when the admissions office kept daily records of applicants' racial/ethnic profile. Mahoney tried to downplay the importance of such reports, but Kennedy persisted in wanting to know if the reports showed how close the school was getting to its critical mass, "which is just a synonym for a number." While she explained the other data included in the reports, Scalia came back to the "critical mass" issue, demanding to know if 2 percent constituted a critical mass. No. Four percent? Before Mahoney could explain her negative response, Kennedy continued this line of questioning to pin down the Michigan counsel on what number the law school was trying to achieve. Eight percent? "Does it stop being a quota because it's somewhere between 8 and 12 [percent], but it is a quota if it's 10? I don't understand that reasoning. Once you use the term critical mass, you're into Quota Land," taunted Scalia. Mahoney was insistent; Michigan did not use fixed numbers. The range for the critical mass depended on the applicant pool's characteristics each year. She cited the law school's undisputed testimony that it had no fixed goal.

Justice O'Connor took up most of the next segment with her concerns over the Michigan plan. She wanted to know how the Court should deal with the open-ended duration of the law school's affirmative action program. Mahoney had the opportunity to give one of her longest explanations without interruption. She noted that, according to the plan, the law school would take race into account as long as necessary "to achieve the educational objectives." The Court should not view the program as permanent, she insisted, because two things could happen that would bring it to an end. One, the number of "high-achieving minorities" will grow so that the law school would not have to take race into account in order to achieve the critical mass. Two, society could evolve to the point where minority status would not make such a "fundamental difference" in a person's life and, therefore, would not be "truly salient to the law school's educational mission." The Court approved the Harvard model in *Bakke*, Mahoney recalled, without a termination point.

O'Connor's line of questioning prompted Rehnquist to inquire about whether statistics showed improvement in minorities being accepted on their own at Michigan Law School without the benefit of quotas. "They're not quotas," Mahoney gently corrected the chief. "Critical mass," he substituted. Data indicated that no blacks were admitted to the Michigan Law School in 1964 (before it first started considering race in recruitment and admissions) and that only a half dozen would be accepted forty years later if race was not considered. Mahoney concluded that progress had been made but not nearly enough to allow meaningful numbers without counting race as a plus.

Justice O'Connor returned to the dialogue, requesting information on how California's law schools were faring since affirmative action had been outlawed in the Golden State by a referendum. Referring to Boalt Hall (the University of California Law School at Berkeley) and UCLA, Mahoney said she thought each had enrolled between zero and seven African Americans. Enrollment of Hispanics was higher because about half of college students in California were in that ethnic category. She added that a "pool problem" existed for African Americans because only about thirty were in the LSAT ranges from which the nation's top ten law schools selected their students.

Kennedy, Rehnquist, and Scalia took up the next few minutes of Mahoney's time to return to the quota issue. Kennedy demanded to know why an "aspiration" to achieve 15 percent minorities was any less a quota if all the applicants who fell within that range were qualified. Mahoney fashioned her answer around the point that the difference between an impermissible quota and a permissible goal was the flexibility of the latter. She reminded the justices that the *Johnson* case involving the use of gender in affirmative action "said that the line between a quota and a goal is in fact whether or not you have to automatically and blindly promote people in order to meet the goal or whether it is a factor that is taken into account and that's exactly what occurs here." The chief justice was curious about how the Michigan Law School arrived at different percentages from year to year. Did they make a conscious decision? Flip a coin? No, counsel responded, the percentage was something in between — not a fixed number and not totally random. Instead, the percentage was "responsive to the applicant pool. They look at the applicants, they are looking for a variety of factors on a holistic basis and they find the applicants that they think are going to bring the most in toto to the law school class, but it is not measured against a specific numerical target. And the district court did not find otherwise."

Still, Scalia pressed Mahoney on the use of race and ethnicity in the admissions process. She pointed out that in *Bakke* the seats that the medical school set aside for minorities could not be assigned to whites. Such was not the case at UM Law School. Whites were "considered on their merits just like every other applicant." Scalia zeroed in on the obvious: "But they aren't just like every applicant. Some applicants are given a preference because of their race." Counsel could not rebut that truism, so she noted that minorities did indeed receive "extra weight" in their applications "because they have something unusual and important to bring to the class." But every applicant had the chance to write an essay about what diverse elements he or she could contribute.

Justice Ginsburg lobbed a sympathetic query that allowed Mahoney once again to compare favorably the Harvard model and the Michigan program. She contended that the law school examines all the "potential contributions to diversity" that an applicant could make. "And what the evidence shows in this case is that it is common for white applicants to be admitted with lower grades and test scores than even minorities who are rejected." Scalia jumped back in to declare his absolutist/textualist position that the Constitution prohibits discrimination on the basis of race. (But the Court's equal protection jurisprudence said otherwise; the government *could* use racial classifications for a compelling state interest as long as the means to achieve that interest were narrowly tailored.) So Mahoney told Scalia the question was whether the kind of racial preference used by Michigan was indeed prohibited. Of course, in her side's view, it was not.

Justice Stevens returned to O'Connor's concern over the "terminal point" for affirmative action because, he said, everyone hoped that "someday race will be a totally irrelevant factor in all decisions." He also wanted to know if such programs "actually generate racial hostility particularly on the part of the excluded members. And that in turn delays the ultimate day we are all hoping for." Mahoney had the opportunity to elaborate on this point. She contended that the key to avoiding hostility was to narrowly tailor affirmative action programs "to have very limited consideration of race and not to, for instance, have too great a disparity between the qualifications of the white students who are admitted and the minority students who are admitted under the program." "Most of the minorities who are admitted [by UM Law School] are in the top 16 percent of all LSAT takers in the country. So we're talking about a really exceptional group of students," Mahoney maintained. She also cited Harvard professor Gary Orfield's surveys of Harvard and Michigan law school students, which overwhelmingly supported diversity programs. Scalia, often the Court jester, could not contain himself. "Sure, they're in already!" he quipped. But he was deadly serious. He suggested that researchers should survey students who were rejected from prestigious institutions only to see "visibly less qualified" applicants accepted. "If you think that is not creating resentment," he insisted, "you are just wrong." Mahoney deftly sidestepped the resentment issue and, instead, focused on whether minorities feel "stigmatized" by affirmative action. She asserted that minorities support such programs and that the experiences they bring to the study of law are appreciated by their white counterparts. So "historic stereotypes" of minorities are not perpetuated.

Justice Breyer wanted to move beyond quotas to ask, under Powell's decision in *Bakke*, what other limits must affirmative action plans follow to pass constitutional muster. Mahoney cited a trio: (1) "flexible consideration of the diversity contribution of every potential student"; (2) acceptance of minorities only if they are "well qualified" so that they can succeed; and (3) only a slight burden on rejected applicants. She proposed statistics to prove the latter. Ninety-five percent of all admissions decisions made at the law school each year "are not affected by the consideration of race." She concluded that the burden was "small and diffuse" and, while "not one to be minimized," was outweighed by the compelling interest of serving "students of all races and our nation."

Justice Ginsburg asked if Mahoney knew what the plaintiff's increase in chance of admission would have been without affirmative action. She responded that she did not know for Barbara Grutter, but that across the class it would have been about 5 percent. Mahoney posited that Grutter would not have been admitted under a race-blind system, but the case record did not contain a definitive answer to that issue.

Scalia fired one last shot, declaring, "I don't know any other area where we decide the case by saying, well, there are very few people who are being treated unconstitutionally. I mean, if this indeed is an unconstitutional treatment of this woman, because of her race, surely, it doesn't make any difference whether she is one of very few who have been treated unconstitutionally." The chief justice rescued his former clerk. "I think you can regard that as a statement rather than a question," he told Mahoney with a note of amusement in his voice. A grateful counsel exclaimed, "Thank you, Your Honor!" as chuckles rippled through the courtroom and her time expired.

Kolbo had two minutes remaining to make his rebuttal. He picked up the theme of Scalia's final salvo to emphasize that "the Constitution protects the rights of individuals, not racial groups." As an individual, Grutter was the victim of discrimination. He also stressed the "indefinite, ongoing, unlimited" nature of the Michigan program, which ran afoul of the Court's precedents, requiring racial preferences to be used for "remedying identified discrimination" in a manner that was not "unlimited, so amorphous, indefinite with respect to time."

Exactly one hour after it had begun, the oral argument ended with Rehnquist's stock, unadorned announcement, "The case is submitted."

Next on tap were Gratz's and Hamacher's appeals. Back to the podium came Kirk Kolbo to argue on behalf of the applicants rejected by the University of Michigan College of Literature, Science, and the Arts. He described the undergraduate admissions policy as "facially and flagrantly" discriminatory on the basis of race. His litany of the affirmative action plan's main characteristics put them directly at odds with the Court's ruling in *Bakke*. The UM "systems featured separate admissions guidelines for different races, protected or reserved seats in the class for select minorities, that is blacks, Hispanics, and Native Americans, racially segregated wait lists, and a policy of never automatically rejecting students from their preferred minority groups while doing so for others."

As she had in Grutter's case, O'Connor initiated the questioning, this time with what she labeled the preliminary matter of whether Hamacher had "standing," the judicial requirement that a plaintiff have a personal, concrete injury that courts can remedy with a judgment. (If Hamacher did not have standing, he could not represent the class of similarly situated plaintiffs, as the district court had originally certified him to do.) Stevens then monopolized the first minutes of the second oral argument with specific inquiries about how Hamacher's facts fit into the litigation. Once he was denied admission at UM, he enrolled at Michigan State and said that he would reapply to UM under its transfer policy, so Stevens demanded to know if that policy was the same as the regular admissions procedure. Kolbo claimed that the two were "essentially the same with respect to consideration of race" but admitted that the transfer policy was not before the Court. Stevens's persistence forced Kolbo to backtrack from his claim that the two policies were exactly the same. Scalia jumped in to declare that Hamacher had standing, but he might not be "entitled to relief." Kolbo disagreed; Hamacher would be entitled to "damages." Hamacher's counsel explained that, because his client had already graduated from another university in the intervening five years since the case was first filed, he would obviously not seek admission to UM as part of his relief, should he prevail in the suit, but he would be entitled to damages for being illegally rejected by Michigan. Recalling this part of the oral argument in a 2006 discussion, Kolbo explained that "the standing question did somewhat surprise us."

Ginsburg observed that the district court found unconstitutional the UM program under which Hamacher had applied, but it upheld the subsequent plan in place after his application. This subject opened an opportunity for Kolbo to reiterate the constitutional deficiencies in both plans, and he added that the "fundamental problem with the diversity rationale is that it depends upon the standardless discretion of educators." He pointed to the fact that universities discriminated against, or favored, different groups according to "shifting fashions." For example, in the *Bakke* case, the University of California at Davis Medical School gave preference to Asian American applicants, but they were excluded from the Michigan affirmative action program.

What difference did standards make to his argument? Kolbo was asked by Breyer. Race could be used in admissions or not, the justice suggested. Kolbo responded that the Court had previously made clear that one component of a compelling interest was "independent, ascertainable standards," as in "remedying identified discrimination" with a narrowly tailored program.

Did Kolbo's argument apply to public and private universities, as well as the employment realm? Ginsburg wanted to know. He acknowledged that private universities should be subject to the same nondiscrimination standards, under Title VI, as public institutions. But he refused to move into the world of employment, even admitting that "we are not suggesting an absolute rule forbidding any use of race under any circumstances." Stevens replied that Kolbo seemed to be saying "that the only permissible use of race is as a remedy for past discrimination." "I would not go that far," Kolbo responded. There ensued a lengthy colloquy with Justice Ginsburg, who presumed that voluntary affirmative action programs, like the one affirmed by the Court in the 1979 *Weber* case, would be invalidated if Kolbo's side prevailed. Again, Kolbo did not apply his argument to employment.

Breyer brought the discussion back to the point raised at length in the *Grutter* argument, namely, what was the Court to make of so many parties telling it that racial diversity was crucial in business, law, and the military, and, without it, "the country will be much worse off"? Kolbo disagreed that such considerations trumped the constitutional right to equal protection. So university presidents and deans can do nothing about underrepresented minorities in their schools? Kennedy asked. They cannot use racial preferences, which injure innocent people and are prohibited by the Constitution, Kolbo insisted. His day in court was over; now Ted Olson returned to the rostrum, again on behalf of the United States government as an amicus for Gratz and Hamacher.

In the undergraduate case, Olson managed to present three paragraphs from his prepared remarks, in contrast to the one sentence he articulated in the law school argument, before the questions commenced. This opportunity allowed him to stress the separateness of the procedures for preferred minorities, as opposed to all other applicants to Michigan's CLSA. He declared that the university admitted accepting all qualified underrepresented minorities. Olson described the 20-point bonus they received for their race/ethnicity as equivalent to a whole grade point, nearly twice the award for a perfect SAT score, and six times higher than the points given for an outstanding application essay. In fact, he asserted that the mega-bonus was unnecessary because every qualified candidate who received it was admitted. "It might just as well be an admissions ticket," Olson posited. He also reported UM's concession that its first undergraduate affirmative action program, invalidated by the district court, had "used separate grids, separate qualifications, separate standards, and protected seats." Furthermore, Olson observed, the university stipulated that its replacement policy had changed "only the mechanics, not the substance of how race and ethnicity were considered in the admissions process."

Stevens now cut the solicitor general off to point out that the changes were significant enough to convince the district court judge that the new program was constitutional. Of course, Olson responded that the federal government "respectfully" disagreed with the lower court's determination to uphold the revised affirmative action plan. Souter followed up his colleague's point to note that the university's revisions resulted in a narrowly tailored design. But Justice Kennedy supported Olson's claim that the university had stipulated that it had not changed "the substance of how race was considered." Correct, said Olson, who then told the Court that it only needed "to look at the operation of the system."

So Ginsburg and Souter asked for clarification on the 20-point bonus and how it applied to preferred minorities, athletes, and applicants of low socioeconomic status. Olson confirmed that an applicant could receive only one such bonus even if he or she fell into more than one of the three categories. "This plan violates every standard that this Court has set for the examination of racial preferences," Olson told the justices. "It is a thinly disguised quota because there's . . . — Justice O'Connor put it this way in *Croson* — a segment of the class reserved exclusively for certain minority groups." Moreover, Olson continued, the UM policy was based on "the stigmatizing notion that if you are a certain race, you think a certain way or if you're a certain race, you have certain experiences that are common."

Souter pointed to the study by Bok and Bowen, refuting that affirmative action stigmatized students. In addition, couldn't UM be proving to the student body that points of view do not correlate with race? Olson said the university was assuming that race/ethnicity determined viewpoint. Stevens explained that he thought the university was arguing that it had to have enough members of certain groups on campus to vary viewpoints. The solicitor general described the UM rationale as "self-contradictory." First, the university ascribes certain characteristics to applicants based on race; then, it argues that enough members of these racial categories have to be on campus so students will see how varied they are within the groups. Breyer launched into a lengthy rebuttal, stating that the university wanted a diverse student body to rid people of stereotypes and produce a better educational experience for everyone. Olson maintained that the university posited several justifications for its program, but that the Supreme Court had equated racial preferences with racial stereotyping, which is divisive and damaging to the goal of eliminating the negative results of racial discrimination.

Ginsburg then went down a highly controversial path in her next question, one that asked the nation's premier advocate to address the "global problem" of affirmative action and comment on whether the United States should consider what Canada, the European Union, and South Africa, and their courts, have done in this policy area.

(Conservatives have reacted adversely to Supreme Court justices citing foreign authorities in their opinions.) Olson did not take on the
dispute over whether the justices should look to precedents in other
countries, but he observed that no other nation had our history, our
Fourteenth Amendment, or our body of judicial interpretation on
racial preferences. Scalia, who is one of the most outspoken opponents
of citing foreign authorities, asked if the countries that had adopted
"racial entitlements" had ever eliminated them and achieved a "color-
blind society or has it been the road to a society that has percentage
entitlements for the various races." "Sadly," Olson replied, he believed the latter description was correct.

The solicitor general concluded his ten minutes with a pithy summation that Michigan could maintain its "elitist . . . selection process
without regard to race, or it may achieve the racial diversity it seeks
with race-neutral compromises in its admissions standards. But the
one thing it may not do is compromise its admissions standards or
change its admission requirements for one race and not another. This
is forbidden by the Equal Protection Clause of the Constitution." He
had withstood the barrage of questions almost solely from the liberal
wing of the Court.

Now the University of Michigan had thirty minutes to defend its
undergraduate affirmative action program. The task fell to John Payton of Wilmer, Cutler, and Pickering, an elite Washington law firm.
He announced that he wanted to set the record straight on "the educational judgment of the University of Michigan that the educational
benefits that come from a racially and ethnically diverse student body
are crucial for all of our students." Those benefits did not depend on
an assumption that "all African Americans think alike." He then
started to describe the majority of UM undergraduates as eighteen-
year-olds, two-thirds of whom were Michiganders, and one-half of
whom hailed from Detroit or its suburbs.

The barrage from the conservative faction on the Court began with
questions from the chief justice about the nature of the UM student
body. Payton portrayed the state of Michigan's racial profile as "very
segregated," with the city of Detroit "overwhelmingly black" and its
suburbs and the rest of the state "overwhelmingly white." Students from
both racial groups "have rarely had experiences across racial or ethnic
lines," he contended, and he gave a lengthy statement of how students

interacted with each other on campus and learned to counter previous stereotypes about those different from themselves. The critical-mass concept, Payton reasoned, was crucial to preventing isolation among minorities and feelings of tokenism. Rehnquist then initiated an inquisition about "a meaningful number" and the critical mass. Payton defined the latter as "when you have enough of those students so they feel comfortable acting as individuals." The chief justice asked how the university knew that. Payton responded that educators knew it from the students they see. Do the professors at UM spend considerable time with their students? Rehnquist asked. Payton responded affirmatively, and he cited the research of UM professors Raudenbush and Gurin, which indicated that the university had just approached critical mass in recent years so that students interacted productively in a variety of contexts. Scalia wanted to know if the Ann Arbor campus accommodated minorities in dormitories set aside just for them. Payton said no and reiterated the school's need for meaningful numbers and a critical mass of minorities so that "education, understanding, produces citizens and leaders in our complex society."

Kennedy once more commented that the Michigan program looked to him just like a "disguised quota." "I believe it's not a quota at all," said Payton, and he attempted to explicate the process. He claimed that admissions counselors read every application completely and assigned points according to the selection index's criteria, including race. Scalia interrupted, "But none of that matters," because preferred minorities who were "minimally qualified" were accepted. Payton returned to his theme that all the applications were read in their entirety, evaluated according to all the factors in the index, assigned the requisite points, and accepted on that basis. A counselor could also flag a file for reconsideration by the Admissions Review Committee.

Rehnquist then unleashed a cascade of queries for the UM counsel. He asked Payton to explain why his brief indicated that the CLSA might not be able to give the high volume of applications the type of individual attention the law school could to its smaller number of applicants, but now he was claiming that "every single application for admission to CLSA is read individually." Payton went with the latter claim, repeating that some applications were read twice.

What constituted an underrepresented minority? the chief justice inquired. Michigan used the same definition for the term as the federal government, was Payton's response. What was that? demanded Rehnquist. Three minority groups, said Payton, but he did not identify them. The chief asked for "a more direct answer" about how African Americans and Hispanics were deemed underrepresented. In the applicant pool, Payton offered. Underrepresented compared with what? probed Rehnquist. Payton elaborated, using the example of African Americans who constituted a "very small pool . . . that are qualified to the extent that we require students to be . . . to do the work at the University of Michigan." If UM did not take race into account, it would not be able to admit "the critical mass necessary for the educational benefits that we want." The chief justice probed further, asserting that underrepresentation "sounds like something almost mathematical" and that the university had a percentage it was using. Payton denied that a percentage was in play, only a "sufficient number of minority students." "What is a sufficient number?" was the inevitable question posed by the chief. When Payton did not answer explicitly, Rehnquist tried again, "I asked you, what is a sufficient number?" "Yes," Payton replied unhelpfully. He had strained the chief's patience, which was known to be taxed on the bench when counsel did not respond adequately to his inquiries. Now an exasperated Rehnquist insisted, "An answer — would you answer it!" A sufficient number achieved the critical mass, which was not a "fixed precise number," Payton tried in response to the chief's outburst. The counsel added that African Americans, Hispanics, and Native Americans were underrepresented.

Now Scalia took up the conservative attack, using the same tactic he had tried with Maureen Mahoney. "Why don't you lower your standards?" Scalia suggested. Instead of Mahoney's argument that the school should not have to choose between academic excellence and diversity, Payton claimed that UM was not accepting "students that aren't qualified," seemingly in direct contradiction to his response to Rehnquist that the pool of African American students with the qualifications to do the work at UM was too small to achieve a critical mass. Therefore, race had to be taken into account to accept a sufficient number of blacks. Amazingly, Scalia did not zero in on the discrepancy; rather, he repeated that UM should lower its acceptance standards. "You don't have to be the great college you are, you can be a lesser college if that value [of diversity] is important enough to you," the anti–affirmative action justice suggested. Payton rambled about the superb universities in America and finally settled on an assertion: "I think we get to decide what our mission is. I think the Constitution gives us some leeway in deciding what our mission is and how we define ourselves."

Justice Breyer broke the string of Rehnquist/Scalia hardballs. He resurrected Justice Kennedy's question about the UM selection index's point system and wanted to know if it met Powell's requirement of "individualized consideration" set out in *Bakke*. Breyer, as he is inclined to do, posed a detailed hypothetical in which Michigan had two candidates: the white applicant is an outstanding athlete and economically disadvantaged; the black has neither characteristic. Under the UM admissions policy, each candidate would receive one 20-point bonus, so, if they tied in their total points, Breyer wanted to know if the nod would go to the minority, without "individualized consideration." Payton responded that both files would receive such consideration; in fact, both might be sent to the Academic Review Committee for a second reading. Seventy percent of the applications it reviewed each year were from white candidates, and the committee could ignore the index scores altogether, according to the university's counsel.

Scalia reemerged to ask if Payton could cite an example of a "minimally qualified" minority who received the 20-point bonus for race and was rejected. At first Payton said he did not know, but, when pressed by Scalia to say whether rejection of such candidates was a reality or merely a theory, the counsel said that, although the record showed "virtually all" minority students were admitted because of preferences, he was certain some were not. He just could not recall one.

Souter tried to refocus the discussion on the fact that Michigan had to accept a higher percentage of minority applicants in order to get the diverse "mix" it desired. Payton returned to his critical-mass argument. So Souter queried him on UM's definition of the concept beyond "token terms." As Payton had done earlier in the session, he cited Professors Roudenbush's and Gurin's documentation of how diversity was working effectively on the Ann Arbor campus. Did the admissions committee use a percentage or specific number? Souter asked. No, replied Payton. Ginsburg requested the origin of the term *critical mass*, recalling that she knew of its sociological use in reference to recruiting women to law school so that they would "feel welcome" and not be considered "curiosities" or be "representatives of their sex." (As one of only a small number of women at Harvard and Columbia

Law Schools, both of which she attended in the 1950s, she certainly had experienced both of those latter feelings.) Payton cited Justice Powell's discussion of the Harvard model with its goal of "meaningful numbers" of minorities to avoid "the dynamics of isolation" that Ginsburg mentioned.

Breyer was still troubled by the numbers, pointing to the law school's testimony that 5 percent minority was too few and 10 percent might be enough in terms of critical mass. "What do I do with that testimony?" pleaded Breyer. "There's a false precision that everybody wants," Payton observed. In the last four years, the undergraduate college had ranged from 12 to 17 percent minority, and Payton said those figures seemed to produce the "educational benefits" of diversity that UM wanted.

"When does all of this come to an end?" Scalia asked, repeating O'Connor's earlier question. The university's attorney reported that "we all certainly expect it to come to an end," but he looked back with surprise over the quarter century since *Bakke* to note how segregated Michigan still was. He offered hope that "the test score gap . . . is narrowing," and the pool of qualified minorities was increasing, but he could not specify an end point for affirmative action.

Justice Kennedy, noted for his self-described propensity to "brood" over difficult cases, was still stuck on the quota issue. He asked if the Court would carry the "burden" of suggesting alternative policies (such as "individualized assessment") if the justices struck down the law school system and the CLSA's 20-point bonus because they "looked just too much like a quota and . . . quotas are impermissible." Payton responded that he could not envision how the UM system could be any more "individualized" in its assessment of applications. With time running out in the oral argument, he managed a clear, yet emotive, summation of his side's position. If diversity was a compelling interest, then the critical mass was crucial to its achievement. Justice Powell's vision of diversity was still necessary in 2003. "This is of enormous importance and correct, not just to the University of Michigan, but I'd say to all of higher education and I think to our country as a whole to be able to do things that bring us together, that bring us understanding, that result in tolerance and . . . make us . . . closer to the day that we all look forward to when, in fact, we are beyond some of these problems we've been discussing rather intensely here today."

If only those words could have constituted Payton's concluding remarks; instead, they became his penultimate point when an unfamiliar bass voice wafted over the sound system. The only African American on the Supreme Court, and the only justice to have benefited from affirmative action in education (at Yale Law School), Clarence Thomas, is typically silent during oral argument. He had sat through two hours of intense questioning on the heated topic of racial preferences utterly mute. Off the bench, Thomas has explained his characteristic silence on the bench, "My grandmother [who raised him] told me, 'You can't talk and listen at the same time.' If I wanted to talk a lot, I'd be on the other side of the bench." He has also noted that his use of the African American Gullah dialect of coastal Georgia while he was growing up had tainted his accent and made him self-conscious in public speaking as a college student. Yet in the Michigan cases he spoke at the very end of the 120-minute debate. He asked Payton, who is also African American, "Do you think that your admissions standards overall at least provide some head wind to the efforts that you're talking about?" Misunderstanding the metaphor "head wind," which blows *against* the subject as it attempts to move forward, Peyton replied, "Yes, I do," indicating that Michigan alumnae of all backgrounds were changing their communities after graduating with degrees from UM. Thomas, telling Payton, "You may have misunderstood me," posed Scalia's question in each of the two cases: couldn't UM adjust its admissions standards if diversity meant so much to it? Thomas acknowledged that Michigan did not want to choose between being "an elite school and the whole diversity issue," but he wanted Payton at least to accept "there is a tension" between the two goals. The counsel responded that nonselective schools could be "completely undiverse," so lower admissions standards did not ensure diversity. Thomas then posed the final query of the session, "Would the same arguments with respect to diversity apply to [historically black colleges]?" With time running out, Payton wanted to know if Thomas meant could such colleges benefit from racially and ethnically diverse student bodies? Then he hurriedly closed with an oxymoron that historically black colleges "have diverse student bodies."

Kolbo had reserved three minutes for rebuttal in this case, and he took the opportunity to present almost two pages of text with the luxury of no "justice interruptus." Ironically, it was not until minute 57 of the *Gratz* argument that the young woman who had appealed her case all the way to the Supreme Court heard her name mentioned in the courtroom for the first time. The policy in play when she applied was designed "to admit all qualified minority students," Kolbo reported that Michigan had conceded. He said the record was also "undisputed" that UM arrived at the 20-point bonus for race because a statistical analysis revealed that it would produce the same results as the old procedure, namely, admitting all qualified minorities. He then zeroed in on the fatal flaw of the policy, under *Bakke*'s standards. It created a two-track system, one in which "it's not enough if you're Jennifer Gratz or Patrick Hamacher to be merely qualified to get admitted to the university. To be admissible is not simply enough because of their skin color. If, however, you are a member of one of the [underrepresented] minority [groups], and you meet those minimum qualifications, that's sufficient. If that's not a two-track system, I can't imagine what one would actually look like."

On the matter of an end point for racial preferences, Kolbo suggested that they might actually "create perverse incentives" against improving minority test scores. He also declared that Michigan had resolved the tension between selectivity and diversity by placing the burden "on the backs of the constitutional rights of individuals like Jennifer Gratz and Patrick Hamacher." As far as the critical-mass concept was concerned, Kolbo insisted that it was "too amorphous, too ill-defined, too indefinite, just like the role model theory, just like the remedy for societal discrimination, too indefinite to support" the compelling state interest standard.

At two minutes past noon, Chief Justice Rehnquist thanked the university's counsel and, with the same routine statement he used at the end of *Grutter*, submitted the undergraduate case for the Court's anxiously awaited decision. A signal that the cases were anything but routine, however, came as soon as the justices left the bench. The tribunal immediately made available to the public an audiotape of the oral argument, which C-SPAN and NPR broadcast without delay. In the age of ubiquitous media, this gesture might seem unremarkable, but the Court had offered such expedited access to its proceedings only one other time — for the two oral arguments in the momentous 2000 presidential election dispute.

CHAPTER 7

"Diversity Is a Compelling State Interest"
Justice Sandra Day O'Connor Upholds
Affirmative Action

The oral arguments completed, the cases submitted, the next step for the nation's highest court was to discuss and vote on the outcome in the Michigan litigation. The justices' long-standing tradition is to gather in "conference" on the day of the argument, or no more than a few days later, to perform this fundamental task. Since the current Court building opened in 1935 (before then, the tribunal met in the Capitol across the street), the justices have had a formal conference room in which to meet. It is located on the east side of the white marble building, adjacent to the chief justice's chambers. Like most of the Court's formal rooms, it is paneled in exquisite honey-colored wood. The sanctum sanctorum contains a portrait of the ubiquitous "Great Chief Justice," John Marshall, and a long table around which the justices gather, with the chief justice at the head. As is typical of Supreme Court procedure, the discussion operates according to seniority. The chief justice, who is "first among equals" (though in Rehnquist's case he was also most senior in tenure, as well as chief), chairs the conference and guides the conversation. Rehnquist was noted for his efficient, but affable, leadership of these meetings, in contrast to his predecessor, Chief Justice Warren Burger, whose personality and intellect made him a less capable steward. Chief Justice Rehnquist recalled on camera in the Court's informational film that, when he became chief in 1986, he vowed that no justice would be allowed to make several comments on a case until everyone had the opportunity to say at least one thing about it. He remembered that when he had been among the junior justices, the rambling nature of the conferences meant it took considerable time for him to have an opportunity to comment.

Conference protocol dictates that the chief opens the discussion, and colleagues then make their comments, starting with the most senior associate justice, who has been Justice Stevens since Harry Blackmun retired in 1994, and continuing down to the most junior, who was Justice Breyer when the Michigan cases were discussed in April 2003. No one else is allowed in the conference room when the justices are performing their judicial duties. If a knock comes at the door, the most junior member of the Court answers it; he also is responsible for pouring beverages for his colleagues. Justice Breyer quipped in September 2005, anticipating the first new justice to join the Court in eleven years after the retirement of O'Connor, that he had become adept at serving coffee since arriving at the tribunal in 1994! After the chief determines that the discussion has run its course (for Rehnquist, who tolerated few tangents, this time would come sooner rather than later), he casts the first vote and asks his colleagues to state their positions, again from most senior to most junior associate.

When the outcome of the case is determined, seniority once more enters the picture. If the chief is in the majority, he may assign the "opinion of the Court" to himself, or he has the prerogative to assign it to an associate justice of his choosing in the majority. If the chief is in the minority, the power to select the opinion writer transfers to the most senior associate in the winning faction. Once the majority opinion is assigned — an extremely important choice because the opinion that speaks for the Court becomes the law of land — its author and his or her clerks (each justice may hire four) begin to work on drafts, which in turn are circulated among the majority for revisions. This process can take at least several months as drafts crisscross back and forth among the justices' chambers. Justices can choose to "join" the draft at any time, with or without suggested changes. Dissenting opinions go through the same process. Because all votes are considered tentative until the Court's opinion is officially announced, justices may change their minds during the process. Thus, the author of a 5:4 opinion has an especially delicate task in trying to hold the majority together until it agrees on one opinion. At worst, a vote can drift to the minority side, making it the winner with a new five-person majority. Or the majority from the initial conference vote might hold, but be unable to offer an opinion on which all five agree. This outcome leads to plurality "judgments" and/or concurring opinions, resulting in less clarity for the law. Such was the muddled result in *Bakke*, when no opinion's rationale attracted five votes.

In a nutshell, what was on the table for the justices to decide in the University of Michigan cases? Simply put, it was whether the affirmative action policies in the undergraduate college and the law school violated the Fourteenth Amendment's equal protection clause or Title VI of the 1964 Civil Rights Act. Under the Court's equal protection standards, government use of racial/ethnic classifications can withstand the required strict judicial scrutiny only if the classification exists to further a compelling state interest and the use of the classification is narrowly tailored to provide a close fit between the classification and the state interest.

Using these criteria, the Court had before it a plethora of approaches offered by the parties in the cases and the record number of amici briefs submitted. The following serves as a guide for the questions the Court had to ponder in its ruminations:

I. What might constitute compelling reasons to use race/ethnicity in university admissions?
   A. Remedy a history of general *societal* discrimination (against minority groups)
   B. Remedy a history of *institutional* discrimination (perpetrated by the university itself against minority groups)
   C. Remedy *specific instances* of discrimination (against identifiable minority individuals)
   D. Create a diverse student body
      1. What could make diversity a compelling state interest?
         a. Combating racial/ethnic stereotypes
         b. Fostering racial/ethnic understanding
         c. Creating a range of ideas/viewpoints
         d. Producing educated citizens/leaders for a pluralistic society
         e. Credentialing diverse members of the law profession
      2. What sources support the benefits of diversity?
         a. U.S. Supreme Court precedents (*Sweatt v. Painter* [1950], outlawing racially segregated public law schools; *Brown v. Board of Education* [1954], invalidating racially segregated primary and secondary schools; *Regents of the*

University of California v. Bakke [1978], upholding affirmative action in professional schools, but finding quotas invalid)

    b. Congressional findings (legislative record in civil rights acts and other laws)

    c. Social science research

    d. U.S. Department of Education interpretations

    e. Amici briefs in *Grutter* and *Gratz*

II. What kinds of affirmative action policies might be narrowly tailored (individualized, competitive, modest in scope, no undue burden on nonminorities)?

    A. Setting aside seats for minority applicants

    B. Achieving a "critical mass" of minority students

    C. Using a two-track admissions system (one for minorities; one for nonminorities)

    D. Using race/ethnicity, along with other factors (e.g., geographic origin, life experience) as a "plus" in an applicant's file

    E. Awarding bonus points to an applicant on the basis of race/ethnicity

    F. Placing no time limit on the use of racial/ethnic considerations

    G. Favoring only racial/ethnic groups that are deemed "underrepresented" in the student body

    H. Using alternative means for increasing minority enrollment, such as

        1. Expanded recruiting and outreach

        2. "Percentage plans" (taking the top 10 [or other figure] percent from all high schools in the state for acceptance in the state universities)

        3. Lower academic selectivity/standards

        4. Socioeconomic criteria

        5. "Experiential diversity"

The Court was expected to hand down its decisions on these complicated and nuanced issues by the end of its term in late June. As it was still proceeding through the opinion-writing process, the Sixth Circuit Court of Appeals surfaced again as part of the controversy in the Michigan cases. On May 28, Judge Alice Batchelder, one of the angry dissenters in the 5:4 *Grutter* decision by the appellate tribunal, upholding the Michigan Law School, in May 2002, issued a memorandum formally accusing the chief judge of her circuit, Boyce Martin, of manipulating the case as it worked its way through the appeals court. She repeated the accusations raised in her dissent, and that of her colleague Judge Danny Boggs in the *Grutter* ruling. Judicial Watch, a conservative organization that investigates the courts, posted the memo on its Web site. The group had filed a formal complaint against Judge Martin in January 2003. Federal judges rarely, if ever, give on-the-record interviews in pending cases and certainly not to criticize their colleagues. Yet Martin felt compelled, in light of Batchelder's new and very public attack, to speak to the *Washington Post*'s Supreme Court correspondent Charles Lane, saying he was "angry" at his colleague for not allowing him to reply formally to her charges, which he denied in the interview. The *Post* reported that Martin "accused Batchelder and other conservatives of trying to delegitimize the 6th Circuit's ruling to increase the chance it will be overturned." The chief judge, who had written the majority opinion validating the Michigan law school's affirmative action policy, stated that his colleagues had "chosen to embarrass me to influence the Supreme Court." He denied all of the memo's accusations and said he had violated none of the court's internal rules for sitting on the three-judge panel to hear procedural motions in Grutter's suit. In fact, he described how the clerk of the court drew Martin's name at random from slips of paper containing the names of all eleven judges on the circuit. Batchelder declined to respond to the *Post*'s interview with Martin. Her memo recommended no punishment for him, and she wrote that corrective measures had been taken, presumably inside the court, and that Martin's chief judgeship would soon expire. Indeed, on October 1, 2003, a new chief—Martin's adversary, Judge Boggs—would replace him. Reporters have noted that, three years after the replacement, acrimony continues to characterize the Sixth Circuit. One correspondent commented that the conflict will continue at least as long as Martin, who is in his early seventies, and Boggs, who is nine years younger, remain on the bench. Though the Sixth Circuit stretches from Tennessee to Michigan, geography offers no buffer for the warring jurists. Both Boggs and Martin are based at the federal courthouse in Louisville, Kentucky.

They could have taken a cue from their colleague, Judge Ronald Lee Gilman, who agreed to speak to Lane about the animosity on the

Sixth Circuit. Gilman, a Clinton appointee to the federal bench, had voted with the dissenting Republican-appointed judges to strike down the UM Law School admissions policy. Yet Gilman declared to the press that "to say Martin manipulated the process is totally unfair. We all need to be more tolerant and collegial and not assume the worst of each other's intentions."

Curt Levey, speaking for the conservative Center for Individual Rights that had initiated the lawsuits against the University of Michigan, commented to the *Post* that Batchelder's memo only "vindicates what we were saying all along. The delay in hearing our petition [for an en banc hearing] was inexplicable."

The public dustup over the law school case disclosed new information on why the undergraduate decision never made it out of the court of appeals. After hearing oral argument in *Gratz* on the same day it heard *Grutter*, the en banc nine-person court took a tentative vote. Martin, who voted to uphold the undergraduate affirmative action program, as he had the law school's, attempted to write the majority opinion to that effect in *Gratz*, paralleling his action in *Grutter*. Unlike in the law school case, however, Martin's opinion could not hold five votes to cement a majority. He told Lane that a majority was still eluding him when the U.S. Supreme Court took the unusual action of granting Gratz's petition for a writ of certiorari in December 2002, without a decision from the court immediately below.

Less than one month after Batchelder released her memo, all eyes turned to the Supreme Court for a ruling in the politically charged cases. Monday, June 23, 2003, was the penultimate scheduled Opinion Day of the Supreme Court for its 2002–2003 Term. Though the Court never announces in advance which cases it will hand down, the much-anticipated decisions were likely to be announced on this sultry morning in the nation's capital before the Court recessed for the summer. At the ready were national news correspondents, packed into the courtroom's press box, as well as broadcast satellite dishes and spotlights, erected on the sidewalks around the Court building. The journalists and spectators were not disappointed.

After decisions in two other cases were delivered from the bench, Justice O'Connor intoned to a hushed audience, "I have the opinion of the Court to announce in *Grutter v. Bollinger.*" The outcome was immediately clear from the start of her summary, which began by declaring that the use of race in admissions by the University of Michigan Law School was narrowly tailored to achieve the compelling state interest of diversity. She then cited Justice Powell's *Bakke* opinion as the guide for determining the compelling nature of a diverse student body. From the bench, O'Connor listed the benefits that studies have shown to accrue from diversity in education, particularly for citizenship, military leaders, and the law profession. Using race as a plus, she announced, did not constitute a quota or a two-track system. Rather, the Michigan Law School policy gave "individualized, holistic" review to all applications and did not unduly harm nonminorities, O'Connor opined. Race-neutral admissions decisions did not produce the educational benefits of diversity. She observed that a quarter century had passed since the Court had handed down *Bakke* and concluded with the caveat that, in another twenty-five years, affirmative action should no longer be necessary. As is customary after the justice writing the majority opinion announces the result, O'Connor named the colleagues who joined her and those who dissented. Not surprisingly, the justices who voted with O'Connor to create the winning majority upholding the law school's plan were from the Court's liberal wing (Stevens, Souter, Ginsburg, and Breyer). The dissenters were equally predictable and included the Court's conservatives (Rehnquist, Scalia, and Thomas). Kennedy, who occasionally votes with the liberals, remained consistent in his skepticism of affirmative action and filed a dissent.

O'Connor produced more details in her thirty-two-page opinion for the Court in *Grutter*. She spent nearly the first one-third of the decision narrating the facts in the case record. From her reliance on the law school's description of its policy, it was clear how O'Connor and her colleagues in the majority arrived at a ruling in UM's favor. The opinion for the Court reported that the law school, one of the highest rated in the nation, followed an admissions policy that attempted to achieve student body diversity in compliance with the *Bakke* decision. Admissions officials gave each applicant's file a "flexible assessment" of all factors and did not limit the meaning of diversity to race and ethnicity, but the policy did attempt to include, via a plus factor, a critical mass of the now-familiar three underrepresented minority groups within the student body.

When she turned to the merits of the case, O'Connor inevitably had to confront the complexity of *Bakke*. She accepted the fact that the decision "produced six separate opinions, none of which commanded a majority of the Court," as she had noted at oral argument. The only holding that garnered five votes in *Bakke* was that a "state has a substantial interest that legitimately may be served by a properly devised admissions program involving the competitive consideration of race and ethnic origin." Thus, in *Bakke* the Court had reversed a lower tribunal's ruling that prohibited the University of California at Davis Medical School from using race as a consideration for any applicant. Despite the "splintered decision in *Bakke*," O'Connor explained that Powell's opinion rendering the Court's judgment "has served as the touchstone for constitutional analysis of race-conscious admissions policies. Public and private universities across the nation have modeled their own admissions programs on Justice Powell's views on permissible race-conscious policies."

O'Connor's opinion delineated those elements of the UCD Medical School's rationale for affirmative action that Powell rejected: (1) remedying the deficit of minorities in medical schools and the profession, (2) remedying societal discrimination, and (3) increasing the number of doctors to work in "underserved" communities. Creation of a diverse student body was the only reason for the use of race in admissions that Powell approved, and he based this rationale on academic freedom protected under the First Amendment.

The *Grutter* majority opinion stated that the Court did not have to determine whether Powell's opinion in *Bakke* was binding under the Court's precedents setting criteria for determining when a judgment was controlling. Instead, O'Connor simply declared that "today we endorse Justice Powell's view that student body diversity is a compelling state interest that can justify the use of race in university admissions." She then turned to Fourteenth Amendment equal protection analysis, citing her own majority opinion in *Adarand* that "government may treat people differently because of their race only for the most compelling reasons." Her plurality opinion in *Croson* explained that the Court applies "strict scrutiny to all racial classifications to 'smoke out' illegitimate uses of race by assuring that [government] is pursuing a goal important enough to warrant use of a highly suspect tool. . . . Not every decision influenced by race is equally objectionable and strict scrutiny is designed to provide a framework for carefully examining the importance and the sincerity of the reasons advanced by the governmental decisionmaker for the use of race in that particular context."

In addition to using *Bakke* as the foundation for the majority's ruling in *Grutter*, O'Connor emphasized that the law school's diversity rational for considering race in admissions was not foreclosed by the Court's affirmative action cases decided since *Bakke*. "We have never held that the only governmental use of race that can survive strict scrutiny is remedying past discrimination. Nor, since *Bakke*, have we directly addressed the use of race in the context of public higher education. Today, we hold that the law school has a compelling interest in attaining a diverse student body."

The Court deferred to the university's "educational judgment that such diversity is essential to its educational mission." O'Connor wrote that the law school and its amici (those groups that had submitted friend-of-the-court briefs supporting it) had substantiated its claims about the benefits of diversity to the Court's satisfaction. Deferring to the school's sense of its own mission, the Court also assumed that UM was acting in "good faith," without "a showing to the contrary." For example, the majority accepted the university's goal of achieving a critical mass of minorities, defined by the law school's understanding of when enough African Americans, Hispanics, and Native Americans were on campus to achieve the educational mission. The school did not establish a specific number or percentage to attain its goal.

The numerous amici who supplied evidence of diversity's many educational benefits bolstered the *Grutter* opinion. O'Connor specifically listed the American Educational Research Association, 3M, General Motors, and "the high-ranking retired officers and civilian leaders." They argued that diversity in education results in a more effective workforce, management corps, and military. "We agree," the Court declared, "that '[i]t requires only a small step from this analysis [in the military brief] to conclude that our country's other most selective institutions must remain both diverse and selective.'" In addition, the Court recalled its previous acknowledgment of "the overriding importance of preparing students for work and citizenship, describing education as pivotal to 'sustaining our political and cultural heritage.' . . . Moreover, universities, and in particular, law schools, represent the training ground for a large number of our nation's leaders." Half of the state governors, more than half of U.S. senators, and more than one-third of U.S. congressmen hold law degrees. A half dozen of the highly selective law schools have produced 25 of the 100 U.S. senators, 74 of the more than 100 federal courts of appeals judges, and 200 of the more than 600 federal district court jurists, as the Association of American Law Schools brief reported. O'Connor asserted that leaders are viewed as legitimate by the citizenry if the institutions that train them are seen as open to students of all races and ethnicities. "All members of our heterogenous society must have confidence in the openness and integrity of the educational institutions that provide this training," O'Connor declared.

The majority accepted the Michigan Law School's testimony that it did not believe all minorities have the same viewpoints; rather, the Court said, the university attempted to diminish such stereotypes among the student body: "Just as growing up in a particular region or having particular professional experiences is likely to affect an individual's views, so too is one's own, unique experience of being a racial minority in a society, like our own, in which race unfortunately still matters." The statement reflected O'Connor's background, depicted in the 2002 memoir of her childhood, *Lazy B: Growing Up on a Cattle Ranch in the American Southwest*, where she recounted her early years on her family's ranch in Arizona. As the book's summary explains, life on the "rugged frontier" "helped make [O'Connor] the woman she is today." One of her proudest achievements was her election to the Cowgirl Hall of Fame several years before her retirement from the Court.

The majority opinion found that "the law school's admissions program bears the hallmarks of a narrowly tailored plan." Its search for a critical mass did not constitute a quota. The varied range of preferred minorities from 13.5 to 20.1 between 1993 and 2000 convinced five justices that it was "inconsistent with a quota." Moreover, the "highly individualized, holistic review of each applicant's file" and "giving serious consideration to all the ways an applicant might contribute to a diverse educational environment" were determinative. In a bad omen for the university's *undergraduate* admissions policy, however, the Court declared, "Unlike the program at issue in *Gratz v. Bollinger*, the law school awards no mechanical, predetermined diversity 'bonuses' based on race or ethnicity." The majority opinion also reported that "all underrepresented minority students admitted by the law school have been deemed qualified."

O'Connor's opinion directly rejected Grutter's argument, reiterated by the solicitor general for the United States, that race-neutral programs could achieve the same educational benefits of student body diversity that the race-based program employs. "We disagree," O'Connor wrote. The narrow tailoring requirement also did not demand that institutions experiment with every possible race-neutral alternative. "Nor does it require a university to choose between maintaining a reputation for excellence or fulfilling a commitment to provide educational opportunities to members of all racial groups." So much for Scalia and Thomas's demands at oral argument that UM could avoid racial discrimination by simply being less selective. Yet the Court interpreted narrow tailoring as requiring "good faith consideration of workable race-neutral alternatives to achieve the kind of diversity the university wants," and it accepted the court of appeals' view that the law school had considered such alternatives. O'Connor particularly dismissed the "percentage plans" advocated by the United States' brief and adopted by the public undergraduate institutions in Texas, Florida, and California. "The United States does not . . . explain how such plans could work for graduate and professional schools."

O'Connor then quoted her dissenting opinion in *Metro Broadcasting, Inc. v. Federal Communications Commission*, stating that racial preferences may not "unduly burden individuals who are not members of the favored racial and ethnic groups." She continued, "We are satisfied that the law school's admissions program does not" because it provided individualized review to each admissions candidate, which weighed "the possible diversity contributions of all applicants."

Coming to the end of her historic opinion, O'Connor stated that "all governmental use of race must have a logical endpoint." She mentioned the possibility of "sunset provisions" in affirmative action admissions policies. "We," she wrote for the Court, "take the law school at its word that it would 'like nothing better than to find a race-neutral admissions formula' and will terminate its race-conscious admissions program as soon as practicable. . . . It has been 25 years since Justice Powell first approved the use of race to further an interest in student body diversity in the context of higher education. Since that time, the number of minority applicants with high grades and test scores has indeed increased. We expect that 25 years from now, the use of racial preferences will no longer be necessary to further the interest approved today."

On the very basic question that the Court had agreed to answer, O'Connor responded for the majority that the Fourteenth Amendment's "Equal Protection Clause does not prohibit the law school's narrowly tailored use of race in admissions decisions to further a compelling interest in obtaining the educational benefits that flow from a diverse student body." Therefore, Grutter's statutory claims under the Civil Rights Act of 1964 failed as well. "The judgment of the Court of Appeals for the Sixth Circuit, accordingly, is affirmed." All of the lawsuits, money, interest groups, words, emotions, demonstrations, and controversy (including in the Sixth Circuit itself) came down to that final sentence of Justice O'Connor's "opinion of the Court." In 1953 Justice Robert Jackson observed about the Supreme Court, "We are not final because we are infallible, but we are infallible only because we are final." Questions of infallibility aside, the Court's ruling in *Grutter* was final. Its opinion was now the law of the land.

Justice Ginsburg's brief concurrence took issue with the twenty-five-year "sunset" of affirmative action. She cited international treaties to support her position, which would raise a firestorm in Congress and among conservative talk-radio hosts who lambasted her use of "foreign" legal authority, despite the fact that the treaties were ratified by the United States. After citing statistics to indicate the continuing racial separation and bias in America, she concluded, "From today's vantage point, one may hope, but not firmly forecast, that over the next generation's span, progress toward nondiscrimination and genuinely equal opportunity will make it safe to sunset affirmative action."

In dissent, Chief Justice Rehnquist accepted that in "limited circumstances . . . drawing racial distinctions is permissible," but they had to be narrowly tailored. He found that Michigan Law School's critical-mass goal was, in reality, "a naked effort to achieve racial balancing," which was not narrowly tailored to meet its compelling interest. He also parted company with the majority's application of strict scrutiny, which he thought was "unprecedented in its deference." He had pressed Maureen Mahoney at oral argument to explain how the law school arrived at its critical-mass percentage. Clearly, he was not persuaded by her answer that the university based it on the nature of the applicant pool each year and an individualized analysis of what kind of diversity each applicant could bring to the student body. His dissent pointed to the law school's claim that it wanted to achieve a critical mass of *each* underrepresented minority group. Yet the statistics that his opinion provided noted that their numbers in the student body varied from 1995 through 2000. During that time, the law school admitted between 1,130 and 1,310 applicants, of which between 13 and 19 were Native American, between 91 and 108 were African American, and between 47 and 56 were Hispanic. During the same five years, enrollment of Native Americans fell to a low of 3 students. How could that figure constitute a critical mass, the chief asked. UM provided no answers in the record to explain the disparities in numbers among the three favored minority groups. The chief's explanation was that the law school simply made offers to members of the selected minority groups "in proportion to their statistical representation in the applicant pool." This process was in direct violation of the Court's ban on unconstitutional "racial balancing." Rehnquist concluded his dissent with an attack on the Court's acceptance of the law school's vague assurance that its affirmative action plan is not permanent. "Thus, an important component of strict scrutiny — that a program be limited in time — is casually subverted."

Scalia and Thomas each wrote pointed dissents reflecting their consistent opposition to affirmative action. Scalia labeled as "anticonstitutional" racial preferences in state educational institutions. He took aim at the majority with his typically acerbic pen: "The University of Michigan Law School's mystical 'critical mass' justification for its discrimination by race challenges even the most gullible mind. The admissions statistics show it to be a sham to cover a scheme of racially proportionate admissions." He reiterated his point from oral argument that the law school's "allegedly" compelling state interest resulted not from the "fabled" critical mass but from the UM's desire to remain prestigious, despite the fact that its "normal" admissions standards excluded most blacks and other minorities. He declared, "If that is a compelling state interest, everything is."

In a dissent that equaled the majority opinion in length, Thomas, after quoting the nineteenth-century black abolitionist Frederick Douglass, wrote, "Like Douglass, I believe that blacks can achieve in every avenue of American life without the meddling of university administrators." The statement revealed his bitterness over racial politics in America, particularly racial preferences. After receiving an undergraduate degree in English from the College of the Holy Cross, from which he graduated ninth in his class in 1971, Thomas won a scholarship to Yale University Law School through its affirmative action program. In his courses, he received mostly passes on Yale's grading scale of honors, pass, low pass, and fail. He appeared to fit in academically and socially, but years later he described his "rage" and loneliness at feeling snubbed by whites who viewed him as an affirmative action token and ignored by blacks with more elite backgrounds. In his third year in law school he interviewed with law firms but again felt he was treated differently because of his race. He had hoped to return to his native state of Georgia to work against the injustices he had witnessed in his childhood, but he was rebuffed by the major law firms there. He still recalls the upset that welled up inside him at the time when all he had to show for his efforts were the "barren husks of rejection letter after rejection letter."

Now he was the sole African American on the nation's highest court and the author of a lengthy dissent in the nation's most important affirmative action case in a quarter century. He admitted that because he wished "to see all students succeed whatever their color, I share, in some respect, the sympathies of those who sponsor the type of discrimination advanced by the University of Michigan Law School." The Constitution, however, does not tolerate an admissions policy that "ripens into racial discrimination. Nor does the Constitution countenance the unprecedented deference the Court gives to the law school, an approach inconsistent with the very concept of 'strict scrutiny,'" Thomas asserted.

Turning the tables on the UM Law School program, he noted that no one would tolerate a university that had generally low admissions standards but applied higher standards to black applicants. The language turned sharper. "Racial discrimination is not a permissible solution to the self-inflicted wounds of [the law school's] admissions policy," he proclaimed, reflecting his and Scalia's line of questioning at oral argument. Then Thomas resorted to the kind of skewering that he and Scalia use in their respective opinions when attacking the liberal decisions of their colleagues: "The majority upholds the law school's racial discrimination not by interpreting the people's Constitution, but by responding to a faddish slogan of the cognoscenti."

Thomas said he could agree with one element of Justice O'Connor's majority opinion in *Grutter* — that "racial discrimination in higher education will be illegal in 25 years." (Never mind that she had written that the Court expected racial preferences would no long be "*necessary,*" not illegal, in a quarter century.) Thomas wrote that he had to dissent from the Court's opinion "because I believe that the law school's current use of race violates the Equal Protection Clause, and the Constitution means the same thing today as it will in 300 months."

The only rationale Thomas could discern for deeming government use of race as a "pressing public necessity" was "to provide a bulwark against anarchy, or to prevent violence." "The Constitution abhors classifications based on race," he wrote, "not only because those classifications can harm favored races or are based on illegitimate motives, but also because every time the government places citizens on racial registers and makes race relevant to the provision of burdens or benefits, it demeans us all."

Throughout the dissent, Thomas referred to the law school's "educational benefits" theory as "classroom aesthetics," and he chastised the majority for its "failure to justify its decision by reference to any principle," including the Court's own precedents. He called "unfounded" O'Connor's "wholesale adoption" of Powell's opinion in *Bakke*.

"For the immediate future . . . the majority has placed its *imprimatur* on a practice that only weakens the principle of equality embodied in the Declaration of Independence and the Equal Protection Clause," Thomas declared. He then concluded his dissent with Justice John Marshall Harlan I's famous lone dissension in the 1896 case of *Plessy v. Ferguson:* "Our Constitution is color-blind and neither knows nor tolerates classes among citizens." *Plessy,* which upheld (7:1) Louisiana's Jim Crow law for railway cars, proclaimed the high Court's "separate but equal" doctrine. Governments did not violate the equal protection clause by separating blacks and whites as long as the accommodations were (theoretically) equal, according to the Court's decision in the Louisiana case. Harlan's plea for color blindness in constitutional interpretation was a voice crying in the wilderness. Not until the Supreme Court's landmark ruling in *Brown v. Board of Education,* fifty-eight years after *Plessy,* did the justices, led by Chief Justice Earl Warren, unanimously repudiate the doctrine that racial segregation (even if facilities were genuinely equal) was constitutional. Ironically, as affirmative action moved toward color-conscious policies in the 1970s, it was *conservative* opponents of racial preferences (like Clarence Thomas) who harkened back to Harlan I's *liberal* defense of color blindness.

Justice Kennedy's brief dissenting opinion accepted Justice Powell's formulation of the "correct rule for resolving this case," but Kennedy believed that the majority in *Grutter* had failed to apply strict scrutiny. Instead, wrote Kennedy, the Court had simply accepted "the University of Michigan Law School's assurances that its admissions process meets with constitutional requirements." He agreed with Chief Justice Rehnquist's dissent that the "concept of critical mass is a delusion used by the law school to mask its attempt to make race an automatic factor in most instances and to achieve numerical goals indistinguishable from quotas." Kennedy had made this point in oral argument, and the responses from Maureen Mahoney obviously did not change his position. He also was not convinced by her explanation of the daily admissions reports. Kennedy wrote that the consultation of these reports by law school officials "suggests there was no further attempt at individual review [of applications] save for race itself." Finally, the majority's perplexing twenty-five-year expiration on affirmative action dismayed him: "Neither [Barbara Grutter] nor other rejected law school applicants will find solace in knowing the basic protection put in place by Justice Powell will be suspended for a full quarter of a century." So, even though Kennedy was willing to accept Powell's view of allowing "appropriate consideration" of race in higher education to produce diversity in furtherance of its educational mission, he could not cast his vote with the majority for the reasons he delineated in dissent.

When Rehnquist declared that he had the opinion of the Court to announce in *Gratz v. Bollinger*, affirmative action supporters knew that their narrow 5:4 victory in *Grutter* would not be repeated in the undergraduate case. Indeed, O'Connor, as she foreshadowed in her *Grutter* opinion, joined the chief justice, Scalia, Kennedy, and Thomas in the ruling to invalidate Michigan's undergraduate admissions plan. In classic Rehnquist style, his announcement from the bench was succinct. The 20-point bonus award by UM's undergraduate college to underrepresented minorities was *not* narrowly tailored to meet its diversity interest. Justice Powell in *Bakke* had required individual assessment of applicants, and he demanded that no single character-istic in a candidate's file should determine admission. UM's review of applications was not individualized, and admissions officers' option of "flagging" applications for additional review could not save the pol-icy from its illegal flaws. Justice Breyer concurred in part and dis-sented in part, making the vote in favor of Gratz 6:3. In full dissent were Stevens, Souter, and Ginsburg.

The chief took the first third of his twenty-eight-page majority opinion to delineate the convoluted facts in the undergraduate case. Before he could address the merits of the litigation, however, he had to decide the procedural matter raised by Justice Stevens at oral argu-ment: Hamacher's standing (although no party had broached the sub-ject at any point in the lawsuit, the chief observed). The Court ruled that Hamacher had standing because he had suffered a past injury from his initial rejection by the University of Michigan and a prospective injury from his intention to apply as a transfer student at the time the district court certified him as the representative of the plaintiff class. Moreover, the university's reliance on race to create diversity was the same in both the general admission policy and the transfer procedure.

Now the majority opinion could turn to the substance of *Gratz*. It had to begin with a reference to *Grutter*, which now was the control-ling precedent in higher education affirmative action cases. Diversity constituted a compelling interest, so the UM undergraduate policy did not fail equal protection analysis under that criterion, but the plan still had to be narrowly tailored. On this point, the policy did not pass constitutional muster because of the automatic 20-point bonus, "one-fifth of the points needed to guarantee admission, to every single 'underrepresented minority' applicant solely because of race." It also precluded the individualized consideration required under Justice Powell's *Bakke* ruling and typified in the Harvard model, appended to Powell's opinion. The automatic distribution of 20 points "to every single applicant from an 'underrepresented minority' group . . . has the effect of making 'the factor of race . . . decisive' for virtually every minimally qualified underrepresented minority applicant," the Rehn-quist opinion argued. The option of "flagging" application files for individualized review could not save the policy. The case record did not even indicate how many applications received such review. "Addi-tionally, this individualized review is only provided *after* admissions counselors automatically distribute the university's version of a 'plus' that makes race a decisive factor for virtually every minimally qualified underrepresented minority applicant."

Nor was the Court sympathetic to UM's argument that the sheer volume of applications prevented the individualized consideration of the sort the law school used for its far fewer applicants and upheld by the Court in *Grutter*. "Administrative challenges," Rehnquist wrote, do not "render constitutional an otherwise problematic system."

Therefore, the university's race-based policy for freshmen admissions was *not* narrowly tailored to meet the educational benefits of a diverse student body. The affirmative action program's violation of the Fourteenth Amendment's equal protection clause and Title VI of the 1964 Civil Rights Act, as determined by the majority, reversed that portion of the district court's ruling in favor of UM's revised policy.

Justice O'Connor filed a brief concurring opinion, perhaps feeling the need to explain her votes for the divergent results between *Grutter* and *Gratz*. She emphasized the "mechanized selection index score" in the undergraduate case, which stood "in sharp contrast to the law school's admission plan [that] enables admissions officers to make nuanced judgments with respect to the contributions each applicant is likely to make to the diversity of the incoming class." She concluded that "the university, of course, remains free to modify its [undergraduate admissions] system so that it does so."

Thomas filed a succinct concurring opinion to reiterate his absolutist position that "a state's use of racial discrimination in higher education admissions is categorically prohibited by the Equal Protection Clause." In a one-paragraph statement, Breyer announced that he was joining the judgment of the Court but not its majority opinion. He also joined a portion of Justice O'Connor's concurrence, as well as a segment of Ginsburg's dissent. He agreed with the latter that in applying the equal protection clause, the government "may properly distinguish between policies of inclusion and exclusion."

Stevens based his dissent directly on the procedural issue he had raised at oral argument. He concluded that neither Gratz nor Hamacher had standing to seek prospective relief by prohibiting the University of Michigan from using racial preferences in its freshman admissions policy. Barbara Grutter, Stevens noted, maintained that she had not attended any other law school and wanted to be admitted to UM Law School, if she had won her case. Instead, both Gratz and Hamacher had already enrolled in other institutions before they filed their lawsuit, and they never reapplied to the Ann Arbor campus again. (Indeed, they had both graduated from their alternative schools.) Thus, there was no "forward-looking relief" for them, and Stevens would have dismissed their case.

Souter joined Stevens's opinion but also filed a separate dissent to say that, the standing issue aside, he disagreed with the substance of the majority's decision. "I think [the freshman admissions system] is closer to what *Grutter* approves than to what *Bakke* condemns, and should not be held unconstitutional on the current record." He believed that the undergraduate admissions policy, "through the selection index system, [considered] all of the characteristics that the college thinks relevant to student diversity for every one of the student places to be filled [and therefore] fits Justice Powell's description of a constitutionally acceptable program." "It suffices for me," wrote Souter, "as it did for the district court, that there are no *Bakke*-like set-asides and that consideration of an applicant's whole spectrum of ability is no more ruled out by giving 20 points for race than by giving the same points for athletic ability or socioeconomic disadvantage." He also found that the "percentage plans," suggested as alternatives by the United States, were just as race conscious as the UM point system but deliberately obfuscated that fact. Souter, employing his wry New England wit, said he would "be tempted to give Michigan an extra point for its own frankness."

Ginsburg's dissent no doubt reflected her own experience with discrimination. After graduating first in her Columbia Law School class of 353 students (only 12 were women) in 1959 (she had transferred from Harvard Law School to be in New York with her husband), her job search was complicated by the fact that she was "a woman, a mother, a Jew — the kiss of death," as one of her friends described Ginsburg's status in the distinctly WASP male world of corporate law. In the early 1960s she accepted a professorship at Rutgers Law School, where she was one of only two women faculty members. In fact, there were only twenty female law professors throughout the entire country. Eventually, she began teaching a course on women and the law and became head of the Women's Rights Project for the ACLU, where she fought for gender equity through public interest litigation.

Her dissent in *Gratz* began with the observation that the Court in *Grutter* had acknowledged the authority of educational institutions to use race in admissions decisions. She took issue with the Court's insistence that the same standard of review must apply to "all official racial classifications." Such consistency, she argued, "would be fitting were our nation free of the vestiges of rank discrimination long reinforced by law. But we are not far distant from an overtly discriminatory past, and the effects of centuries of law-sanctioned inequality remain painfully evident in our communities and schools." Unemployment, poverty, health care, neighborhoods, and schools "remain racially divided," Ginsburg asserted, providing a wealth of statistics to support her claim. "The racial and ethnic groups to which the [undergraduate] college [at UM] accords special consideration (African Americans, Hispanics, and Native Americans) historically have been relegated to inferior status by law and social practice; their members continue to experience class-based discrimination to this day."

The Court had deemed racial classifications a "suspect category" requiring strict judicial scrutiny, not because they were always unconstitutional, but because they usually had been used, "to our national shame, . . . for the purpose of maintaining racial inequality." Ginsburg proffered her theory that the Court could "distinguish between policies of exclusion and inclusion," because "where race is considered 'for the purpose of achieving equality,' no automatic proscription is in order." Just as she had in her *Grutter* concurrence, Ginsburg cited universal human rights documents to bolster her argument. For the reasons delineated by Justice Souter in his dissent, she saw "no constitutional infirmity" in the UM undergraduate admissions policy. She approved of the "full candor" that institutions with affirmative action policies exhibited, and she concluded that it was preferable to "achieving similar numbers [of minorities] through winks, nods, and disguises."

A mere two years after the Michigan affirmative action cases came down, Justice Breyer published a slim volume, *Active Liberty: Interpreting Our Democratic Constitution*, based on a series of lectures he delivered at Harvard in late 2004. He defined "active liberty" as the nation's sharing of its sovereign authority with its citizens. Interpretation of the Constitution, he maintained, should consider not only those tenets known as "originalism," that is, text, history, tradition, and precedent, but also the purpose of the text, its language and values, and the consequences of judicial decisions. It is unusual for Supreme Court justices to comment on the substance of their decisions soon after they are rendered. In the common-law tradition, judicial decisions are to speak for themselves and not depend on the unofficial explanation of justices after the fact. Yet Justice Breyer penned a short chapter on *Grutter* for his 2005 book. He explained that Justice O'Connor's majority opinion in *Grutter*, with which he agreed, reflected the principles of active liberty, as he defined them. These principles, he wrote,

find some form of affirmative action necessary to maintain a well-functioning participatory democracy. They say that an interpretation of the Equal Protection Clause that would outlaw the law school's affirmative action program is an interpretation that, from the perspective of the Constitution's basic democratic objectives, would not work. Too many individuals of all races would lack experience with a racially diverse educational environment helpful for their later effective participation in today's diverse civil society. Too many individuals of the minority race would find the doors of higher education closed; those closed doors would shut them out of positions of leadership in the armed forces, in business, and in government as well; and too many processes are *theirs*, not *ours*. If these are the likely consequences — as many knowledgeable groups told the Court they were — could our democratic form of government then function as the Framers intended?

Breyer's last point was particularly clever in light of "original," or "Framers', intent" advocates, who argue that the Constitution should be interpreted as those who framed it originally intended. The fundamental governing document should not be updated by judicial fiat, originalists argue. Yet Breyer writes that, by considering the consequences of judicial decisions, judges can apply the Constitution's text and principles to contemporary problems, while complying with the Founders' intentions.

No doubt, Breyer was particularly susceptible to the inclusion rationale that Justice Ginsburg used to support affirmative action in both *Grutter* and *Gratz*. (Breyer, however, concurred with the judgment of the *Gratz* majority reversing the district court's ruling upholding the revised affirmative action policy in *Gratz* for the reasons Justice O'Connor set forth in her concurring opinion. The 20-point bonus and its mechanistic application obviously made him uncomfortable.) He had spoken over the years about how his father had been excluded from clubs at Stanford University because he was Jewish, and Justice Breyer referred to his Jewish heritage in a 1995 speech at the Holocaust Museum in Washington, noting that the rule of law in Nazi Germany had collapsed and failed to save victims of Hitler's Third Reich. In race cases prior to *Grutter* and *Gratz*, Breyer had voted to uphold set-asides for minority businesses in federal contracts and race-based "majority-minority" voting districts. His book concluded about *Grutter*: "When faced with one interpretation of the Equal Protection Clause that, through efforts to include, would facilitate the functioning of democracy and a different interpretation of the Equal Protection Clause that, through perceived exclusion, might impede the functioning of that democracy, is it surprising that the Court majority chose the former?"

Of course, it did so by only one vote and produced a split result between the outcomes of the two University of Michigan cases. Even Breyer, who seemed so certain about the basis for his vote in *Grutter*, had come to a splintered conclusion in *Gratz*. What reactions to the two landmark decisions awaited the justices among the various groups with a stake in the affirmative action debate?

CHAPTER 8

"Affirmative Reaction"

In the Wake of *Gratz* and *Grutter*

Starting at the very top of the American government hierarchy, President George W. Bush took the high road by praising the Supreme Court's decisions in the Michigan cases. "I applaud the Supreme Court," Bush said in a prepared statement on the same day the rulings came down, even though the law school outcome was a major defeat for his administration, which had argued that both affirmative action plans were illegal. "Today's decisions seek a careful balance between the goal of campus diversity and the fundamental principle of equal treatment under the law. . . . Like the Court, I look forward to the day when America will be a color-blind society," the president observed.

Bush's counterpart at the University of Michigan, President Mary Sue Coleman, who was at the Court when the decisions were announced, exclaimed, "This is a tremendous victory for the University of Michigan, for all of higher education, and for the hundreds of groups and individuals who supported us. The Court has provided two important signals. The first is a green light to pursue diversity in the college classroom. The second is a road map to get us there." On the Ann Arbor campus, minority students rallied in celebration of the rulings, carrying signs that read, "Race is a factor because racism is a factor."

On the steps of the Supreme Court, white UM students protested with placards proclaiming, "Judge not by race" and "Diversity is *no* excuse for racism." They reflected the disappointment of the Center for Individual Rights, which admitted that the lawsuits they had so doggedly pursued fell short of their expectations. Not totally defeated, however, CIR spokesperson, Curt Levey, described the Court's split decision as creating "a pretty fine line they [universities] have to walk."

Elaine Jones, the director-counsel of the NAACP Legal Defense and Educational Fund, who had drawn conservatives' ire after she contacted Senate Judiciary Committee staff regarding the Michigan cases and encouraged a delay on Sixth Circuit judicial nominations, was exuberant over the outcome: "We were supposed to go down [to defeat] on Michigan. We won! Sixty-five corporations said they were for diversity!"

Some scholars joined in the celebration of diversity and even declared that the Court's decisions in the two cases were not "split," "as initially reported in the press." Vikram David Amar, for example, a public law professor at the University of California's Hastings College of Law in San Francisco, wrote that the cases "were a clear victory for diversity-based racial affirmative action, with a roadmap outlined in *Grutter* for how to take advantage of that victory."

Amar was correct in that the law school ruling was broader in scope than a first glance might indicate. O'Connor had garnered a majority (albeit a precarious one that could be overturned in a future case, especially after her 2006 retirement and replacement by conservative justice Samuel Alito) for the proposition that racial/ethnic diversity in higher education constitutes a compelling state interest. Even Rehnquist had to accept that premise in *Gratz*, as did Justice Kennedy in his *Grutter* dissent, because O'Connor's ruling now constituted the controlling precedent. Yet, in contrast to Amar's view, the victory for affirmative action proponents was not complete. The narrow tailoring requirement still had to be met according to *six* justices (including Breyer). Nonindividualized, mechanistic, point-based procedures were clearly unconstitutional in the Court's eyes.

To the extent that the Michigan cases produced divided decisions, they reflect the paradox in public opinion. A 2003 Pew Research Center survey discovered that Americans approved 2 to 1 "programs designed to increase the number of black and minority students." Yet the same survey reported that Americans disapproved 3 to 1 "giving [minorities] preferential treatment." Andrew Kohut, director of the Pew Research Center, reported that it was striking how closely the Court's decisions reflected the public's beliefs on this controversial issue. "The Court comes across as temperate, reflecting the complexity of opinion in the public itself," Kohut remarked. The *Washington Post* commented that Justice O'Connor possessed a knack in her two decades on the high tribunal of "landing pretty near the spot where the public uneasily settles." Her biographer and *USA Today* Supreme Court correspondent Joan Biskupic argues that O'Connor was particularly adept at identifying and seizing the middle ground among the justices and then using her prodigious political and personal skills to forge an opinion on that point. As Biskupic notes, "O'Connor came to the Court knowing how to count votes. She was the only [justice to have previously served as an] elected politician on the Court during her time there." Her mentor, Justice Powell, was equally talented at splitting the difference between liberal and conservative positions among his colleagues and creating a compromise that often matched (or perhaps helped mold) public opinion. His work as head of the Richmond school board during the turbulent 1950s, and presidency of the American Bar Association, no doubt served him well in honing his statesmanship.

Linda Greenhouse, Pulitzer Prize–winning Supreme Court correspondent for the *New York Times*, labeled the results in the Michigan cases an "unapologetic embrace" of diversity as a compelling state interest, far beyond Justice Powell's vision in *Bakke*. O'Connor's opinion took affirmative action from the classroom to "civic life" and "American society." Greenhouse speculated that after the Court granted certiorari in *Grutter* and *Gratz*, the justices recognized the high stakes at issue (especially after a record number of amici briefs appeared on their doorstep). They would have to decide the cases "in the full glare of public attention." Greenhouse declared that the Court took a "societal reality check" and asked itself how it would look to the country if it struck down affirmative action, especially when the overwhelming majority of amici briefs (particularly from the Fortune 500 companies) favored it. She noted that, in contrast, most of the anti–affirmative action briefs were submitted by conservative interest groups, which a majority of the justices might have perceived as more partisan or ideological and less "real world" in their outlook.

Immediately after the Court announced its decisions, higher education administrators, lobbyists, and lawyers began to identify the rulings' ramifications. Those institutions that had policies in place similar to the validated Michigan Law School program could maintain the status quo. Those that used more arbitrary, formulaic preferences for minority applicants were on notice that they had to alter their now illegal procedures. According to Constantine Curris, president of the American Association of State Colleges and Universities, the Court's rulings were "essentially an affirmation of policies that most institutions have followed." "This is clearly a win for the higher education community," reported Scott Palmer, formerly with the U.S. Department of Education, but in 2003 a lawyer who consulted with colleges and universities to guide them on how to establish constitutional programs. He emphasized that "now you're in a discussion of *how* you do race-conscious affirmative action, not *whether* you do it."

Michael A. Fletcher reported for the *Washington Post* that "most colleges and universities accept the vast majority of applicants." The average acceptance rate across the nation is 70 percent. Less selective schools set relatively low minimum standards for test scores, GPA, and high school courses; applicants under that floor are automatically rejected. Those who rate highly on the trio of criteria are usually accepted. In between the high and low standards fall students whose files will receive individual attention, when race and other factors that lead to diversity are considered.

Shelden Steinbach, general counsel for the American Council on Education, an interest group for higher education, observed just after the Michigan decisions were released that "very few schools . . . replicate the University of Michigan's undergraduate admissions program. The hand writing has been on the wall for almost a decade, and most universities have amended their admissions processes so as to provide a full-file review of each individual candidate." In that sense, the hard work of the CIR, and other opponents of rigid race-based admissions policies, had already paid off even before the Michigan decisions were announced.

As George Washington University president Stephen Trachtenberg explained, "Michigan's going to have to spend a little money and hire a bigger admissions crew and actually read all the applications — like we do." His procedural prediction was correct, but his "little money" comment was more than understated. Two months after the Court's ruling in *Gratz*, banning the use of the point-based selection index, UM announced that it expected to spend between $1.5 and $2 million to hire and train additional staff for reading applicant files.

In August 2003 the University of Michigan announced its new affirmative action policy for undergraduates, jettisoning the point-based index repudiated by the Court. According to the *Philadelphia Inquirer*, applicants for the entering first-year class of 2004, and transfer students, were given the option of reporting their race/ethnicity on their application, but that factor would be considered "holistically" with the entire file, according to UM provost Paul Courant. Would-be "Wolverines," the university's sports mascot, would be asked to supply more information on their socioeconomic background. They would also provide a short answer about their views on diversity. "We continue to believe in gathering a group of students that are very bright but different from one another — students from all walks of life and backgrounds," Courant declared. Part-time readers and admissions counselors were to peruse each application separately and make recommendations on admission. The two recommendations from each reader then would go to a manager, who made the final decision. A review committee was established to arbitrate any disagreements among the readers and managers. The new undergraduate selection process was modeled on the UM Law School policy.

After Michigan's announcement of its new undergraduate affirmative action procedure, the Center for Individual Rights warned that it would keep a close eye on the policy's implementation. Terry Pell, the CIR's president, vowed, "If race continues to trump most other admissions factors, the new system will be just as illegal as the system the Court struck down."

Michigan discovered, not surprisingly, that devoting more attention to each applicant's dossier took considerably longer than its invalidated bonus-point plan. By mid-November 2003, UM had admitted only one-third (500) as many students (for 2004 fall admission) as it had by the same time the previous year, when it had selected 1,500 applicants. The university detected another difference in its new admissions program, which it blamed on the prolonged lawsuits against the university. In March 2004 it reported a 23 percent decline in blacks, Hispanics, and Native Americans seeking admission to the undergraduate college. Of course, the university did not cite negative publicity about racial tensions on the campus, which appeared in the media during the litigation process, as a potential reason for a drop in minority applications.

In 2005 UM's director of undergraduate admissions Theodore Spencer happily noted that African American applicants increased by 12.8 percent. "We had work to do," Spencer admitted, "to dispel whatever myths there were about the lawsuit, including those that said that we changed our applications to prevent minority students from coming." The university increased its efforts to recruit more students, especially African Americans and Hispanics. Admissions officers held workshops on completing the new application for high school students and their guidance counselors. Michigan's president, Mary Sue Coleman, visited four churches in black communities to "welcome students and open her arms wide to let them know that they're invited to apply," according to a UM spokesperson.

While keeping the rate of admission nearly the same between 2004 and 2005 (a little over half of black applicants were admitted each year, and three-quarters of Hispanics were accepted), Michigan's undergraduate program raised its proportion of African Americans in the 2005 freshman class to 6.9 percent from 5.8 percent and its rate of Hispanics from 4.4 percent to 5 percent. Native Americans held constant at 1 percent. The undergraduate admissions director maintained that "academic quality did not slip at all in any of the categories. We were aware of that and wanted to make sure that didn't happen."

True to his word in the immediate aftermath of the *Gratz* ruling, the CIR's Terry Pell continued to evaluate Michigan's admissions procedures. UM "is doing what it ought to be doing: encouraging more students to apply and to attend once they're admitted," Pell commented about the 2005 data. "The numbers are consistent with what the university is saying, and that's all good news. [But] if Michigan continues to experience the sort of disparity in which the black dropout rate is twice that of whites, it will be almost conclusive proof it is continuing to use two different standards for admissions." The university has attributed the difference in retention rates across racial lines to financial and other nonacademic factors.

Carl Cohen, the University of Michigan philosophy professor whose initial investigation of UM's admissions procedures paved the way for the historic affirmative action litigation, also watches the undergraduate admissions policy "as closely as [he] can." "Most of what they do," he noted in 2006, "goes on behind closed doors. I cannot say whether the procedures approved [by the Supreme Court] for the law school are truly being adopted in the undergraduate context. That claim is made, of course. I am skeptical, but I have no evidence that shows the claim to be unwarranted."

The *Gratz* decision forced another major state institution, the University of Massachusetts at Amherst, to abandon its point-based admissions system that was similar to Michigan's. U.Mass. resigned itself to the fact that the Supreme Court decision would require the school to spend more time reviewing the 16,000 applications it receives each year.

Other universities, public and private, began to rethink their minority recruiting efforts in the wake of *Gratz*. Initially, admissions officers did not believe their outreach programs fell under the Michigan ruling striking down the undergraduate point-based index, but they began to worry about the broader interpretations of the decision. Their minds were not eased when conservatives argued that the Michigan undergraduate ruling applied not only to admissions procedures but also to minority outreach programs. Anti–affirmative action groups claimed such programs were unconstitutional; they threatened new legal action and filed complaints with the U.S. Department of Education. Conversely, admissions officers asserted that race-specific efforts to woo minorities to their campus were legal because students still had to apply and be accepted, but the *Washington Post* reported in November 2003 that "rather than risk protracted litigation and legal bills that could run into the millions of dollars [Michigan had spent more than $10 million defending both lawsuits], they are quietly altering their programs to make them less racially exclusive." Such a response demonstrates the power of interest group litigation, the mere threat of which can produce the outcomes desired by the litigating organizations.

Amherst College in Massachusetts reported that its heavily subsidized trips to campus for minority students in the past had resulted in about 70 percent of the 170 attendees receiving admissions offers, with a yield of approximately one-third (or 39 enrollees out of 119 offers made). As of 2004, Amherst dropped its special open houses for "students of color" only and began including low-income whites, along with minorities, in its reconstituted campus visits. Amherst's dean of admissions said the post-*Gratz* era felt like a "war, and we are in the middle of it." His college was proud of its minority outreach efforts that had changed Amherst from virtually an all-white school a generation earlier to one-third minority by the dawn of the twenty-first century. Now the college would have to expand its definition of diversity to include students beyond those in racial/ethnic minority groups. Mount Holyoke, the nation's oldest women's college, followed suit. MIT opened its previously all-minority summer school program to whites after conservative groups threatened a lawsuit. A similar seven-week program for minorities at Princeton's Woodrow Wilson School of Public Policy and International Affairs, in place since 1985, was put on hold and then reopened in 2005 to all students interested in public service and committed to "cross-cultural issues." Williams College expanded a graduate fellowship and prefreshman program to include all races. Carnegie Mellon University did the same with a full-tuition scholarship and summer program in math and science. The university now includes other criteria in achieving diversity, such as whether a prospective student is the first to pursue higher education in his or her family.

Smaller schools like Amherst worry that they could become resegregated by not being allowed to use their successful minority recruitment programs. The Amherst admissions dean observed, "We are less well known than places like Harvard, Yale, and Princeton, and therefore we have to work harder to become a diverse place. We can't just be passive and expect to attract top students from outside the Northeast." Statistics affirm his concern over keen competition for highly qualified blacks and Hispanics. The College Board, which administers the SAT, reported that only 1,877, or 1.5 percent, of blacks who took the test in 2003 scored higher than 1300 (on the scale of a perfect 1600); only 72 African Americans achieved a score above 1500. Of all SAT-takers in 2003, about 10 percent (148,024) scored higher than 1300, and 13,897 earned scores above 1500. Amherst, like many other colleges, identifies promising minority recruits in data purchased from the College Board. Students who take the SAT can list their race/ethnicity on a questionnaire that accompanies the test.

Like many white students, minorities, especially from low-income households, particularly where parents did not attend college, agonize over paying for higher education. When the school is a prestigious, northeastern, private college, like Amherst, the cost per year can surpass $40,000. Amherst had provided generous financial aid packages to minority students in the past, but those were also placed in jeopardy by the *Gratz* ruling.

By early 2006 the conservative interest group Center for Equal Opportunity had sent challenges to 200 colleges and universities over scholarships reserved for minorities and women. The center claims that more than 150 schools responded by expanding their aid programs to cover nonminorities, though no government or nonpartisan private organization maintains such statistics. The American Association of State Colleges and Universities estimated that hundreds, perhaps thousands, of scholarships and fellowships had been awarded on the basis of race, and that half of the colleges in America reviewed and/or revised their minority aid programs.

As with admissions procedures after *Gratz*, many universities were trying to get out ahead of expensive legal challenges to their race-based funding. Some schools, however, already faced action from the U.S. Department of Justice (DOJ) or Department of Education (DOE). Southern Illinois University, for example, negotiated a consent decree with DOJ to open its graduate fellowships, originally designated for minorities and women, to whites and men. Pepperdine University Law School, with Kenneth Starr as its dean, and hardly a bastion of liberalism, had to negotiate with the DOE over racial criteria in its programs. In early 2006 the massive State University of New York system made $6.8 million in scholarship funds open to all students, rather than just minorities for whom the dollars had been designated.

Some changes were symbolically awkward, as in the case of Washington University in St. Louis, which was also under a legal threat of intervention from the DOE. The school had to open to whites a minority-only scholarship that had been endowed in honor of the university's first black dean. In the initial year after the change, twelve of the forty-two recipients were white. Not surprisingly, such programmatic revisions rankle liberal civil rights groups. Theodore Shaw, director-counsel of the NAACP's Legal Defense and Educational Fund, scoffs at the charge that minority-targeted funding injures white students. He fumed to the *New York Times*, "How is it that they conclude that the great evil in this country is discrimination against *white* people? Can I put that question any more pointedly? I struggle to find the words to do it because it's so stunning." Yet cognizant of the legal realities forcing university administrators to reconfigure their programs, Washington University's College of Arts and Sciences dean identified another reality of trying to achieve diversity: "It will take more time, it will take more creativity."

Looking at the goal of collegiate careers — graduation — the University of Virginia touts a high rate of completion for its black students.

The *Journal of Blacks in Higher Education* reported in 2006 that, for the twelfth consecutive year, U.Va. achieved the highest six-year graduation rate for African American students among major public institutions. Eighty-six percent of black students who had enrolled at Virginia in 1998 graduated by 2004. The nationwide rate for African Americans in the same time period was only 42 percent. The next-highest rates for other flagship state universities were 70 percent for the University of California at Berkeley and the University of New Hampshire, and 69 percent at the University of North Carolina at Chapel Hill. U.Va. points to several reasons for its consistent success, including recruiting black students who are qualified to succeed in its rigorous academic program. The university may benefit from a high school graduation rate for blacks in Virginia that, at 64.1 percent, is almost 13 points higher than the national rate for African American high schoolers. U.Va. also provides financial aid to students who otherwise might not be able to afford college and assigns students to "peer advisers" who help them transition from high school and succeed in college. Virginia's president John Casteen credits black students themselves for their high graduation rate at U.Va. "I think it is something students do. They succeed." Of course, that is a politic statement when affirmative action opponents continue on the warpath against race-based collegiate programs.

Despite abolishing its point-based affirmative action admissions system in 1999 under threats from the Center for Equal Opportunity and the Center for Individual Rights, the University of Virginia has been successful in enrolling a diverse student body. For its class of 2009, "Mr. Jefferson's University," which ranks among the top twenty-five schools in the nation, received almost 16,000 applications. It offered admission to nearly 6,000 (38 percent). More than 3,000 (53 percent) accepted. Ten percent of the class is African American, 10 percent Asian American, and 4 percent Hispanic. Five percent of the class is classified as "international."

In the state of Michigan anti–affirmative action warriors turned to the grassroots political process as a next step in eliminating racial preferences. Their goal was to place an amendment to the state's constitution on the ballot that would ban such preferences in university admissions, state hiring practices, and contracts. They needed 317,757 signatures to bring the amendment up for a voter referendum. Aiding the effort was Ward Connerly, a black regent of the state university system in California and founder of the American Civil Rights Coalition, who had successfully moved a similar policy (Proposition 209) through the Golden State in 1996 and the state of Washington two years later.

The movement brought a familiar name back to Michigan — Jennifer Gratz — to lead the new charge against affirmative action. As executive director of the Michigan Civil Rights Initiative, the former plaintiff declared, "I absolutely believe that treating people differently because of skin color is wrong." Gratz had left her native state in 2001, three years after she received her degree in math from UM's Dearborn campus. She eventually moved north of San Diego, California, with her new husband, and became a software trainer for a vending machine company. When asked by the *Washington Post* how her rejection from the University of Michigan, where she had hoped to study forensic science, changed her life, she replied, quite logically, "I can't tell you exactly how my life would be different because I wasn't given the opportunity." Nevertheless, she articulated the differences between the Ann Arbor campus, one of the more beautiful collegiate settings in the country, and the commuter Dearborn campus, with only four or five classroom buildings and the "U-Mall," with cafeteria tables, where all the nonresident students (there were no dorms) kill time between classes. Beyond collegiate ambience and aesthetics, Gratz also mentioned that UM brings recruiters to the Ann Arbor campus from the top firms in the nation, whereas at UM-Dearborn recruiters come only from the Detroit metropolitan area. Her first job out of college was with a credit union, and she continued to live with her parents. She adds, however, "I'm not an angry or bitter person." With only a slight edge, she wished well the minority students who were accepted under the UM affirmative action program. "They've been given an opportunity to go to an excellent school. Good for them," she remarked in 2003. Gratz continues her avid support for the Wolverine football team and wears a University of Michigan sweatshirt as a tangible expression of her loyalty. She once met the team's coach at an airport while traveling and told him how she watches the nontelevised UM games on her computer.

Back in Michigan for the next anti–affirmative action battle, Gratz helped field e-mails and phone calls and assisted organizers of the ballot referendum in raising $600,000. They felt upbeat about their chances when a January 2004 poll by the *Detroit News* showed 64 percent of Michiganders against racial preferences. The countereffort was led by a pro–affirmative action consortium called Citizens for a United Michigan, headed by retired general Michael Rice. "We have to get the word out not to sign these petitions. [The amendment] will have far-reaching effects. . . . We are asking people not to throw their signature away in a shopping mall," Rice reported.

Democratic governor Jennifer Granholm campaigned against the signature effort and argued that, if the new amendment was added to the state's constitution, fewer women and minorities would be hired in Michigan government, and state universities would see a drop in diversity. On Martin Luther King Jr. Day in 2004, Granholm joined a news conference with Detroit's Democratic mayor Kwame Kilpatrick and leaders from the NAACP and the Southern Christian Leadership Conference to speak against Connerly's initiative. Kilpatrick had previously spoken out against him: "We will stand up to [Connerly], stand up to all who oppose affirmative action." Detroit's NAACP chapter president, the Reverend Wendell Anthony, followed suit, stating, "We won't allow them to put a black face on a red, white, and blue problem. If we sit quietly and don't speak up, we are in trouble." Representative John Dingell (D-MI) wrote a letter to Connerly bluntly declaring, "The people of Michigan have a simple message to you: go home." The California regent and successful entrepreneur not only did not leave, he contributed $500,000 of his own funds to the anti–affirmative action campaign.

According to University of Michigan's general counsel, Marvin Krislov, a successful outcome for Connerly's movement "could be devastating in terms of our ability to have a diverse student body." He worried that even outreach programs to recruit women and minorities could be banned under the amendment, which would not allow the state of Michigan to "discriminate against, or grant preferential treatment to, any individual or group on the basis of race, sex, color, ethnicity, or national origin" in public employment, university admissions, or contracting.

Opposition to the amendment became bipartisan when Granholm's Republican opponent in the 2006 gubernatorial race, Dick DeVos, spoke out against the measure. Groups working to defeat the initiative included the American Arab Chamber of Commerce, the Michigan Catholic Conference, the Michigan Jewish Conference, and the United Auto Workers. *USA Today* reported that Connerly's attempts to ban affirmative action had stalled after his successes in California and Washington. Florida Republican governor Jeb Bush labeled him "divisive" when Connerly took his antipreferences campaign to the Sunshine State. He also failed in his 2003 effort to persuade California voters to pass his Proposition 54, which would have prohibited the state from collecting racial data. Controversy surrounding Connerly continued right up to election day 2006 in Michigan, when a video appeared on the Internet depicting him accepting support for the amendment from the Ku Klux Klan. On the video, he commented that if the KKK "thinks that equality is right, God bless them. Thank them for finally reaching the point where logic and reason are being applied, instead of hate."

Republican state representative Leon Drolet, of suburban Detroit, who also supported the amendment, accused its opponents of "using weapons of mass distraction," a pun on the reason the United States gave for invading Iraq in March 2003. The old split between urban and suburban Detroit over race was rearing its ugly head again. But Ron Edwards, a black talk-show host in the Detroit suburbs, who supported the amendment, took a stand not unlike Justice Clarence Thomas's view of affirmative action. Edwards, quoted in the *Washington Post*, reported that he teaches his children to be self-reliant and not to depend on preferences. Otherwise, he said, women and minorities will not know whether they progressed on their own merit or as a result of affirmative action. "If you want to hurt a racist," he concluded, "succeed."

Like Jennifer Gratz, former plaintiff Barbara Grutter joined in the effort to pass the antipreferences amendment. After her loss in the litigation to gain admittance to the UM Law School, she never enrolled in law school. Instead, Grutter teamed with a political scientist at Michigan State University to establish the organization Toward a Fair Michigan, whose objective was to arrange for debates and discussions about the ballot initiative around the state. She called on Professor Cohen, with whom she had developed a close friendship, to speak in favor of the amendment. He reported that he did so "with enthusiasm" but was concerned that the corporations, unions, and universities that were aligned against the initiative were outspending its supporters by a ten-to-one margin.

Cohen need not have worried. In the November 7, 2006, referendum, the anti–affirmative action amendment garnered 58 percent (or 1.8 million) of Michiganders' votes. Those voters who supported the constitutional amendment to end preferences had exercised a potent civic duty: they had overturned a decision of the nation's highest court. Ward Connerly, beaming over his victory, declared that the Supreme Court's decision in *Grutter*, upholding racial preferences in the University of Michigan Law School's admissions, "is history." Jennifer Gratz, now completely victorious in her decade-long fight against UM's affirmative action program, proclaimed that it was time for the university "to stop trying to manipulate the outcomes and start treating people equally." "I had said all along," she observed, "that the people of Michigan would pass [the amendment] overwhelmingly."

Opponents of the amendment also responded swiftly. UM's president Mary Sue Coleman vowed, "We will not be deterred." "We believe so strongly in affirmative action," she told a rally on the Ann Arbor campus the day after the election, "[that] we went before the United States Supreme Court to defend its youth, and we prevailed. Today I pledge that we will continue that fight. We will do whatever it takes to defend diversity at the University of Michigan." By Any Means Necessary (BAMN), a coalition of civil rights activists, immediately filed suit in Detroit's U.S. District Court, attempting to enjoin implementation of the amendment. BAMN argued that the proposal had appeared on the ballot fraudulently (because signers of the referendum petition had been misled) and constituted a violation of the equal protection clause — to no avail. Under Michigan law, the amendment went into effect on December 22, 2006, forty-five days after the election. Governor Granholm asked the Michigan Civil Rights Commission to identify, by February 23, 2007, any state laws that might be affected by the new amendment banning preferences based on race, gender, color, ethnicity, or national origin in employment, education, or contracts.

As the anti–affirmative action amendment campaign had been under way in Michigan, the Sixth Circuit Court of Appeals returned to the spotlight on the issue. Republicans in the House of Representatives began to investigate Judge Boyce Martin for alleged misconduct in his handling of the *Grutter* and *Gratz* appeals. In turn, Democrats accused the political opposition of using undue political pressure against the judiciary. Sixth Circuit judges reported in the *Washington Post* that staffers of the House Judiciary Committee had visited unannounced the Cincinnati base of the court and demanded to interrogate two Democratic-appointed judges. They refused. The staffers also requested internal, confidential documents from the court, saying they were investigating the charges made by Judge Alice Batchelder the previous year accusing Chief Judge Martin of manipulating the outcome of the *Grutter* litigation.

Judge Damon Keith, a Jimmy Carter appointee who had taken senior status on the Sixth Circuit, told Charles Lane of the *Post* that the Republicans were "mad at our court because they lost, and they won't let up. It's unbelievable." Keith pointed out that the Supreme Court's ruling in *Gratz* had returned the case to the district court in Michigan to carry out the results of the decision in the plaintiffs' favor. For example, Judge Duggan had to determine legal fees owed to the winning side. That phase of the lawsuit could return to the Sixth Circuit on appeal; thus, the Judiciary Committee staff was investigating, and bringing political pressure to bear on, a case that was still pending. A senior committee staff member explained: "We're not trying to reargue the case. We're concerned about the integrity of the process." Committee chair James Sensenbrenner Jr. (R-WI) would not comment to the *Post* on the matter, but staffers said the committee was simply exercising its oversight authority over the federal judiciary. Because impeachment proceedings begin in the House of Representatives, in its Judiciary Committee, impeachable offenses by federal judges would first be considered in that committee. Judge Martin commented to the *Washington Post*, "I'm confident that I've done nothing that was contrary to what the statute required me to do as chief judge [of the Sixth Circuit]." By the time the Judiciary Committee staffers arrived at his court in the fall of 2003, his chief judgeship tenure had expired (as of September 30).

One year after Gratz's lawyers won at the U.S. Supreme Court, they filed a motion back in the U.S. District Court for the Eastern District of Michigan, Southern Division, for attorneys' fees and costs under the Civil Rights Attorneys' Fees Awards Act of 1976. Judge

Patrick Duggan, who had decided the *Gratz* case at trial, now had to determine how much to award for the plaintiffs' expenditures from 1997 through their 2004 motion, including charges by at least sixteen lawyers from three different law firms, including the Center for Individual Rights. Plaintiffs requested $2,071,352.84. Duggan reduced that figure to account for what he identified as an incomplete victory at the high court, "vague billing entries," disallowance of costs related to the intervenors, excludable fees for public and media relations, duplication of attorneys' efforts, and unreasonable charges (such as the compact disc of the Supreme Court's "greatest hits" [oral arguments]). Duggan also concluded that "defendants [the University of Michigan] should not bear the costs for plaintiffs' attorneys to stock their libraries" with books on affirmative action. In an opinion issued on January 27, 2005, Duggan awarded a total of $671,997.75 to the plaintiffs for attorneys' fees and expenses, a final figure that was $1,399,355.09 less than the originally requested total.

Despite approval of the Michigan constitutional amendment banning affirmative action in the Wolverine State, *Grutter* was still the law of the land in thirty-three states that had not banned preferences. Law schools nationwide did not suffer the admissions and financial aid upheavals that befell undergraduate institutions after *Gratz*. Yet racial preferences in law school admissions remained controversial. In 2005 UCLA law professor Richard Sander published an article in the *Stanford Law Review*, where he argued that affirmative action in law school admissions actually *decreases* the number of black lawyers because many African Americans attend law schools that are at least a rung above their capabilities, resulting in poor grades and bar exam failures. Other studies indicate that without affirmative action in America's law schools, the number of African American attorneys might drop anywhere from 9 to 35 percent. Even critics of the Sander article, and there are many, agreed that disparities between black and white graduation rates and bar exam pass rates were "alarming." Despite the fact that the number of African American attorneys had grown from 4,000 in 1970 to 40,000 in 2006, data from 1991 (the one year for which Sander's critics maintain that reliable statistics exist) show that about 40 percent of blacks did not successfully complete law school, or did so but did not pass the bar exam. The corresponding figure for white law students was only 17 percent. The question, of course, revolves around causality. Are racial preferences to blame for the disparities in outcomes? Or something else? For example, one sociologist blames the law school environment for differences in African American and white student performance. Yet neither that argument nor Sander's applies to the selective law schools, some scholars assert. As the University of Michigan maintained in the *Grutter* litigation, its highly ranked law school successfully graduates students of all races and effectively prepares them for the bar exam and legal careers. This debate is no more likely to end than is the more general one over affirmative action. Yet, as Ed Johnson, a research economist at the Bureau of Labor Statistics, told the *New York Times,* Sander's controversial thesis can be a useful tool in exploring the role that racial preferences play in preparing American lawyers.

Debates on preferences often become mired in the compensatory view of race. Minorities argue that they are owed restitution for their suffering at the hands of the majority or, as the Supreme Court would put it, compensation for *general societal* discrimination against *groups* or for *specific identifiable* prejudice against *individuals.* Justice Powell and his protégée, Justice O'Connor, crafted a wholly different rationale for affirmative action based on their vision of higher education (undergraduate, graduate, and professional schools) that was free to be diverse under the First Amendment's academic freedom guarantee (or, as Justice Breyer put it, an "active liberty" interpretation of the Constitution). In her *Grutter* opinion, O'Connor expanded Powell's vision beyond campuses to encompass an image of a diverse American society (produced by diverse higher education) that is informed and engaged in civic life, productive and creative in the global business climate, and confident and secure in an effective military.

Yet, by suggesting the twenty-five-year "sunset" on affirmative action in higher education, O'Connor opened another chapter in racial/ethnic awareness, if not preferences. In order to reach a time, in the next quarter century, when higher education will not have to use race/ethnicity as a plus, and can still create a diverse student body, the entire American educational system will have to concentrate on raising the academic performance of minority students. UCLA provides a contemporary example of what could happen if race/ethnicity drop out of the admissions process, without improvement of primary and secondary schools that serve primarily black students. In June

2006, UCLA reported that its first-year class of 4,852 students for the upcoming fall would have only 96 blacks, or 2 percent of the class. The *Los Angeles Times* noted that UCLA was the alma mater of such celebrated African Americans as Jackie Robinson and Ralph Bunche and is located in a county that is 9.8 percent black. Of the 96 blacks who were due to enroll in fall 2006, 20 of them are recruited athletes. Current undergraduates at the university complained about the low number of blacks expected to arrive on campus as freshmen. Chancellor Albert Carnesale admitted, "Clearly, we're going to have to meet this crisis by redoubling our efforts, which have not yielded the results we'd like to see." He cited the common lament that academically selective schools have trouble attracting, admitting, and enrolling qualified black students.

Administrators appreciate the problem's complexity, but observers of the UCLA situation focused on the results of Connerly's Proposition 209, banning race-based decisions in university decisions, and the fact that minorities often attend schools that are in low socioeconomic neighborhoods and have fewer resources. Although Connerly touts the partnerships between higher education and K–12 schools that formed in the aftermath of "Prop. 209" as a means "to create a competitive pool of minority students," the Los Angeles school district, second largest in the nation, has the sixth worst graduation rate (44.2 percent) of the fifty largest school districts in the nation. These data from 2002–2003 showed that the overall graduation rate in the United States was 69.6 percent, with Asian Americans at 77 percent, whites at 76.2 percent, Hispanics at 55.6 percent, and blacks at 51.6 percent. Black males' rate was 44.3 percent. Of the nation's fifty largest school districts, three graduate less than 40 percent of their students: Detroit, which has the lowest rate of all fifty districts, is at 21.7 percent, Baltimore at 38.5 percent, and New York City at 38.9 percent. Obviously, such statistics do not bode well for producing students who are prepared to undertake higher education.

Lisbeth B. Schorr, director of the Pathways Mapping Initiative of the Project on Effective Interventions at Harvard University, has specifically linked policies for reducing disparities between black and white students and the Supreme Court's *Grutter* opinion. She calls the proposed policies "The O'Connor Project," another indication of how the Supreme Court's first female justice left her stamp on law and society. Schorr advocates "intervening early to eliminate the need for racial preferences in higher education." She argues, "Justice O'Connor's expectation is realistic if, and only if, the nation acts promptly to put in place the measures that would eliminate, or substantially reduce, racial disparities that occur between birth and young adulthood." The good news, according to Schorr, is that knowledge already exists about how to reduce the disparities, but the theory must be translated into practice and then — now the bad news — applied through a unified political will among white and black leaders and constituencies in order to effectuate the policies.

Schorr proposes a quartet of approaches that, she asserts, can reduce or eliminate racial disparities and make racial preferences at universities obsolete. These include (1) reducing racial disparities in birth outcomes, most notably through improved medical care in minority communities; (2) decreasing racial disparities in school preparedness through better access to health care, as well as improved home environments and child care; (3) shrinking the disparate racial outcomes of K–12 education by attracting better teachers, promoting strong interrelations among teachers, parents, and students, reducing class size, and increasing expectations for academic success; and (4) decreasing racial differences in the transition from childhood to young adulthood through revisions in the foster care and juvenile justice systems, and strengthening minority communities, as well as their economies and families. In short, Schorr emphasizes "the importance of education, family responsibility, and social justice" in meeting the goals she has delineated.

Appropriately, when Justice O'Connor retired in 2006, she redoubled her efforts to create the kind of active, informed civic community that her *Grutter* opinion envisioned. In a March 2006 commentary, coauthored with former Colorado governor Roy Romer, she expressed her concern that "most young people today simply do not have an adequate understanding of how our government and political system work, and they are thus not well prepared to participate as citizens. . . . A healthy democracy depends on the participation of citizens, and that participation is learned behavior; it doesn't just happen." Highlighting the pluralistic theme of *Grutter*, O'Connor and

Romer insisted that "understanding society and how we relate to each other fosters the attitudes essential for success in college, work, and communities. . . . [F]ailing to hone the civic tools of democracy will have economic consequences." As coleaders of the National Advisory Council of the Campaign for the Civic Mission of Schools, O'Connor and Romer advocated that American education must emphasize civics, as well as math and science. (The controversial No Child Left Behind Act, centerpiece of the Bush II education policy, concentrates on promoting math, science, and reading skills. Educators complain that increased time spent in teaching to standardized tests in these core subjects has given short shrift to government, history, and civics in the curriculum.)

With O'Connor pursuing her post-Court career and, sadly, caring for her husband of more than fifty years, who suffers from Alzheimer's disease, what is the judicial future of her affirmative action legacy? When President George W. Bush nominated U.S. Court of Appeals Court judges John Roberts (D.C. Circuit) and Samuel Alito (Third Circuit) to the Supreme Court in 2005, members of the Senate Judiciary Committee quizzed them about their views on adhering to precedent, especially those with which they might disagree. Of course, they offered the traditional response that stability in the law requires judges to adhere to past decisions.

Two cases that the Court accepted on appeal in June 2006 will test their commitment to that common-law tradition. *Parents Involved in Community Schools v. Seattle School District No. 1 et al.* and *Meredith v. Jefferson County Board of Education et al.* (in metropolitan Louisville, Kentucky) placed before the justices the question of whether school districts can voluntarily use race to assign children to public schools in order to assure their racial diversity. Plaintiffs in each case, a parents' advocacy group in Seattle, and a mother in Louisville, argue that such assignments unconstitutionally penalize white and/or Asian American children. The Ninth and Sixth Circuits, respectively, upheld the plans in each city. The justices, who only need to muster four votes to accept a case for review, rejected a similar appeal in December 2005, before O'Connor left the bench in January 2006. It is improbable that the four liberal justices who stood with her in *Grutter* to affirm diversity as a compelling state interest in higher education (Stevens, Souter, Ginsburg, and Breyer) would jeopardize that ruling a few years later with O'Connor's seat filled by conservative Justice Alito. Rehnquist's conservative stance on affirmative action is unlikely to be negated by his onetime clerk and protégé, Chief Justice John Roberts. Scalia and Thomas assuredly would be eager to have another crack at establishing their anti–affirmative action positions as the law of the land. Justice Kennedy, who sometimes plays the swing voter, has little in his record that would point to a vote *for* the race-based school assignments — with one possible exception. He is just as concerned about American civic society as is Sandra Day O'Connor, frequently speaking at home and abroad about the importance of the rule of law and the contributions of lawyers to American democracy. Could he possibly be swayed by arguments demonstrating that students, communities, and businesses benefit from diversity in K–12 education? As did lawyers in the *Grutter* and *Gratz* litigation, attorneys before the Supreme Court in the Seattle and Louisville cases might be well advised to aim their arguments at the potential swing voter — this time Kennedy.

The Bush administration did just that. In its briefs for the Louisville and Seattle cases, siding with the parents against race-based school assignments, the solicitor general (Paul Clement, who replaced Ted Olson) quoted Justice Kennedy's dissent in *Grutter*. In the Michigan Law School case he had announced his opposition to affirmative action procedures that "perpetuate the hostilities that proper consideration of race is designed to avoid." A majority of the Court could also distinguish the facts in the *Grutter* precedent, involving a selective law school, from the K–12 public schools at issue in the Kentucky and Washington litigation. Moreover, strictly speaking, the Seattle and Louisville cases do not involve affirmative action (defined as racial preferences in employment or admissions decisions).

Yet the justices referred to the *Grutter* and *Gratz* precedents frequently in the December 2006 oral arguments in the public school cases. While affirmative action proponents carried "Fight for Equality" signs and shouted "Equal education, not segregation" at the Court's doorstep, Justice Kennedy observed from the bench that the Court had barred "outright racial balancing" in the higher education race cases three years earlier. "That seems to me what you have here [in the race-based school assignment policies]," he asserted. On the front plaza outside the Court's majestic facade, the CIR's Terry Pell, hoping for a win that had eluded his public interest law firm in *Grutter*, commented, "Regardless of how well-motivated, allowing the state to engineer racial mixing only creates racial stereotypes and increases racial tension. The court needs to put an end to state-mandated tinkering with race." As this book goes to press, Justice Kennedy's swing vote may determine the future of race-based decisions in American public education.

When asked about her role as a tiebreaker on the high court, Justice O'Connor would typically downplay her influence. She continued this theme at a talk to the Ninth Circuit Conference soon after her retirement announcement in the summer of 2005. She recited a poem aimed at those who inflate their contributions to the world:

> Take a bucket, fill it with water,
> Put your hand in, up to the wrist
> Pull it out, and the hole that's remaining
> Is a measure of how you'll be missed.
> The moral in this quaint example
> Is do just the best that you can,
> Be proud of yourself, but remember,
> There is no indispensable woman.

The verse's homespun wisdom must appeal to the Arizona cowgirl. Yet it hardly captures the demonstrable impact the first woman justice had on Supreme Court decisions during her quarter century on the high tribunal. Whether her precedent in the University of Michigan Law School affirmative action case will endure as long as her iconic image remains to be seen. (The *Grutter* ruling lasted only a little over three years in the state that spawned the litigation.) It is difficult to picture American society in the early twenty-first century, however, without some version of O'Connor's commitment to diversity. The dilemmas and ironies of affirmative action undoubtedly will persist. From grassroots ballot initiatives to the U.S. Supreme Court, American voters and judges will face the challenge of resolving the prolonged tension between color-blind and color-conscious approaches to race in the nation's education system.

CHRONOLOGY

Gratz et al. v. Bollinger et al., 539 U.S. 244 (2003)
Grutter v. Bollinger et al., 539 U.S. 306 (2003)

1964	Civil Rights Act passed by Congress and signed into law by President Lyndon Johnson. Title VI bars discrimination based on race, color, sex, or national origin in all institutions receiving federal funding.
1974	U.S. Supreme Court "moots" *DeFunis v. Odegaard*, the first education affirmative action case to reach it on appeal, because the white plaintiff had nearly completed his studies at the University of Washington Law School.
1978	U.S. Supreme Court announces 5:4 judgment in *Regents of the University of California v. Bakke*, allowing race to be used in admissions decisions as a "plus," among other factors, to achieve the compelling state interest of diversity, but invalidating rigid quotas.
1981	President Ronald Reagan appoints Sandra Day O'Connor to be the first woman justice on the U.S. Supreme Court, after pledging to do so in his 1980 presidential campaign.
1995 and 1997	White students Jennifer Gratz (1995) and Patrick Hamacher (1997) apply to the University of Michigan's undergraduate college and are rejected.
1996	The Center for Individual Rights (CIR), a conservative public interest law firm, wins its lawsuit against the University of Texas Law School's use of racial preferences in admissions. The U.S. Supreme Court denies Texas's appeal from the Fifth Circuit in *Hopwood v. Texas*.
1996	University of Michigan philosophy professor Carl Cohen receives, and makes public, the previously confidential race-based admissions policy from the UM Admissions Office under his Freedom of Information Act request.
1997	The CIR files suit on behalf of Gratz and Hamacher in the U.S. District Court for the Eastern District of Michigan, challenging the UM undergraduate college's affirmative action program.

1997	Barbara Grutter, a white law school applicant at the University of Michigan, is rejected.
1997	The CIR files suit in the U.S. District Court for the Eastern District of Michigan on behalf of Grutter against the UM Law School, challenging its use of racial preferences in admissions.
2000	U.S. District Court judge Patrick Duggan hears oral argument in the trial of *Gratz et al. v. Bollinger, et al.* (Bollinger was president of UM.)
2000	Judge Duggan invalidates the UM undergraduate admissions affirmative action policy in use from 1995 through 1997 because its grid system separated minorities and nonminorities into different pools for consideration and reserved seats for underrepresented minorities. He upholds the post-1997 point-based "selection index," which gave underrepresented minorities a 20-point bonus, because it operated like Justice Powell's "race-as-a-plus" model in *Bakke*.
2001	U.S. District Court judge Bernard Friedman presides over the trial of *Grutter v. Bollinger et al.*
2001	Judge Friedman's opinion strikes down the UM Law School's affirmative action policy of giving preference to underrepresented minorities because its rationale for doing so (achieving a diverse student body) was not a compelling state interest as required under Fourteenth Amendment equal protection analysis.
2001	En banc panel of nine judges from the Sixth U.S. Circuit Court of Appeals in Cincinnati hears oral argument in both the *Gratz* and the *Grutter* case.
2002	Chief Judge Boyce Martin Jr. hands down 5:4 en banc ruling in favor of UM Law School, arguing that the affirmative action policy at issue meets the guidelines set out in Justice Powell's *Bakke* opinion. Bitter dissents accuse Martin of manipulating the circuit's internal proceedings to arrive at his narrow vote in favor of racial preferences.
2002	Grutter's lawyers submit a petition for a writ of certiorari to the U.S. Supreme Court. Despite having no ruling from the Sixth Circuit after almost a year, Gratz's

attorneys also file a certiorari petition with the high court. It accepts both petitions.

2003   The Bush administration is divided on the cases but ultimately decides to submit friend-of-the-court briefs against affirmative action in both disputes.

2003   The Supreme Court justices hear oral argument in *Gratz* and *Grutter* on April 1. Thousands of demonstrators gather around the Court building, with most expressing support for affirmative action.

2003   On June 23 the Court announces both decisions: 5:4, with Justice O'Connor writing the opinion of the Court in *Grutter*, the majority agrees that diversity in higher education is a compelling state interest and that the UM Law School's policy of viewing race as a plus in its "holistic" and "individualized" review of applications comports with Justice Powell's understanding of "narrow tailoring" under strict judicial scrutiny; 6:3, with Chief Justice Rehnquist expressing the Court's opinion in *Gratz*, the majority strikes down the UM undergraduate affirmative action policy's point-based "selection index" for its failure to provide "individualized" readings of applicants' files, which violates "narrow tailoring."

2003   The University of Michigan changes its undergraduate admissions procedures to comport with the law school's policy upheld by the high court. The CIR vows to keep close watch on implementation of the new program.

2005   Gratz (UM-Dearborn) and Hamacher (Michigan State) have long ago graduated from their alternative universities, but U.S. District Court judge Duggan awards their attorneys $671,997.75 in fees and expenses, considerably less than the $2,071,352.84 requested.

2005   Chief Justice William Rehnquist dies. President George W. Bush appoints conservative U.S. Court of Appeals (D.C. Circuit) judge John Roberts Jr. to replace him.

2006   Justice O'Connor retires from the Supreme Court, and President George W. Bush appoints Samuel Alito Jr., a conservative judge from the Third U.S. Circuit Court of Appeals to her seat.

2006   The Court accepts appeals, and hears oral argument, in two cases challenging the voluntary use of race in student assignment to schools (K–12) by Seattle, Washington, and Louisville, Kentucky, school districts.

2006   Michigan voters approve 58 percent to 42 percent a state constitutional amendment to disallow racial, gender, color, ethnic, or national origin preferences in education, government hiring, and government contracts (as California did in 1996). Jennifer Gratz returns to Michigan from her home in California to lead the ballot initiative as executive director of the Michigan Civil Rights Initiative. Barbara Grutter also campaigns for the amendment as the founder of Toward a Fair Michigan, based at Michigan State University.

RELEVANT CASES

Adarand Constructors, Inc. v. Peña, 515 U.S. 200 (1995)

Brown v. Board of Education, 347 U.S. 483 (1954)

City of Richmond v. J. A. Croson Co., 448 U.S. 469 (1989)

DeFunis v. Odegaard, 416 U.S. 312 (1974)

Firefighters Local Union #1784 v. Stotts, 467 U.S. 561 (1984)

Firefighters v. Cleveland, 478 U.S. 501 (1986)

Fullilove v. Klutznick, 44 U.S. 448 (1980)

Griggs v. Duke Power Co., 401 U.S. 424 (1971)

Hopwood v. Texas, 84 F.3d 750 (5th Cir. 1996)

Jett v. Dallas Independent School District, 490 U.S. 701 (1989)

Johnson v. Santa Transportation Agency, Santa Clara County, 480 U.S. 616 (1987)

Lorance v. AT&T Technologies, 490 U.S. 900 (1989)

Martin v. Wilks, 490 U.S. 755 (1989)

Meredith v. Jefferson County Board of Education et al., No. 05-915 (2007)

Metro Broadcasting Inc. v. Federal Communications Commission, 497 U.S. 547 (1990)

Parents Involved in Community Schools v. Seattle School District No. 1 et al., No. 05-908 (2007)

Patterson v. McClean Credit Union, 491 U.S. 164 (1989)

Regents of the University of California v. Bakke, 438 U.S. 265 (1978)

Sheet Metal Workers v. EEOC, 478 U.S. 421 (1986)

Sweatt v. Painter, 339 U.S. 629 (1950)

United States v. Paradise, 480 U.S. 149 (1987)

United Steelworkers of America v. Weber, 443 U.S. 197 (1979)

Wards Cove Packing Co. v. Atonio, 490 U.S. 642 (1989)

Wygant v. Jackson Board of Education, 476 U.S. 267 (1986)

BIBLIOGRAPHIC ESSAY

Note from the series editors: The following bibliographic essay contains the primary and secondary sources that the author consulted for this volume. We have asked all authors in the series to omit formal citations in order to make our volumes more readable, inexpensive, and appealing for students and general readers. In adopting this format, Landmark Law Cases and American Society follows the precedent of a number of highly regarded and widely consulted series.

In 1994–1995 I had the honor of serving as a judicial fellow at the Supreme Court of the United States. The experience of spending a year soaking up the atmosphere of the institution from the inside, attending oral arguments, and seeing justices in a variety of roles has given me a multifaceted view of the tribunal. Justice Lewis F. Powell Jr. and Justice Sandra Day O'Connor, who play starring parts in my narrative, were kind enough to grant me interviews in the mid-1980s, along with Justice William J. Brennan Jr., Justice William H. Rehnquist, and Justice John Paul Stevens, which set me on my path of getting to know justices' ideologies and personalities from a closer perspective than books can provide. Research that I have performed in the Justice Harry Blackmun Papers at the Library of Congress offered an invaluable look at how justices operate behind the scenes as they craft decisions.

My stint as a judicial fellow also provided the good fortune of making long-standing friendships and professional associations with Court staff. General William Suter, clerk of the Court, has been unfailingly helpful in procuring seats for oral arguments in landmark cases, including the subjects of this book: *Gratz v. Bollinger* and *Grutter v. Bollinger*. The arguments are available in audio and text on Northwestern University's "Oyez" Web site, but nothing compares to witnessing them in person. I was also fortunate to see both decisions announced from the bench. Through the Supreme Court Summer Institute for Teachers, cosponsored by Street Law and the Supreme Court Historical Society, I worked with Maureen Mahoney, who argued *Grutter* for the University of Michigan Law School, in presenting the UM cases to teachers for their moot court exercise in 2003. In addition, direct responses to me from Ms. Mahoney's opponent at oral argument, Kirk Kolbo, and from Professor Carl Cohen at the University of Michigan, were a boon to the research.

The Web is a treasure trove of primary sources, upon which this book relies for original analysis. FindLaw is a free Internet service that contains petitioner, respondent, reply, and amici briefs. The site also offers opinions from the U.S. Supreme Court, the U.S. courts of appeals, and the U.S. district courts. Briefs filed by the U.S. solicitor general are available on his office's Web site. In addition to the Library of Congress, university law libraries in all regions of the country serve as repositories of Supreme Court briefs and opinions. The Supreme Court's Web site contains its opinions. The Sixth U.S. Circuit Court of Appeals played a controversial role in the Michigan cases; its Web site is useful for learning the cast of characters on that bench through biographies of each judge and a short history of the circuit. The Center for Individual Rights, which initiated the lawsuits against the University of Michigan, provides descriptive material about its mission on the Web. A simple Google search produced interesting content by and about Carl Cohen, the University of Michigan philosophy professor who started the long journey toward the Supreme Court for the affirmative action cases with a Freedom of Information Act request to the UM Admissions Office regarding its use of racial preferences.

Three books on affirmative action provide detailed background material on the history, events, and court cases that preceded the Michigan litigation. My predecessors in the Landmark Law Cases and American Society include Howard Ball's *The* Bakke *Case: Race, Education, and Affirmative Action* (Lawrence: University Press of Kansas, 2000), and Melvin I. Urofsky's *Affirmative Action on Trial: Sex Discrimination in* Johnson v. Santa Clara (Lawrence: University Press of Kansas, 1997). A brilliant overview of racial preferences and their context in civil rights history is Terry H. Anderson's *The Pursuit of Fairness: A History of Affirmative Action* (New York: Oxford University Press, 2004). John David Skrentny's *The Ironies of Affirmative Action: Politics, Culture, and Justice in America* (Chicago: University of Chicago Press, 1996) provides a sophisticated analysis of racial politics. Reporter Greg Stohr, of Bloomberg News, produced an early journalistic account of the UM litigation in *A Black and White Case: How Affirmative Action Survived Its Greatest Legal Challenge* (New York: Bloomberg Press, 2004). The outline for my book on the Michigan cases originated in my chapter, "Affirmative Action in Higher Education: *Gratz v. Bollinger* and *Grutter v. Bollinger*," in Gregg Ivers and Kevin T. McGuire, eds., *Creating Constitutional Change: Clashes over Power and Liberty in the Supreme Court* (Charlottesville: University Press of Virginia, 2004). Crucial research cited approvingly by affirmative action advocates, and criticized by opponents, is William G. Bowen and Derek Bok's *The Shape of the River: Long-Term Consequences of Considering Race in College and University Admissions* (Princeton, NJ: Princeton University Press, 1998). See also University of Michigan law professor Terrance Sandalow's article on the Bowen and Bok study, "Minority Preferences Reconsidered," *Michigan Law Review* 97 (May 1999): 1874–1927. Malcolm Gladwell's "Getting In: The Social Logic of Ivy League Admissions," published in the October 10, 2005, issue of the *New Yorker*, explains the sad history of anti-Jewish quotas at Harvard College starting in the 1920s. Timothy Egan's feature story in the January 7, 2007 *New York Times*, "The Asian Campus," explores whether "Asian-Americans are being denied spots in top colleges to keep their members in check," ("Education Life," Section 4A, pp. 24–27, 35). UCLA law professor Richard Sander asserts that affirmative action in law schools actually produces fewer black lawyers in his *Stanford Law Review* article, "A Systematic Analysis of Affirmative Action in American Law Schools" (Spring 2005). A 2006 critique of his conclusions may be found in "The Real Impact of Eliminating Affirmative Action," by David L. Chambers, Timothy T. Clydesdale, William C. Kidder, and Richard O. Lempert, available on the University of Michigan Law School Web site. (Lempert was on the faculty committee that produced the UM Law School affirmative action plan in 1992.) Ward Connerly, the California entrepreneur and former regent in the California university system who spawned successful anti–affirmative action movements in California, Washington, and Michigan, has published a memoir, *Creating Equal: My Fight against Race Preferences* (San Francisco: Encounter Books, 2000). Nathan Glazer's *Affirmative Discrimination: Ethnic Inequality and Public Policy* (Cambridge, MA: Harvard University Press, 1987), is a sociologist's argument against the use of racial preferences. One of the first comprehensive studies of *Bakke*, its background, and meaning was Allan Sindler's Bakke, DeFunis, *and Minority Admissions: The Quest for Equal Opportunity* (New York: Longman, 1978). *Toward an Understanding of* Bakke, published by the United States Commission on Civil Rights in 1978, was my introduction to the University of California at Davis Medical School case. It contained a brief analysis of the case, as well as all of the opinions, totaling 157 pages. In addition, the booklet featured federal guidelines on affirmative action policy. The volume formed a primer for my very first job as an affirmative action compliance officer.

Material on the Kennedy administration's civil rights record can be found in Robert Dallek's insightful biography, *An Unfinished Life: John F. Kennedy, 1917–1963* (New York: Back Bay Books, 2003); Irving Bernstein's admiring policy analysis, *Promises Kept: John F. Kennedy's New Frontier* (New York: Oxford University Press, 1991); and Nick Bryant's critique, *The Bystander: John F. Kennedy and the Struggle for Black Equality* (New York: Basic Books, 2006). Two books provide documentary sources on the Kennedy presidency: Harold W. Chase and Allen H. Lerman, eds., *Kennedy and the Press: The News Conferences* (New York: Crowell, 1965); and Theodore C. Sorensen, ed., *"Let the Word Go Forth": The Speeches, Statements, and Writings of John F. Kennedy, 1947 to 1963* (New York: Delacorte Press, 1988). Jason Sokol's *There Goes My Everything: White Southerners in the Age of Civil Rights, 1945–1975* (New York: Knopf, 2006) provides a comprehensive summary and analysis of the turbulent post–World War II South. Before his nomination to the Fourth U.S. Circuit Court of Appeals, Judge J. Harvie Wilkinson III, Justice Powell's first law clerk, penned *From* Brown *to* Bakke: *The Supreme Court and School Integration, 1954–1978* (New York: Oxford University Press, 1979). To mark the fiftieth anniversary of the *Brown* decision in 2004, the Supreme Court Historical

Society sponsored *Black, White, and* Brown: *The Landmark School Desegrega-tion Case in Retrospect* (Washington, DC: CQ Press, 2004), edited by Clare Cushman and Melvin I. Urofsky.

Henry J. Abraham's *Freedom and the Court: Civil Rights and Liberties in the United States*, 8th ed. (Lawrence: University Press of Kansas, 2003), on which I have the honor of serving as the junior author, contains a classic analysis of race cases before the nation's high court. Louis Fisher's *American Constitutional Law*, 4th ed. (Durham, NC: Carolina Academic Press, 2001) is an excellent casebook by the premier political scientist at the Congressional Research Service.

A collection of essays with a liberal bent by the major players at the University of Michigan (Patricia Gurin, Jeffrey S. Lehman, Earl Lewis) is entitled *Defending Diversity: Affirmative Action at the University of Michigan* (Ann Arbor: University of Michigan Press, 2004). For a description of racial tensions on the UM campus in the 1980s from a conservative author, see Dinesh D'Souza, *Illiberal Education: The Politics of Race and Sex on Campus* (New York: Free Press, 1991). An edited work by Paul Berman, *Debating P.C.: The Controversy over Political Correctness on College Campuses* (New York: Dell, 1992), offers context for the discussions of race and gender on campuses in the Reagan era. David Riddle's article on the busing controversy in Michigan during the 1970s — "Race and Reaction in Warren, Michigan, 1971 to 1974: *Bradley v. Milliken* and the Cross-District Busing Controversy," *Michigan Historical Review* 26 (Fall 2000): 1–49 — is superb. "Michigan Quick Facts" from the U.S. Census Bureau, available online, provide demographic data for the state. Enrollment data, including statistics categorized by race and ethnicity, are available on the University of Michigan Library Web site.

Preview of United States Supreme Court Cases, published online and in hard copy by the American Bar Association's Division for Public Education, offers detailed, yet highly readable, summaries of cases coming before the U.S. Supreme Court. Douglas W. Kmiec wrote the preview of *Gratz* and *Grutter*, "Does the Constitution Allow Universities to Consider Their Applicants' Race?" in the 2003 edition, pp. 350–362. Vikram David Amar published "Equal Protection: Racial Minorities in the 2002 Term," as the 2003 *Preview*'s analysis of the Court's decision in the UM cases, pp. 475–483. His entry drew my attention to how Justice O'Connor wove her concern for civic engagement into her opinions. Brian Deese summarized the Seattle and Louisville race-based school-assignment cases in the 2006 edition of *Preview*, pp. 165–171. Justice Stephen Breyer's collection of lectures, *Active Liberty: Interpreting Our Democratic Constitution* (New York: Knopf, 2005), applies his jurisprudential theories to *Grutter v. Bollinger*. A fascinating policy response to the Michigan decisions is Lisbeth B. Schorr's "The O'Connor Project: Intervening Early to

Eliminate the Need for Racial Preferences in Higher Education," *Judicature* 88 (September–October 2004): 92–96.

Joan Biskupic's first-rate biography, *Sandra Day O'Connor: How the First Woman on the Supreme Court Became Its Most Influential Justice* (New York: Ecco, 2005), is a splendid portrait of her subject. O'Connor's memoir, coauthored with her brother, H. Alan Day, *Lazy B: Growing Up on a Cattle Ranch in the American Southwest* (New York: Random House, 2002), sets the stage for her pioneering career. Her collection of essays, edited by Craig Joyce, *The Majesty of Law: Reflections of a Supreme Court Justice* (New York: Random House, 2003), contains her thoughts on gender and race and a tribute to Justice Lewis F. Powell Jr. The latter's definitive biographer is John C. Jeffries Jr.; his book is titled simply *Justice Lewis F. Powell, Jr.: A Biography* (New York: Scribner's, 1994). My volume of brief essays on each member of the Rehnquist Court, *"The Supremes": Essays on the Current Justices of the Supreme Court of the United States* (New York: Peter Lang, 2001), is the source of biographical and judicial philosophy. I used material from my book *A "Representative" Supreme Court? The Impact of Race, Religion, and Gender on Appointments* (Westport, CT: Greenwood, 1991) in discussing presidential use of a form of affirmative action in making Supreme Court appointments. Mark Tushnet's *A Court Divided: The Rehnquist Court and the Future of Constitutional Law* (New York: Norton, 2006) is a stimulating analysis of the justices' ideologies, including O'Connor's.

Because of my proximity to the nation's capital, my daily newspaper of choice is the *Washington Post*. Supreme Court correspondent Charles Lane published detailed reports of the University of Michigan cases at all stages. His coverage of the public political rift on the Sixth Circuit was invaluable to placing that story in the larger context surrounding the litigation. Lane's *Post* colleague Anne Hull wrote "A Dream Denied Leads Woman to Center of Suit," a lengthy feature story on Jennifer Gratz, published on February 23, 2003. I also relied on stories in the *New York Times*, the *Washington Times*, and *USA Today*. *New York Times* Supreme Court reporter Linda Greenhouse and her counterpart at *USA Today*, Joan Biskupic, were the Henry J. Abraham Distinguished Lecturers at the University of Virginia in 2004 and 2006, respectively, during which they each shared their insights on the affirmative action decisions and Justice O'Connor's role in them.

Bork, Robert, 33–34
Bowen, William, 93
Bradley, Bill, 104
Bradley v. Milliken (1974), 45
Brennan, William J., Jr.
  Bakke and, 24, 25
  employment discrimination and,
    33
  Firefighters and, 30
  Johnson and, 32–33, 96
  Metro and, 35
  Paradise and, 31
  quotas and, 31
  retirement of, 36, 37
  strict scrutiny and, 36
  Weber and, 27
  Wygant and, 50
Breyer, Stephen, 105, 127, 158
  active liberty and, 154–155, 173
  affirmative action plans and, 123
  compelling state interest and,
    176
  conference protocol and, 136
  critical mass and, 132
  diversity and, 110, 125–126
  on Equal Protection Act, 156
  Gratz dissent and, 151, 152, 156
  Grutter opinion and, 141, 155
  individualized consideration and,
    131
  Kolbo and, 113–114, 125
  nomination of, 41
  Olson and, 115
  on original intent, 155
  percent plan and, 116
Brown v. Board of Education (1954),
    31, 51, 89, 149, 183
  Marshall and, 16
  precedent in, 137
  race/education and, 90
  school desegregation and, 2
Bryant, Nick, 8
Bunche, Ralph, 174
Bureau of Labor Statistics, 173

Burger, Warren, 135
  Bakke and, 24
  Fullilove and, 28
  retirement of, 32
  school segregation and, 49
Burns, James MacGregor, 3
Bush, George H. W., 41, 82, 83
  appointment by, 37
  Civil Rights Act and, 36
  quotas and, 37
Bush, George W.
  affirmative access and, 87
  affirmative action and, x, 88, 89
  education issue and, 176
  Michigan cases and, 87, 157
  nominations by, 36, 176
  percentage plans and, 92
  Roberts and, 181
  10 percent plan and, 39
Bush, Jeb, 169
Bush v. Gore (2000), 89
Busing, 46, 48–49, 51
  Democratic Party and, 47–48
  endorsement of, 48
  opposition to, 48
By Any Means Necessary (BAMN),
    170
Bystander, The (Bryant), 8

California Supreme Court, *Bakke*
    and, 23
Campaign for the Civic Mission of
    Schools, 104, 176
Cantor, Nancy, 51, 52
Carnegie Mellon University,
    diversity at, 164
Carnesale, Albert, 174
Carter, Jimmy, 20, 77, 171
Casteen, John, 41, 166
Catholic Church, calming influence
    of, 178
CEEO (Committee on Equal
    Employment Opportunity),
    6–7, 8–9

application by, 60–61, 111
Bakke and, 95
discrimination against, 123
diversity and, 62
interview of, 60
racial considerations and, 82,
  123
statutory claims of, 146
suit by, 139, 180
support for, 109, 110
Grutter v. Bollinger et al. (2003), x,
  60, 64, 71, 72, 74, 76, 83, 90,
  91, 94
  affirmative action and, 158
  amici briefs in, 90, 98–107, 138,
    159
  appealing, 84–85
  Bakke and, 153
  compelling state interest and, 176
  controversy about, 107, 140
  dissent in, 138–139, 141, 147,
    148, 149, 150, 158
  diversity and, 143
  opinion in, xii, xiii, 140–143,
    145, 146, 149, 151, 154, 155,
    158
  oral arguments in, xii, 180, 181
  precedents from, xii, 81
  race and, 154, 178
  racial preferences and, 170
  swing vote in, 177
Gurin, Patricia, 81, 91, 107, 129,
  131
  on educational environment, 66
  on Michigan students, 54
  NAS and, 67

Hamacher, Patrick, 65, 72, 124,
  134, 181
  amici briefs for, 126
  appeal by, 71, 85, 87, 89
  rejection of, 64, 67
  standing of, 151, 152, 153
  suit by, 58, 59, 63, 179

Harlan, John Marshall, I, 150
  Plessy dissent by, 28, 149
Harper's Weekly, on University of
  Michigan, 52
Harris poll, on affirmative action,
  26
Harvard Law School, 131–132, 153
Harvard plan, 79, 92, 94, 96, 116,
  117, 118, 119, 120, 151
  diversity and, 122
Harvard University, amicus brief by,
  118
Higher education
  affirmative action and, x, 65
  diversity in, 66
  integrating, 9
  segregation and, 70
  strict scrutiny and, 66
  See also Education
"Higher Education: A Plea for
  Making It Accessible, The"
  (Angell), 52
Hill, Anita, 38
Hitler, Adolf, 156
Holocaust Museum, Breyer at, 156
Hopwood v. Texas (1996), 59, 179,
  183
  racial preferences and, 84, 87
House Judiciary Committee, 85,
  171
Humphrey, Hubert, 13, 16, 48

"I Have a Dream" speech (King), 2,
  11–12
Independent Women's Forum,
  amicus brief by, 107
Institute for Justice, 43
Integration, 9, 47, 54, 62
Ironies of Affirmative Action, The
  (Skrentny), 16

Jackson, Robert, 104, 146
*Jett v. Dallas Independent School
  District* (1989), 35, 183

MCAT (Medical College
    Admissions Test), 22, 24
McCarthy, Eugene, 17
McCree, Wade, 24
McDonald, Michael, 44, 63
McGovern, George, 48
Medical College Admissions Test
    (MCAT), 22, 24
Mellon Foundation, 93
*Meredith v. Jefferson County Board of
    Education et al.* (2006), 176, 183
*Metro Broadcasting Inc. v. Federal
    Communications Commission*
    (1990), 35, 42, 145, 183
Michigan Catholic Conference, 169
Michigan Civil Rights Commission,
    170
Michigan Civil Rights Initiative,
    167, 182
Michigan House of Representatives
    Constitution Committee, 57
Michigan Jewish Conference, 169
"Michigan Mandate," 53
Michigan Student Union, blockade
    of, 53
Microsoft, affirmative action and, 88
Middle class, affirmative action and,
    51
Military
    affirmative action and, 97–98, 99,
        100
    diversity and, 98, 99, 112–113
    race-conscious programs and,
        99–100
Military academies
    affirmative action and, 114
    racial preferences and, 113, 115
Military brief, 97–98, 112
    affirmative action and, 113, 114
    recruiting programs and, 115
Minorities, ix, 73
    affirmative action plans and, 61, 79
    enrollment of, 119, 121, 134, 138

higher education costs and, 164
hiring/promoting, 17, 31
isolation among, 129
law schools and, 112
preferred, 90, 126, 129, 147
recruiting/training, 15, 113
restitution for, 173
special education programs for, 43
underrepresentation of, 112,
    129–130, 147, 151, 152
viewpoints of, 144
Minority aid programs,
    reviewing/revising, 165
Minority business enterprises
    (MBEs), 24, 27–28
Mitchell, John, 18
Moore, Karen Nelson, 82, 83
Mount Holyoke, minority students
    at, 163–164
Moynihan, Daniel Patrick, 14
Myrdal, Gunnar, 2, 7

NAACP. *See* National Association
    for the Advancement of
    Colored People
*Naked Racial Preference: The Case
    against Affirmative Action*
    (Cohen), 55
Narrow tailoring, 28, 65, 78, 91,
    106, 108, 110
NAS (National Association of
    Scholars), amicus brief by, 67
National Academy of Engineers,
    amicus brief by, 102
National Academy of Sciences,
    amicus brief by, 102
National Action Council for
    Minorities in Engineering,
    amicus brief by, 102
National Advisory Council
    (Campaign for the Civic
    Mission of Schools), 104,
    176

National Association for the
  Advancement of Colored
  People (NAACP), 6, 44
  antipreferences amendment and,
    168
  Jones and, 157
  LDF of, 77
  Lockheed and, 8
  minority-targeted funding and,
    165
  school desegregation and, 45
  suit by, 46
  Thomas and, 37
National Association of Scholars
    (NAS), amicus brief by, 67
National Association of State
    Universities and Land Grant
    Colleges, 66
National Bar Association, 37
National Council of Black Lawyers,
    38
National Journal, on CIR, 44
National Urban League, 37
Naval Academy Preparatory
    School, minorities at, 99
"Negro Family: The Case for
    National Action, The"
    (Moynihan), 14
Negro problem, 2
New Deal, 4, 19
New Frontier, 4, 6
Newsweek, on affirmative action
    policies, 41
Newsweek poll, on preferences/
    college admissions, 39
New York Times, 59
  on Michigan cases, 159
  on Sander's thesis, 173
  Shaw in, 165
New York Times/CBS poll, on
    affirmative action, 43
Ninth Circuit Conference,
    O'Connor and, 178

Nixon, Richard M., 3, 5
  busing issue and, 48
  Philadelphia Plan and, 17
No Child Left Behind Act, 176
Nondiscrimination, 7, 84, 146
Norris, Alan E., 82

O'Connor, Sandra Day, x, 132
  affirmative action and, 33, 34,
    120–121, 122, 142, 173, 177,
    178
  appeals to, 90–91, 96
  appointment of, 30
  Bakke and, 141–142
  breast cancer and, 34–35
  civic education and, 104
  civic society and, 175, 177
  Croson and, 127
  democracy and, 104, 175–176
  diversity and, 142, 143
  employment discrimination and,
    33
  Equal Protection Clause and, 146
  gender and, 93
  Gratz concurrence and, 152
  Grutter opinion and, xiii, 96,
    140–141, 141–142, 143, 145,
    146, 149, 155, 158, 173, 175,
    181
  Jackson plan and, 51
  legacy of, 144, 176
  Marshall and, 31, 104
  Metro and, 145
  middle ground and, 50, 88, 96,
    110, 158–159, 178
  Olson and, 115
  Paradise dissent and, 32
  percentage plans and, 145
  Powell and, 50, 96, 149, 159
  public service and, 103–104
  on quotas, 32
  racial classification and, 42
  Reagan and, 179